Crisis Systems at t

Grounded in frontline experience and global research, this work unpacks the complexities of defining behavioural health, the challenge of crisis cycling, and the evolving roles of law enforcement and community partners. Written from the unique perspective of a seasoned police officer embedded in the world of behavioural health crisis response, this work offers an insider's examination of the evolving landscape of public safety and mental health intervention.

Drawing on lived experiences, operational insights, and contemporary best practices, the author advocates that police are one component within a broader collaborative, systems-based approach to crisis. Beginning with a foundational understanding of what forms a behavioural health crisis, the book guides readers through a range of response models – from non-police crisis lines and paramedic teams to police co-responder models and police call diversion programs. It critically examines the limitations of police training, the harsh realities of non-clinical outcomes such as tactical disengagement and use-of-force, and broader systemic pressures that shape crisis intervention. Each section ends with a reflective commentary, blending academic insight into frontline pragmatism. The final chapters look ahead, proposing integrated frameworks and collaborative strategies to proactively manage crisis cycling and building more responsive, humane systems.

With a focus on real-world application, informed by both practice and research, this book is an essential resource for policing professionals, behavioural health professionals, policymakers, and students seeking a grounded yet progressive approach to behavioural health crisis intervention.

Glen Blackwell has over 35 years of operational policing experience with the Western Australia Police Force, including a decade focused on the intersection of policing and behavioural health crisis response. Recognised as a leader in this field, he has played a central role in the development, leadership, and training of specialised police and mental health co-responder teams aimed at improving outcomes for individuals in acute crises. He established the agency's behavioural health training role, delivering accredited crisis training for police and mental health clinicians, and revised de-escalation training across the agency. He also held a six-month tenure within Western Australia Health, supervising the Mental Health Emergency Response Line, supporting implementation of recommendations from the Nexus Review.

He holds a Master of Leadership (High Distinction), with his academic work focusing on behavioural health crisis systems and the evolving role of police within this complexity. Being awarded a prestigious Winston Churchill Fellowship enabled him to embed with crisis response teams across North America and the UK – both police-led and civilian – participating in frontline patrols, proactive crisis cycling programs, and advanced crisis training. He is an active member of several international crisis response associations and has presented his work at global conferences. In 2024, he presented a behavioural health crisis policy brief to national leaders at Australia's Parliament House, advocating for more integrated, evidence-based crisis systems. He continues to contribute to policy, training, and research aimed at collaborative systems-based approaches that look beyond acute response to behavioural health crisis management.

Crisis Systems at the Crossroads

A Practical Perspective on Behavioural Health, Policing, and Crisis Systems

Glen Blackwell

Routledge
Taylor & Francis Group
NEW YORK AND LONDON

Designed cover image: Getty Images

First published 2027
by Routledge
605 Third Avenue, New York, NY 10158

and by Routledge
4 Park Square, Milton Park, Abingdon, Oxon, OX14 4RN

Routledge is an imprint of the Taylor & Francis Group, an informa business

ISBN: 978-1-041-26217-6 (hbk)
ISBN: 978-1-041-26216-9 (pbk)
ISBN: 978-1-003-74958-5 (ebk)

DOI: 10.4324/9781003749585

Typeset in Galliard
by Newgen Publishing UK

This book is dedicated to all frontline responders who work around the clock to support people in crisis. Their understanding, experience, and dedication often remain undervalued and underacknowledged in efforts to reform crisis systems. Special recognition is offered to police officers, whose unique role carries added responsibility to respond to volatile and often dangerous situations that no other sector has capacity to manage and do so with a commitment to serve and protect those most in need of care. Recognition given as broader discussions continue about how crisis systems should evolve to provide safer and more therapeutic responses in the future.

Contents

Acknowledgements ix
Disclaimer xi

1 Introduction 1
Introduction 1

2 Behavioural Health Crisis and Crisis Cycling 6
Behavioural Health v. Mental Health 6
Chronic Crisis Cycling 10
Behavioural Health v. Suicidality Calls – Are They the Same? 17
Observational Summary 24

3 Community Crisis Response Systems 35
Introduction 35
Crisis Call Lines 35
Community Response Teams 41
Crisis Stabilisation Centres 46
Observational Summary 49

4 Police Crisis Response Systems 59
Introduction 59
Co-Responder 59
Serenity Integrated Mentoring 64
Right Care, Right Person 67
Crisis Intervention Teams 74
Observational Summary 79

5 Non-Clinical Outcomes to Crisis 94
Introduction 94
Tactical Disengagement 94
Judicial Management 100
Tactical Resolution (Use-of-Force) 106
Observational Summary 111

6 The Question of Behavioural Health Training for Police 120
Introduction 120
Diagnostic Specific Knowledge 122
Training Needs To Be Practical, Not Clinical 122
Behavioural Health Training Content 124
Who Should Learn and When? 135
Observational Summary 138
Training Footnote 139

7 Systemic Barriers to Crisis Management 150
Introduction 150
Operational Barriers to Crisis Response 150
"Defund the Police" and Crisis Response 157
Policing as Law Enforcement 160
Observational Commentary 165

8 Evolving from Crisis Response to Crisis Management 174
Introduction 174
Moving beyond Crisis Response 175
Reviewing Current Management Programs 186
Fourth Emergency Service – Behavioural Health 193
Observational Summary 198

9 Conclusion 211
Conclusion 211
Final Observational Summary – Police Role in Crisis 222

Index 229

Acknowledgements

The writing of this text has not been an entirely solo effort. I have been fortunate to receive a great deal of support from colleagues and friends from around the world; many of whom are leaders in their own right within the field of crisis management. Their willingness to share their experiences, challenges, insights and to even challenge standing assumptions has helped me gain a broader understanding of the local nuances of crisis management across jurisdictions to make this the work it is today.

From a policing perspective, I am particularly grateful to Police Constable Hayley Sherwin OBE of Merseyside Police UK, a leading authority in the United Kingdom within crisis response and proactive crisis ideology who provided practical advice regarding local operational realities. I also thank Western Australia Police Sergeant Mandy Johnson, whose decades of experience and patience allowed her to guide the writing to something accessible and relevant when I would drift, which kept my work grounded. Detective III Liz Reyes of the Los Angeles Police Department, a driving force in their Mental Evaluation Unit in operationalising progressive reform, kindly reviewed the chapter on police response models offering a valuable US perspective.

I also want to acknowledge fellow pracademic Ron Bruno, a US police officer (retired) whose frontline experiences and academic integrity, particularly from being on the board of Crisis Intervention Teams International and establishing Crisis Response Programs and Training, gave valuable assistance with the chapters on Non-Clinical Outcomes and Systemic Barriers to Crisis Management.

Ensuring clinical and academic integrity, I extend my thanks to Professor Amy Watson, an internationally recognised leader in research on police and justice encounters with people experiencing behavioural health challenges, for her review of the opening chapter on defining behavioural health crisis and crisis cycling. I am also thankful to Professor Nick Crofts AM, founder of the Global Law Enforcement and Public Health Association, for reviewing the chapter on evolving from crisis response to crisis management and systems-based approaches. My thanks also go to Dr Hayley Passmore and Dr Julia Butt for their early guidance, with particular appreciation to Julia for her ongoing support in clarifying clinical concepts along the way.

I also wish to acknowledge the Winston Churchill Trust – Australia, whose support made it possible to build the international relationships and experiences that form the foundation of much of this work. The opportunity to travel as a Churchill Fellow broadened my understanding of crisis systems globally and the subsequent fellowship that enabled me to attend Australia's Parliament House provided a unique platform to engage with national leaders to discuss crisis reform.

I am also grateful to the team at Routledge for their trust in this project, particularly senior editor Ellen Boyne, who recognised the importance an operational practitioner's perspective could make within a complex and challenging topic.

I thank my wife Anita and son Theodore who have supported me throughout this journey. They endured long period of absences as I travelled the world and equally long periods of me locked away taping at the keyboard. They also kept me sane reminding me to step outside and walk the dogs, go to the beach, or go mountain biking together.

Disclaimer

The views, recommendations, and opinions expressed in this work are those of the author and do not necessarily reflect the position of the Western Australia Police Force or any Australian Police agency nor do they necessarily reflect the position of those individuals who kindly gave their time in reviewing the work prior to publication. The author has at all times attempted to ensure the accuracy of the contents and commentary does not equal an opinion expressly of those organisations acknowledged within the work.

1 Introduction

Introduction

Since Marc Abramson's 1972 examination of what he claimed was the criminalisation of mental health, crisis response has been written about extensively.[1] Many texts explore how systems have been developed and evaluated, or suggest reform, while other texts debate who should – or should not – respond when a crisis call is made. Predominately these works have been written by academics, psychologists, clinicians, or political policy specialists – contributions which offer valuable insight into crisis. Yet their perspectives are often gained from a level of separation from the imminent, dynamic, complex, and at times dangerous realities that real-world crisis calls present to frontline responders to navigate.

This book offers a different perspective.

Drawing on over 35 years of operational policing, including a decade of specialising in behavioural health crisis systems, I have helped establish co-responder programs, responded in both general duties and specialist crisis roles, developed and delivered training for police, co-responder teams and postgraduate students. I have also spent time seconded into a health department mental health crisis call centre, serving as a team leader assisting implementation of systems change post a practice review. These experiences provide a practical understanding and insight into how crisis calls begin, how they evolve, and how they are resolved – sometimes successfully, sometimes not.

This practical knowledge is supported by academic research. My postgraduate studies focused on policing and behavioural health crisis, and a Winston Churchill Trust Fellowship enabled me to observe, patrol, and train with police and non-police crisis teams across North America and the United Kingdom. These opportunities enabled a rare, first-hand experience of international approaches to crisis management, built ongoing professional connections, and helped my perspective to remain informed by practitioners on the global frontline.

DOI: 10.4324/9781003749585-1

Accordingly, I bring the perspective of a *pracademic*: someone who has been at the sharp end of crisis response while also examining the research on these systems. I have negotiated with individuals armed and volatile, de-escalated people actively suicidal, dealt with distressed families, resuscitated those reached too late, and navigated the complexity of collaborating with services supporting individuals who cycle through crisis. Real-world experiences that ground academic analysis and observational works.

As such, this text will not completely present itself as an academic study or a comprehensive guide for jurisdictions to follow carte blanche. Too often works calling for universal change fail to understand jurisdictional pressures, or the dynamic, and unpredictable nature of crisis calls. They also can reinforce the divisive debate around who is 'best placed' to respond, particularly when it comes to the role of police. A debate which frequently calls for the removal of police completely from crisis response, yet ignores the realities faced by communities and first responders.

As Baldry and Dowse (2013) observed, in terms of this debate, the police are placed in a paradoxical position.[2] Health and social services call for the police to reduce their role, yet they regularly turn people in crisis away – leaving the police as the only agency unable to refuse engagement, even as they are criticised for doing so and held to account if they do not.

This book also acknowledges that crisis is not clinical, linear, or predictable. Some situations are best managed by non-police responders; others will always require police intervention. To address this complexity honestly, the text engages with topics that may be confronting: suicide, intimate partner violence, substance use, police use-of-force (including deadly force), and coronial inquiries. Subjects are not included for emotive effect but as they are key to understanding crisis in its entirety and its impact on communities.

Some perspectives in this work may challenge assumptions made by earlier research work. This does not dismiss their value, rather, the aim of this book is to broaden those conversations by integrating research with lived operational practice. The following chapter overviews outline the structure of the text, themes explored, and how this integration is used to guide the reader through a conversation which may challenge current views on crisis response and management.

Chapter 2 – Behavioural Health Crisis and Crisis Cycling

This chapter intends to set the tone for the text, by redefining crisis beyond restrictive diagnostic frameworks and academic terminology such as "Persons with serious mental illness".[3] It questions whether such approaches have hindered rather than help crisis reform.

The chapter also examines whether calls for behavioural health crisis and suicide should be considered as incidents in the same response framework, with a final look at how certain individuals, often referred to as 'frequent flyers', have become locked in patterns of repeated crisis cycling.[4]

Chapter 3 – Community Crisis Response Systems

This chapter reviews non-police response systems through the lens of the United States, Substance Abuse and Mental Health Services Administration framework, which divides crisis management into three key stages:[5]

- Someone to Contact – Crisis Call Lines
- Someone to Respond – Community Responder Teams
- A Safe Place for Help – Crisis Stabilisation Centres

Chapter 4 – Police Crisis Response Systems

Police agencies have not remained a passive sector in crisis response, with demand having a significant impact on resourcing. To address these challenges, they have innovatively adopted programs to improve outcomes. This chapter will review four contemporary models: Co-Responder; Serenity Integrated Mentoring; Right Care, Right Person; and Crisis Intervention Teams, which tackle demand in different ways.

Chapter 5 – Non-Clinical Outcomes to Crisis

Taking a robust and frank discussion, this chapter will examine how not all crisis incidents can be resolved through clinical intervention. Looking at how contemporary policing agencies and judicial systems are evolving to reduce harm through disengagement, improving therapeutic support in courts and candidly discussing the realities of police tactical engagement.

Chapter 6 – The Question of Behavioural Health Training for Police

As the call for reducing the role of policing in crisis escalates, parallel calls are made to improve police training for when they must respond. Such calls are often followed by recommendations for training sessions to be built around specific diagnostic profiles and intersecting societal factors. This chapter seeks to explore the viability, practicality, and benefit such recommendations have for police response.

Chapter 7 – Systemic Barriers to Crisis Management

Crisis management reform is often impeded by a series of influencing factors of sectors own making or factors created beyond their control. This chapter will explore how political agendas such as "Defund the Police" or policing's own "Peelian Principles" have either helped or hindered progress. It will also explore operational barriers that can contribute to reducing the effectiveness of response systems, or indeed cancel the opportunity for progress.

Chapter 8 – Evolving from Crisis Response to Crisis Management

The author brings together the common themes arising from the preceding chapters and discusses why the future of crisis work lies beyond traditional interventionist programs. It examines how communities, governments, and sectors need to view crisis through a systems-based thinking lens.

Rather than offering a generic guide for all communities, this chapter raises systems-based thinking as a framework which promotes local adaptations, through shared responsibility and understanding. By reimagining crisis beyond the limitations interventionist models create, communities can build systems that improve outcomes for individuals and communities and strengthen the system as a whole.

The final section of this chapter raises the question whether the time has come for communities to establish a fourth emergency service, alongside police, fire, and ambulance, dedicated to behavioural health crisis.

Chapter 9 – Conclusion

This book offers the observations, insights, and experiences that over three and a half decades of frontline crisis response bring. It deliberately challenges many narrowed or politically driven approaches that have shaped crisis debates and policy. It calls for a fuller appreciation of the complexities that drive crisis and equal complexity of outcomes that follow. Acknowledging policing is not always the right sector to address every crisis, the text will recognise that at times police remain the only ones capable to respond.

These realities from the frontline reinforce a central message: to meaningfully progress from crisis response to crisis management requires collaboration, not exclusion.

Notes

1 Ballard, E., & Teasdale, B. (2016). Reconsidering the criminalization debate: An examination of the predictors of arrest among people with major mental disorders. *Criminal Justice Policy Review*, *27*(1), 22–45. https://doi.org/10.1177/0887403414561255
2 Chappell, D. (Ed.). (2013). *Policing and the mentally ill: International perspectives.* Routledge. www.routledge.com/Policing-and-the-Mentally-Ill-International-Perspectives/Chappell/p/book/9780367866730

3 Slate, R.N., Frailing, K., Johnson, W.W., & Buffington, J.K. (2021). *The criminalization of mental illness: Crisis and opportunity for the justice system* (3rd ed.). Durham, NC: Carolina Academic Press; Mansour, H., Mueller, C., Davis, K.A.S., Burton, A., Shetty, H., Hotopf, M., Osborn, D., Stewart, R., & Sommerlad, A. (2020). Severe mental illness diagnosis in English general hospitals 2006–2017: A registry linkage study. *PLoS Medicine, 17*(9), e1003306. https://doi.org/10.1371/journal.pmed.1003306

4 Akins, S., Burkhardt, B. C., & Lanfear, C. (2015). Law enforcement response to "frequent fliers": An examination of high-frequency contacts between police and justice-involved persons with mental illness. *Criminal Justice Policy Review*. Advance online publication. https://doi.org/10.1177/0887403414559268; House, A. (2023). Serenity integrated mentoring and the high intensity network: A scheme that raises serious questions for practice and governance in UK psychiatry. *BJPsych Bulletin*, *47*(1), 1–4. https://doi.org/10.1192/bjb.2022.6

5 Substance Abuse and Mental Health Services Administration. (2025). *Model definitions for behavioral health emergency, crisis, and crisis-related services* (HHS Publication No. PEP24-01-037). U.S. Department of Health and Human Services. https://988crisissystemshelp.samhsa.gov/sites/default/files/2025-08/SAMHSA_Model_Definitions_508_080525.pdf

2 Behavioural Health Crisis and Crisis Cycling

Behavioural Health v. Mental Health

To understand behavioural health crisis response, it's important to first understand the concepts that shape current approaches to crisis response and management. Central to this text is the intentional use of the term *Behavioural Health Crisis* rather than *Mental Health Crisis*. While this might seem semantic or a technical difference, it actually represents a critical shift in how these types of crises are understood, classified, and managed both within academic research and operationalisation of practice in the real world.

This text purposely uses the term *Behavioural Health Crisis* to provide a broader and more accurate framing of the diverse and complex conditions that trigger crisis-related calls for service. This choice is guided by the author's 35 years of experience in policing, rather than clinical expertise. Over a decade of the author's policing career was devoted to developing, leading, and training co-responder teams composed of both police and health professionals in Australia. This frontline experience means that the diversity of crisis-related calls and the required responses are well understood from a practical perspective.

This perspective was further informed through research, liaison, and first-hand observations of behavioural health crisis response teams, led by both police and non-police, in North America and the United Kingdom. These experiences allowed the author to undertake active frontline work and participate in real-world training, giving unique insights into an array of approaches adopted globally by stakeholders in crisis intervention.

Why Terminology Matters

The terms *Mental Health Crisis* (MHC) and *Mental Health Call for Service* (MHCFS), though still common in operational, academic, and policy

DOI: 10.4324/9781003749585-2

contexts, tend to oversimplify the complex nature of crises encountered by frontline-responders. It implies a diagnostic clarity that doesn't align with what responders see in practice. Police regularly attend crises shaped by psychiatric, neurodevelopmental, cognitive, substance-related, or situational factors – none of which are easily captured by the term mental health alone.

This limited framing can create operational and systemic blind spots. It risks reinforcing medicalised biases and excludes the lived realities of people whose distress may not fit into recognised diagnostic profiles. As the *World Health Organisation* (2022) observed many mental health crisis services systems:

> operate within outdated legal and regulatory frameworks and an entrenched overreliance on the biomedical model in which the predominant focus of care is on diagnosis, medication and symptom reduction while the full range of social determinants that impact people's mental health are overlooked.
>
> (p. XIII)[1]

However, despite such warning, researchers and policymakers still consistently use terms such as *Persons with Serious Mental Illness* (PwSMI) or *Serious Mental Illness* (SMI) to categorise individuals who engage with crisis response systems.[2] Labels typically referring to people with schizophrenia, bipolar disorder, or major depression with psychotic features. However, Australian emergency department (ED) data shows that these diagnoses are a small portion of crisis presentations. With schizophrenia spectrum (ICD-10 – F20–F29) making up 13%, and mood disorders (ICD-10 – F30–F39) about 8%, together representing less than a quarter of all mental health-related ED crisis visits.[3]

In contrast, over half of ED crisis presentations fall into two distinct categories:[4]

- **F10–F19**: Mental and behavioural disorders due to psychoactive substance use (27%)
- **F40–F49**: Anxiety, stress-related, and somatoform disorders (24%)

A further challenge relates to incidents of *Acute Stress,* also referred to as Situational Distress, which often present as suicidal behaviour in individuals with no diagnosed mental illness. The ICD-10 now includes Acute Stress under F40–F49, with Australian Bureau of Statistics recording this as a leading driver of suicidal presentations to EDs and a major contributor to completed suicides.[5] Highlighting emotional crises without prior diagnoses can still be "serious".

Forewarning: The complexity of suicidality and its implications for first-responders will be explored in greater depth later in this chapter.

Substance Use Disorders (SUD) adds another layer to crisis response, often being tasked under "Mental Health" calls. The New South Wales Police Force report that 23% of police-attended incidents involve SUD as a contributing factor[6] and are the second most common factor in suicidal ED presentations, at a rate of 28.2% of all deliberate self-harm cases.[7]

While not all SUD incidents are mental health calls, the seriousness of SUD misuse and overlap with police mental health calls is clear when looking at arrest rates and the justice system.[8] In Australian prisons:

- 65% of inmates report substance use issues.[9]
- 74% experience both SUD and mental health disorders (9% in the general population).[10]
- 60% of individuals with a mental health diagnosis also experience SUD dependence.[11]

Equally significant is how frequent first-responders, particularly police and the justice system, are dealing with those in crisis who lack any formal diagnoses at the time of intervention. Australian prisons data reveal 29% of detainees were found to have a diagnosable disorder during intake, despite no previous diagnosis.[12]

Despite SUD, Acute Stress, and Anxiety having larger impact on ED crisis presentations, and the frequency of police dealing with the undiagnosed, they remain underrepresented in discussions. Instead, less common but more "serious" diagnoses tend to dominate police training, crisis research, and planning. This shows the limits of traditional "serious mental illness" terminology and stresses the need for a broader, more inclusive perspective of behavioural health.

Terminology Change Is Coming

Fortunately, organisations such as the *American Medical Association* and *Centers for Disease Control and Prevention* have adopted *Behavioural Health* as a broader category that includes suicidality, situational distress, mental illness, and substance use disorders.[13] Language that is gaining traction in North America, yet global uptake remains inconsistent or, in many jurisdictions, non-existent.

Adopting the term *Behavioural Health Crisis* recognises a broader range of causation in real-world settings. However, this definition still fails to fully capture how broad and complex crisis calls are for first-responders. For example, in Australia, 11% of all emergency department crisis admissions are for those with organic mental disorders, such as dementia or neurodivergence (ICD-10 – F00–F09).[14] That's a rate comparable with those "serious mental illness" presentations, yet these cases remain outside most mainstream crisis discussions.

The *Australian Royal Commission into Violence, Abuse, Neglect, and Exploitation of People with Disability* identified this gap in addressing disability in a policing context, and its impact on developing inclusive crisis response systems.[15] Dowse and colleagues also noted criminologists and disability scholars have been slow to examine the intersection of disability and policing, despite the growing need.[16] Concerns only echoed in a recent Australian study that revealed 28% of adolescents presenting to children's hospitals in crisis are neurodivergent.[17]

Another limitation of current terminology focus is the risk of *diagnostic shadowing*.[18] This happens when familiar or dominant labels, such as schizophrenia, end up obscuring other contributing factors, or comorbid conditions in assessment by clinical practitioners. For police and first-responders, this challenge arises in what could be called "*social diagnostic shadowing*" – when callers, often family or friends, may unintentionally misrepresent negative behaviours as a 'mental health crisis'. Such as in situations of domestic violence or illicit drug use, where callers believe behaviours will be more socially acceptable or reduce the likelihood of coercive or criminal outcomes.[19]

The Case for Behavioural Health Terminology

These examples illustrate why language matters. Terminology will guide everything from academic literature, and research funding to legislation and emergency response systems. Narrow terms such as *mental health crisis* and *serious mental illness* do not reflect the realities faced by responders in the real world. Such narrow terms risk reinforcing bias, limiting policy, and creating misaligned crisis frameworks at the expense of those with complex needs.

Police and paramedics are tasked with ensuring immediate safety. Their responses are necessarily procedural, such as arrest or involuntary transport, rather than focusing on long-term clinical care. Diagnostic profiling is rarely available or within capacity in the field, and rigid diagnostic labels do little to aid dynamic resolution.

Rather, adopting broader and more flexible terminology, such as *Behavioural Health Crisis* and *Behavioural Health Call for Service*, provides a better reflection of what responder's encounter: often an intersection of mental health conditions, personality disorders, neurodivergence, substance use, trauma, and emotional distress. This reimagining will better represent what first-responders are encountering in the field. That is, police and first-responders are primarily called to manage "*behaviours*" linked to "*health*" related "*crisis*".

Conclusion

Language will significantly shape how policing and first-responders approach active calls for service. However, rigid clinical terms such *mental health calls for service, or serious mental illness,* fail to fully capture how crises eventuate in the real world. With ever increasing calls for crisis response systems to adopt more inclusive and trauma-informed approaches, so too the language used needs to evolve.

The terms Behavioural Health Crisis and/or Behavioural Health Call for Service enable a broader, systems approach to multiple factors contributing to a crisis, such as neurodiversity, mental health, substance use, situational distress, and co-occurring issues. A term that reflects crisis calls are not neat clinical interventions, rather a call for emergency response systems to act upon *Behaviours,* linked to *Health-related Crisis* requiring an immediate, person-centred response.

Behavioural Health Crisis or Behavioural Health Call for Service encourages collaboration across policing, mental health, social workers, behavioural support, advocacy, and more. By acknowledging the complexity of crisis in the language used to research and operationalise it, it builds a response system shaped to meet the needs of individuals, rather than attempting to fit individuals into diagnostic profiles and treatment pathways.

Chronic Crisis Cycling

When someone is experiencing a behavioural health crisis requiring urgent help, it's often the police, not mental health professionals, who show up first. But how did we get here? Discussions focusing on causation often revolve around two key points: the number of mental health beds available and number of individuals with mental and cognitive health issues in the judicial system.[20]

Points which are critical and will be addressed; however, this chapter aims to move beyond them. Consideration will be given to gaps in care, system fatigue, unmet clinical needs, and without blaming, exploring how those frequently subject to crisis calls may unintentionally shape how crises systems evolve. Looking beyond the traditional deinstitutionalisation/criminalisation, we can explore how a range of factors have influenced crisis care systems that have become reliant upon police response.

Deinstitutionalisation or Systemic Gaps in Care – Results in Criminalisation?

Today's discussions on crisis intervention often centre on police fatal use-of-force. While such incidents are tragic and should be scrutinised, they represent the outliers of police behavioural health engagements. A more common and pressing concern of police involvement in crisis interventions is the criminalisation of behavioural health. This sees those with health issues managed in criminal rather than medical settings. The common argument raised to explain overrepresentation of behavioural health in the criminal justice system is deinstitutionalisation: that is, the large-scale reduction of psychiatric hospital beds and closure of long-term mental health institutions from the mid-20th century onward.[21]

Psychiatric bed numbers fell in the United States from approximately 500,000 in the 1950s to fewer than 40,000 by 2014, despite the population roughly doubling over the same period.[22] The United Kingdom experienced a similar decline, and in Australia, it dropped from 45.5 to 27.5 mental health beds per 100,000 people between 1992–93 and 2019–20, without accounting for the decades of reductions prior.[23]

While bed numbers are often used to gauge the capacity of mental health systems, this focus oversimplifies the issue. Research shows a lack of economic, social, and health community-based supports can create "hotspots", which have higher rates of mental illness, substance use, poverty, housing instability, and crime.[24] Often referred to as 'social convergence', this lack of resourcing can see police filling the gaps as default crisis responders.[25]

This reliance on police to fill the gaps in social "hotspots" likely contributes to criminalisation, as without community-based resources to call upon, officers revert to practices relied upon to tackle criminal recidivism, being the justice system. This justice approach likely contributes not just to a rise in use-of-force during engagement, but increased incarceration rates due to systemic gaps in community care.[26]

Incarceration rates have real-world consequences with nearly half Australian and United States prisoners experiencing mental health problems. In England, the numbers are even higher, especially for women, with nearly 70% of female inmates reporting some form of mental illness.[27]

Rates become more troubling for those with neurodevelopmental conditions. Western Australian research found 89% of juvenile detainees exhibited severe neurodevelopmental impairments, and over one-third were diagnosed with Foetal Alcohol Spectrum Disorder (FASD).[28] US research showed twice the rate of autism in prisons as that of the general population, highlighting their vulnerability to criminalisation rather than care when in crisis.[29]

Such systemic gaps in continuous community care, beyond bed counts alone, underscore how systemic failures reinforce a cycle of crisis and incarceration.

The Emergence of Non-Police Crisis Models

Communities have begun to address these gaps in services with a range of alternative, non-police crisis response models. Paramedic Response Teams are crisis units made up of a paramedic and mental health professional, and one such predominant model is San Francisco's Street Crisis Response Team (SCRT) – a notable example that can provide rapid, specialised care without police intervention.[30]

Another model is the Co-Responder Team approach, which pairs police officers with mental health clinicians to respond together to crisis calls. A well-known example is the Los Angeles Police Department's Systemwide Mental Assessment Response Team (SMART), which has been active in providing joint interventions that balance safety and mental health care.[31]

These teams vary in terms of clinical expertise, staffing, mobility, and capacity in removing police completely from crisis response. We'll take a closer look at each of these models, their structures, and how they operate in practice in chapters: *Community Response and Police Response Modalities.*

Crisis Recidivism

One long-term outcome of reduce community supports is crisis recidivism, the repeated use of police, first-responders, and emergency departments by the same individuals. Crisis recidivism tends to get less attention in crisis discussions, partly as it is difficult to measure, and possibly as it may appear to blame people who are already vulnerable. Yet, research shows there is a small cohort of individuals with complex and unmet behavioural health needs that disproportionately create calls for crisis intervention.

Australian research indicates that just 3% of callers to crisis helplines are responsible for 60% of total contacts.[32] Similar studies in policing suggest fewer than 7% of individuals account for nearly a quarter (23%) of behavioural health-related calls, and around one-in-four people contacted by police during a behavioural health crisis had previous incidents under similar circumstances.[33]

A pattern which continues through the crisis care continuum with hospital emergency departments also being heavily impacted by recidivism. Approximately 70% of individuals who present to EDs during crisis return within 28 days with the same or similar concerns.[34] While EDs are designed to be reactive, this level of recidivism risks them becoming de-facto crisis stabilisation centres to fill gaps in long-term community supports, much like policing.

This gap highlights a critical flaw in the system: failure to create effective long-term community supports leads to a revolving door between police encounters, emergency medical care, and the criminal justice system, thus resulting in a cohort of individuals who become locked in a pattern the author refers to as *chronic crisis cycling*.

Defining Chronic Crisis Cycling

Individuals caught in patterns of behavioural health crisis cycling are disproportionately at risk, not only to themselves, but also from or to first-responders, the public, and police. Over time, these individuals tend to become well known to frontline services and may be labelled, sometimes informally, sometimes institutionally, as "Frequent Flyers," "High Intensity Users," or "Chronic Consumers."[35]

While colloquial phrases are common across sectors, they lack precision and definitive definition. Importantly, they risk reinforcing implicit biases amongst service providers and worse stigmatising individuals who are locked in patterns of crisis often through no fault of their own. Evidence from both policing and clinical sectors shows such biases can affect effectiveness of care provision during crisis.

Merino and colleagues (2019) observe that, as mental health services are often provided on a one-to-one basis, clinicians act as gatekeepers to care, parallelling how police are portrayed in much of current academic literature.[36] This gatekeeping means biases attached to chronic crisis cycling can directly impact outcomes, particularly obstruction referrals into long-term community support.

A common starting point in attempting to define *chronic crisis cycling* is to ask, "how often is too often?" But frequency alone is too simplistic for such complexity. High contact rates may signal concern in terms of wellbeing. But what are the drivers, patterns, and risk of a person's crisis cycling? Focusing on numbers alone obscures the complexity and diversity of an individual's needs and the failures preventing long-term wellbeing?[37]

To illustrate the limitations of a frequency-based definition, consider the two contrasting, real-world examples:

- **Individual A** has a diagnosed behavioural health condition and calls emergency services several times a week. These calls typically relate to non-dangerous delusional beliefs – such as imagined emergencies – that increase their sense of distress but do not pose a risk to themselves or others. Often, a brief phone interaction is all that's needed. While their behaviour does create a frequent level of demand on emergency resources, the overall risk profile is minimal.

- **Individual B** also has a behavioural health diagnosis, with chronic suicidality as a key feature. Their behaviours are high risk, often life-threatening, and usually necessitate urgent interventions such as resuscitation or intensive care. However, their crisis interventions occur only monthly or bi-monthly.

Clearly, Individual A interacts more frequently with services, yet the intensity and potential consequences of Individual B's crises are far greater. This comparison highlights a core challenge: the most visible metric (frequency) may not be the most meaningful one when it comes to assessing risk, need, or requirement for pathways into long-term care.

Accordingly, any practical definition of *chronic crisis cycling* must go beyond frequency to also consider *risk*. The author proposes a more useful approach is the application of a structured matrix – one that evaluates not just how often an individual engages with services, but also the level of risk they present – as shown in Table 2.1. Risk, in this context, can be considered across several dimensions:

- **People**: the degree of harm to the individual or others (e.g., none, injury, hospitalisation, death)
- **Reputation**: implications for public trust in sectors and legitimacy of their actions
- **Liability**: potential legal or professional consequences for sectors or individual first-responders, ranging from unlikely to highly probable

Therefore, the author proposes the following as an initial definition to start defining the phenomenon that is Chronic Crisis Cycling:

> Individuals whose repeated interactions with emergency services, particularly police and emergency departments, occurs in the absence of effective long-term care interventions, and which may involve a real and significant risk to themselves, to others, and/or to public safety.

This definition aims not to blame, discriminate, or stereotype, but to frame crisis cycling as a system-level issue that demands thoughtful, multi-sectoral, and multi-faceted management.

What Creates Chronic Crisis Cycling

Chronic crisis cycling is often attributed to deinstitutionalisation, reduced mental health beds, or affecting persons with serious mental illness, but the

Table 2.1 Chronic Crisis Cycling Risk Matrix

[Chronic Crisis Cycling Risk Matrix]							
Consequences			*Resourcing Demand*				
People	Reputation	Liability	Daily	Weekly	Monthly	Quarterly	Infrequently
Death to Self/ Others	National Exposure	Highly Probable	**Extreme**	High	High	High	Moderate
Permanent Disability	Localised Exposure	Probable	High	High	High	Moderate	Moderate
Minor Hospitalisation	Affected Parties	Limited	High	Moderate	Moderate	Moderate	Low
Limited Health Affect	Limited	Unlikely	Moderate	Moderate	Moderate	Low	Low
None	None	None	Moderate	Moderate	Low	Low	Low

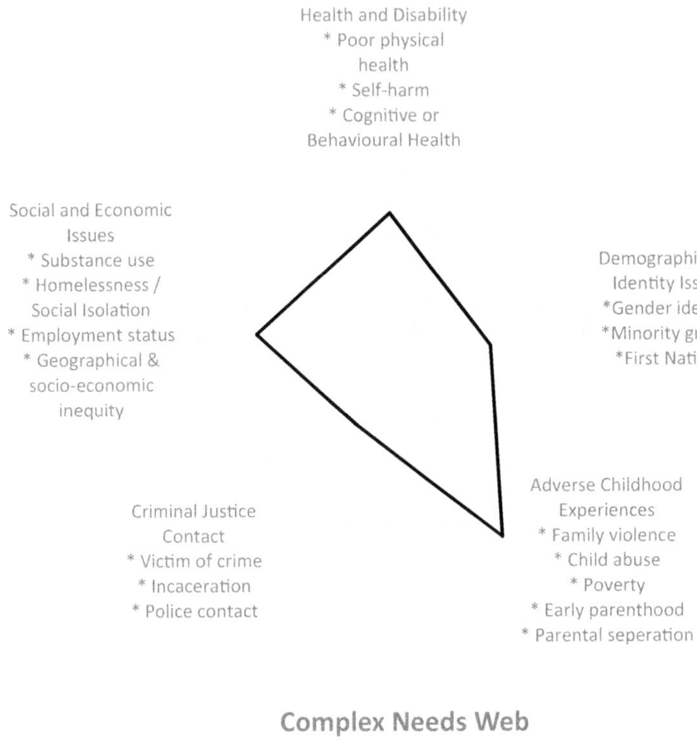

Figure 2.1 Complex Needs Web.

issue is much more complex. Baldry and Dowse (2013) have come up with a powerful way to illustrate this complexity with their "Complex Needs Web".[38] This web presents a visualisation of the interconnectedness of multiple factors, from health and trauma to social and judicial challenges, which impact on a person's pattern of crisis.

The Complex Needs Web as shown in Figure 2.1, reproduced with the consent of the creators, maps 'disadvantageous factors' contributing to an individual's chronic crisis cycling. Visibly identifying these factors assists in holistically understanding the drivers of chronic crisis cycling, challenging assumptions some individuals choose, or fail, when caught in these patterns. Instead, it illustrates the complexity of social needs and service delivery gaps which enable ongoing vulnerability. For many, becoming a so-called 'frequent flyer' is not so much a choice, but systems failure. This re-framing in turn prompts a question: are we building systems to respond to the symptoms of crisis, or are we failing to build systems supporting pathways to wellbeing and break the cycle?

The Impact of Crisis Cycling

Failing to address Chronic Crisis Cycling has real-world negative consequences. Research from Australia identified 67% of prisoners released with co-occurring mental health and substance use disorders were re-incarcerated, compared to 51% among those without such conditions.[39] In Los Angeles, nearly one-third of incarcerated individuals with mental illness were re-arrested and re-incarcerated ten or more times, generally for low-level offending.[40] These patterns illustrate how untreated chronic crisis cycling can lead to disproportionate justice system involvement.

Findings supported by a Connecticut study examining 18- to 21-year-olds with serious mental illness who were already engaged in the justice system. It was reported that while there are established programs aimed to reduce justice involvement in the general population, no such evidence-based interventions existed for this vulnerable group.[41]

Conclusion

As a frontline police officer, who has spent many years responding to behavioural health crisis calls, the author can confirm most officers ask "*Why are we the ones, repeatedly showing up first?*". The question becomes even more poignant when responding to the same individuals again and again who are clearly locked in a cycle of crisis.

Ultimately, impactful reform requires sustained investment in community-based support, shifting from reactive to proactive strategies, and a reimagining how emergency services, including police, recognise patterns of chronic crisis cycling. Until then, police officers and other first-responders will continue as the default long-term care for many vulnerable individuals in our community.

Behavioural Health v. Suicidality Calls – Are They the Same?

This section explores whether suicidality should automatically be treated as a behavioural health crisis requiring police or clinical intervention, or if any interventions are required, from looking at the history of police involvement in suicide, societal expectations, clinical perspectives, and suicide in other contexts. However, before the reader progresses into the section, please take time to read the following content warning.

Content Warning

This chapter contains open discussions of suicide, self-harm, and related case studies. If this material may be distressing, please engage with caution and ensure you have appropriate supports available.
While this chapter explores historical, legal, and social perspectives on suicide, it does not seek to influence readers' personal beliefs. Readers are encouraged to critically reflect and form their own views of suicide and suicidality.

Behavioural Health Calls

Calls for service to police and first-responders involving behavioural health concerns often originate from members of the public, family, or even the individual in crisis. They call because of observing erratic, distressing, or highly unusual behaviours often creating a sense of foreseeable harm. Many of these presentations frequently involve delusional thinking, responses to hallucinations, or other conditions which manifest in observable concerning, or out of character behaviours, or behaviours consistent with cognitive impairment.

From the author's operational experience, such presentations can appear as:

- Individuals reporting repeated burglaries in which no evidence of forced entry is found, but they believe unknown persons enter their homes, moving personal items or consuming food.
- Individuals with cognitive impairment undertaking repetitive and unusual behaviours in high public traffic spaces after becoming separated from carers.
- Callers expressing beliefs neighbours, government agencies, or unknown persons are monitoring or controlling them via electronic means such as the internet or mobile phones.
- Individuals convinced noxious gasses are being pumped into their residence in an attempt to harm or control them.
- A particularly notable example involved a person in an affluent entertainment precinct stabbing motor-vehicles with a large knife whenever occupants entered the vehicle. The individual believed the vehicles were hostile actors attempting to abduct and harm the occupants.

Each of these examples clearly reflect a profound disturbance in perception or cognition, most likely based in some form of psychiatric illness or cognitive impairment. These situations clearly meet the criterion for classification as a behavioural health crisis requiring the support of clinically trained professionals.

However, while such examples can be attributed to psychiatric illness, a substantial proportion of Behavioural Health Calls for Service are triggered instead by expressions or indications of suicidality. It is estimated that up to 20% of police time may be consumed by such calls.[42] Suicidality, whether voiced directly, implied, or inferred from behaviours, often instigates a chain of emergency responses. Police, ambulance, and other first-responders subsequently prioritise such calls reacting swiftly to apprehend the individual, typically under local mental health legislation, evidenced by involuntary transportation rates to hospital emergency department for psychiatric assessment.[43]

However, this practice raises important questions:

- Are police and first-responders over-interpreting their legislative powers and exceeding legal justification? or
- Are first-responders simply relying on overly cautious institutionalised culture driven by a fear of professional liability?

These questions are not merely academic. They explore the limitations of legislation, first-responders' authority, and thresholds for involuntary apprehension. They also raise a broader philosophical debate about autonomy and an individual's right to die, and who has the authority to determine this. If so, what frameworks, legal, clinical, or moral, should guide such decisions? In addition, these questions highlight the existing terminology and call classification under the banner of "Behavioural Health Crisis" may be too broad, potentially leading to implicit bias by first-responders which results in inappropriate interventions. Such questions must be explored to inform future policy, practice, and training.

How Did Suicide Become a Policing Response?

In the early 19th century, suicide was criminalised as "self-murder" and prosecuted as an offence. Sir William Blackstone, a leading English legal scholar of the time, observed to obtain a conviction of such matter's individuals must 'be of discretion and in their senses' or else it is no crime or prosecutable.[44] Once found guilty of 'self-murder', punishment extended beyond the criminal courts: financially, with property forfeited to the English Crown, and spiritually, being denied burial in Christian consecrated grounds for their sins. Subsequently, coronial juries had a tendency to find those who died by suicide were evidently insane, thus negating those spiritual and financial hardships imposed upon surviving families.[45]

Paralleling this criminal debate was the emergence of life insurance and subsequently a section of those covered who died by suicide.[46] This generated further medico-legal debate, as highlighted by the 1861 English case *Horne v Anglo-Australian and Universal Family Life Assurance Company*, where the coroner's jury ruled Mr. Horne had taken his life "*whilst in a state of mental derangement*".[47] However, all agreed death by suicide implied mental illness. James Foulis Duncan, president of the British Medico-Psychological Association, questioned this assumption writing "*cases of suicide may and do occur when the person is not insane, without, at the same time, falling into great inconsistency*".[48]

Despite such medico-legal debates, suicide remained an offence across most countries until the 1960s, a long-time legacy of criminalisation which entwined policing with suicide and its regulation.

Decriminalisation of Suicide but Legal and Medical Conflict Continues

The United Kingdom's *Suicide Act 1961* was tabled in parliament to decriminalise the act of suicide. The political debate was summed up by Member Richard Butler who stated "It is not to allow people to commit suicide... It is to relive people who unsuccessfully attempt suicide from being liable to criminal proceedings".[49] While this legislative change was a global shift in the criminalisation of suicide, the UK Ministry of Health simultaneously directed GPs or Hospitals to automatically refer all attempted suicide presentations for psychiatric assessment, reinforcing suicide as an evidence of mental illness.[50]

This medico-legal conflict continued into the late 20th century, though shifting from criminal to civil law, particularly around wills and insurance. In the Australian case *Shorter v Hodges 14 NSWLR 1988* the court was required to make a ruling after the deceased shot himself shortly after making a will. Acting on psychiatric evidence, the court concluded that suicide does not, by itself, indicate insanity or a lack of testamentary capacity.[51]

Moving away from the medico-legal debate, contemporary research has begun to re-examine the motives and contexts behind suicide in addition to the connection between suicide and behavioural health – with studies such as a recent large-scale psychological autopsy of 3,275 suicides across the globe. The study found while 87.3% of those who died by suicide had a pre-existing mental disorder, it showed nearly 13% did not. Findings which challenge assumptions that suicide is always a symptom of psychiatric illnesses and reinforce the need to view suicide as a nuanced issue, separate from broader behavioural health crisis.[52]

Acceptance of Suicide as a Conscious Action

Voluntary euthanasia, or Medical Aid In Dying (MAID), provides a clear example of societies ability to clearly separate suicidality from mental illness. In jurisdictions where MAID is legal, terminally ill individuals may request medical assistance to end their lives under strict safeguards which ensure the individual is of sound mind and not suffering from a treatable mental illness.[53] Legislations such as California's *End of Life Option Act*, Oregon's

Death with Dignity Act, and New Zealand's *End of Life Choice Act* reflect societies and the states shift in accepting these decisions as autonomy and not mental illness.[54]

This distinction has implications on first-responders and mental health professionals when engaging chronically suicidal individuals, particularly when linked to those with personality disorders and/or unresolved severe complex trauma. A relatively small group remain locked in chronic crisis cycling, experiencing repeated emergency interventions, and hospitalisations, yet exhibit little long-term recovery. Research indicates such interventions can create further trauma, and for some individuals, repeated coercive crisis intervention may erode autonomy and actually exacerbate their distress.[55] Although many individuals with complex trauma meet criteria for mental illness, this does not automatically preclude mental capacity. Though complex PTSD (and some other treatment resistant conditions) are not terminal, they can overwhelmingly diminish quality of life. Raising the ethical question: if the state has relaxed intervention in cases of terminal physical illness, should similar reconsideration be applied to chronic psychological suffering, particularly if current interventions may increase harm?

Another societal delineation of capacity and suicide emerges in the context of intimate partner violence (IPV). Here, suicidality has become a tool of emotional coercion: suicidal statements or suicidal behaviours are not expressions on internal crisis, rather they are used to manipulate or threaten another.[56] With research suggesting this has become one of the most frequent behaviours used by perpetrators of IPV.[57] Direct research of IPV perpetrators has confirmed these actions are often premeditated and calculated, intended to cause emotional and psychological harm on the victim.[58] Governments have adapted to this understanding; for example, in Australia Victoria's *Family Violence Protection Act 2008*, the use of suicidality is recognised as emotional abuse and coercive control, allowing for criminal prosecution of perpetrators.[59]

The following is an excerpt of the Victorian *Family Violence Protection Act 2008* with specific reference to suicide italicised and bold[60]:

> Section 7 Meaning of emotional or psychological abuse
>
> For the purposes of this Act, emotional or psychological abuse means behaviour by a person towards another person that torments, intimidates, harasses or is offensive to the other person.
>
> Examples:
>
> - repeated derogatory taunts, including racial taunts;
> - threatening to disclose a person's sexual orientation to the person's friends or family against the person's wishes;
> - threatening to withhold a person's medication;

- preventing a person from making or keeping connections with the person's family, friends or culture, including cultural or spiritual ceremonies or practices, or preventing the person from expressing the person's cultural identity;
- *threatening to commit suicide or self-harm with the intention of tormenting or intimidating a family member*, or threatening the death or injury of another person.

This *weaponisation* of suicidality creates another layer of challenges for police, mental health professionals, and crisis response systems. Effective crisis systems will require nuanced, trauma-informed, and IPV-aware approach, particularly when responding to suicide threats within known abusive relationships.[61] However, professionals must remain cautious. While threats may be manipulative, they do not preclude the risk of actual suicide. Research indicates individuals who use suicidality coercively may still die by suicide, underscoring the complexity of these cases.[62] Again highlighting how suicidality is a distinctly separate issue to behavioural health crisis.

Do Police Hold a Duty of Care?

Such complexity in understanding suicidality highlights suicide cannot be reduced only to individual cognitive or mental illness. This re-framing challenges long-standing assumptions of suicide and requires renewed exploration of institutional responsibility for suicide response. For police officers (and first-responders), they need to ask if they have a legal or ethical obligation to intervene when someone expresses suicidal thoughts. Considerations such as these create operational tension for police officers: who may feel moral pressure to act, yet become cautious regarding the limits of their authority and legal liability.

When an individual expresses suicidal ideation but appears calm, rational, and has no intention, it is unclear whether police intervention is justified or lawful. These circumstances raise the difficult question about a police officer's "duty of care," and whether they are obligated to prevent harm – a concern not only for officers, but also for the families, friends, and communities seeking help.

A landmark Australian case provides legal clarity.[63] In *Stuart V Kirkland-Veenstra [2009]*, the High Court of Australia considered whether two police officers held a duty of care to a man found sitting in a car with a hose from the exhaust into the cabin.[64] Although presenting as indicators of an apparent suicide attempt, officers noted he appeared calm, lucid, and rational, stating he was going home to his wife. Tragically, he died by suicide shortly after the interaction. The High Court ruled that as officers believed he showed no signs of mental illness, they did not have capacity to invoke powers under mental health legislation. This decision reinforced a key legal principle in Australia: police do not automatically have a duty of care to intervene in cases of suicidality or interfere with an individual's autonomy, unless clear signs of mental illness are present and legal thresholds are met.

This legal stance is not unique to Australia, with United States courts delivering similar rulings. In *Adams v. City of Fremont* [1998], the California Court of Appeal held police officers did not have a legal duty to prevent a man from dying by suicide after their brief interaction.[65] The court emphasised tort law does not impose a duty on police to prevent someone from taking their own life. Highlighting officers must prioritise the safety of themselves and others rather than prevent suicide in the absence of a clear and immediate danger to others.

Tactical Disengagement and Changing Policing Models

In response to these judicial directions and operational realities, some police departments have shifted their approach to calls involving behavioural health crises. One notable example is the Los Angeles Police Department's 2019 adoption of a *Tactical Disengagement* policy.[66] An approach, now adopted by agencies across the US, allowing officers to delay or even avoid engagement when a person in crisis does not pose an immediate threat to others or intervention may escalate the situation. Officers can choose to leave the scene, observe from a distance, or return at a more appropriate time, acknowledging that not every situation requires immediate or coercive intervention.[67] This concept, and its implications, will be explored further in the chapter *Non-Clinical Outcomes to Crisis*

Conclusion: Arrest to Care or Still Arrest

Historically suicide was treated as a crime or "Self-Murder" requiring police to arrest and prosecute. Only to be systematically changed by medico-legal practitioners to a symptom of Mental Illness, changing police responses from criminal to medical.[68] Yet, today's *health* response still more often triggers priority arrival of police or non-police responders, questioning of autonomy and often coercive involuntary medical care, echoing 18th century criminal arrests.

While 18th century directions changed suicide from a crime to a symptom of mental illness, today's courts have shifted and taken a different view. Courts have said that suicidality alone does not automatically infer mental illness. A distinction highlighted by the High Court of Australia finding officers "*could not have apprehended him unless they believed him to be mentally ill*", when dealing with a suicidal person.[69] This requires policymakers and crisis responders to ask whether behavioural health calls and suicide calls are the same, and if police or responders assume obligations under common law or mental health legislation.[70]

This assumption of an obligation has real-world impact on a bigger question, autonomy. Modern ethical debate acknowledges the right of "competent adults of sound mind [to] make legally binding voluntary choices, including the so-called 'death-choice' being the refusal of life-sustaining or life-prolonging treatment as well as suicide".[71] With increased acceptance of medical aid in dying, and emerging understanding of suicide in intimate partner violence, it does not mean discussion of autonomy doesn't create concern and division.

However, modern understanding requires an honest assessment of whether repeated police or clinical interventions, especially coercive interventions, are protecting and improving an individual's wellbeing. Or are such crisis interventions undermining autonomy, creating more harm to the individual and perpetuating stigma of suicidality in society?

This complexity raises an important question. If police are not legally compelled to intervene, and society questions an officer's capacity to override an individual's autonomy, then who should go? Should health services be more assertive in crisis response to suicide calls? Should communities establish non-clinical interventions? Or does society need to accept not every call for suicidality requires a priority response, if at all? Questions which need to be examined to balance safety, respect of an individual's choice, and societal needs.

Ultimately, this discussion encourages readers to critically assess whether a call for suicidal ideation alone justifies police or clinical intervention under the banner of behavioural health. Does suicide require a separate response framework? Or are current reactive interventions simply echoing 18th century persecution? More broadly these questions invite reflection on what alternative frameworks would look like to address suicide less coercively, with more compassion, dignity, and effectiveness.

Observational Summary

The concept of "crisis", particularly as encountered by frontline emergency responders such as police officers, displays in a wide range of behavioural presentations. In these moments, the immediate objective is to ensure the safety of all individuals involved. However, first-responders are increasingly operating within a system heavily influenced by diagnostic classifications and clinical frameworks that do not align with the realities of real-time crisis response.

Emergency personnel, especially police, rarely have the capacity to perform comprehensive clinical assessments during these interactions. Whether the individual is experiencing a cognitive impairment such as Foetal Alcohol

Spectrum Disorder, a schizoaffective episode, substance-induced psychosis, undiagnosed or comorbid conditions, responders are ultimately tasked with managing the behaviours before them, rather than undertaking clinical diagnoses. The overemphasis on clinical diagnostic profiles in research, proposed training frameworks, policies, and clinical supports often hinders rather than helps in these high-pressure scenarios.

To more accurately reflect the nature of these encounters, the term *Behavioural Health Crisis* has emerged as a more practical and inclusive phrase. It captures the behavioural exhibition of a health condition, whether psychiatric, neurodevelopmental, substance-related, or situational-crisis, that prompts an emergency call for service (or BHCFS). This terminology shifts the focus from diagnostic labels to the observable behaviours that require intervention, aligning more closely with the operational realities mandated to police and other emergency responders.

Building on this discussion, it was identified a small cohort of individuals can become repeatedly entangled within crisis response systems. These individuals re-present from one crisis to another and continually remain managed in a reactive system, with little prospect of transition into longitudinal care. Over time, this group has been labelled with stigmatising terms such as "frequent flyers", rather than being acknowledged as individuals with unmet needs. This pattern of chronic crisis cycling would suggest there is a pressing need to be recognised and understood as an emerging distinct sub-group within crisis intervention frameworks, requiring renewed exploration of nuanced support, care pathways, and policy development.

Lastly, the chapter explored a timely topical question for first-responders. Asking is there a difference between behavioural health crisis and suicidality? Behavioural health crisis is a broad category of presentations, clearly defined in a disturbance of behavioural health wellbeing. However, legal and clinical frameworks increasingly recognise that suicidality alone does not necessarily constitute a behavioural health disorder. In some jurisdictions, suicidal thoughts alone have been held as insufficient grounds for involuntary apprehension, challenging assumptions all instances of suicidality justify police action under statutory mental health powers.[72]

Assumptions, challenged within a range of non-clinical contexts, including medical assistance in dying, and intimate partner violence, which in this last point has even been criminalised. Further, we explored what is the actual impact of repeated intervention, on those chronically suicidal individuals locked in a chronic crisis cycle pattern?

As alluded to earlier this renewed understanding raises deep ethical and legal questions for frontline crisis responders: Does the state possess a legitimate mandate to override a person's expressed will to die in the name of protection? If so, what frameworks, legal, clinical, or moral, should guide such decisions? Does suicidality hold a legitimate position under the broader category of behavioural health crisis, or does it demand its own distinct response model, reflective of its unique complexity?

These are not questions with definitive answers, nor are they raised with the intention of resolving the debate. Rather, they are posed to encourage critical reflection and considered dialogue across affected sectors. As jurisdictions seek to build more coherent and collaborative crisis response systems, it is essential for future discussions to differentiate between behavioural health crises, excessive diagnostic profiling and voluntary decisions regarding life and death. Without such distinctions, crisis responses risk becoming ethically inconsistent, legally hazardous, and clinically ineffective.

The challenges outlined here could be attributed, in part, to decades of health systems withdrawing frontline services and fragmentation, compounded by a diagnostic culture that could be perceived to serve the interests of specialised disciplines more than the individuals in crisis. This chapter sets the foundation for a broader exploration of how behavioural health crises are managed, the evolution of specialist intervention models, and the consequences of systemic fragmentation. It argues for a realignment of crisis response systems toward their core mission: safeguarding the wellbeing of vulnerable individuals through timely, appropriate, and coordinated care.

Notes

1 World Health Organization. (2022). *World mental health report: Transforming mental health for all.* World Health Organization. https://iris.who.int/handle/10665/356119

2 Slate, R. N., Frailing, K., Johnson, W. W., & Buffington, J. K. (2021). *The criminalization of mental illness: Crisis and opportunity for the justice system* (3rd ed.). Durham, NC: Carolina Academic Press; Mansour, H., Mueller, C., Davis, K. A. S., Burton, A., Shetty, H., Hotopf, M., Osborn, D., Stewart, R., & Sommerlad, A. (2020). Severe mental illness diagnosis in English general hospitals 2006–2017: A registry linkage study. *PLoS Medicine, 17*(9), e1003306. https://doi.org/10.1371/journal.pmed.1003306

3 Australian Institute of Health and Welfare [AIHW]. (2023). *Mental health services provided in emergency care.* www.aihw.gov.au/mental-health/topic-areas/emergency-departments

4 Australian Institute of Health and Welfare. (2023). *Mental health services provided in emergency care.* Australian Institute of Health and Welfare. www.aihw.gov.au/mental-health/topic-areas/emergency-departments

5 O'Hare, K., Watkeys, O., & Dean, K. (2023). Self-harm and suicidal ideation among young people is more often recorded by child protection than health services in an Australian population cohort. *Australian & New Zealand Journal of Psychiatry, 57*(12), 1527–37. https://doi.org/10.1177/00048674231179652 Bøe, A.S., Mehlum, L., Melle, I., & Qin, P. (2023). Psychiatric disorders

among adult deliberate self-harm patients and subsequent risk of dying by suicide, mental and behavioural disorders and other external causes. *Journal of Psychiatric Research*, *165*, 83–90, ISSN 0022-3956, https://doi.org/10.1016/j.jpsychires.2023.07.011.

6 Fuller, G., Goldsmid, S., & Brown, R. (2016). *Managing intoxicated offenders: Best practice in responding to individuals affected by drugs and alcohol.* www.aic.gov.au/sites/default/files/2020-05/monograph-65.pdf

7 O'Hare, K., Watkeys, O., & Dean, K. (2023). Self-harm and suicidal ideation among young people is more often recorded by child protection than health services in an Australian population cohort. *Australian & New Zealand Journal of Psychiatry, 57*(12), 1527–1537. https://doi.org/10.1177/00048674231179652; Seljenes Bøe, A. S., Mehlum, L., Melle, I., & Qin, P. (2023). Psychiatric disorders among adult deliberate self-harm patients and subsequent risk of dying by suicide, mental and behavioural disorders and other external causes. *Journal of Psychiatric Research*, *165*, 83–90, ISSN 0022-3956, https://doi.org/10.1016/j.jpsychires.2023.07.011.

8 Baser, O., Rodchenko, K., Zeng, Y., et al. (2024). Mental health disparities in young adults with arrest history: A survey-based, cross-sectional analysis. *Health Justice*, *12*(1). https://doi.org/10.1186/s40352-023-00257-2; Watson, A. C., & Fulambarker, A. J. (2012). The crisis intervention team model of police response to mental health crises: A primer for mental health practitioners. *Best Practices in Mental Health*, *8*(2), 71. PMID: 24039557; PMCID: PMC3769782.

9 Australian Institute of Health and Welfare. (2019). *The health of Australia's prisoners 2018.* Canberra: AIHW. doi:10.25816/5ec5c381ed17a; Willis, T., Comartin, E., Victor, G., Kern, L., & Kubiak, S. (2021). Individuals with mental illness who have multiple encounters with law enforcement. *Journal of Offender Rehabilitation*, *60*(2), 117–37. https://10.1080/10509674.2020.1863298

10 Australian Institute of Health and Welfare. (2019). *The health of Australia's prisoners 2018.* Canberra: AIHW. doi:10.25816/5ec5c381ed17a; Willis, T., Comartin, E., Victor, G., Kern, L., & Kubiak, S. (2021). Individuals with mental illness who have multiple encounters with law enforcement. *Journal of Offender Rehabilitation*, *60*(2), 117–137. https://10.1080/10509674.2020.1863298

11 Fuller, G., Goldsmid, S., & Brown, R. (2016). *Managing intoxicated offenders: Best practice in responding to individuals affected by drugs and alcohol.* www.aic.gov.au/sites/default/files/2020-05/monograph-65.pdf; Jaffe, A., Jiang, D., & Huang, D. (2012). Drug-abusing offenders with co-morbid disorders: Problem severity, treatment participation, and recidivism. *Journal of Substance Abuse Treatment*, *43*, 244–50.

12 Forsythe, L., & Gaffney, A. (2012). Mental disorder prevalence at the gateway to the criminal justice system. *Trends & Issues in Crime and Criminal Justice No. 438.* Canberra: Australian Institute of Criminology. https://doi.org/10.52922/ti252064

13 American Medical Association. (2022). *What is behavioral health?* www.ama-assn.org/delivering-care/public-health/what-behavioral-health#; US Centers for Disease Control and Prevention. (2024). *About behavioral health.*

www.cdc.gov/mental-health/about/about-behavioral-health.html#:~:text=Behavioral%20health%20is%20a%20key,and%20behaviors%2C%20and%20substance%20use

14 Australian Institute of Health and Welfare [AIHW]. (2023). *Mental health services provided in emergency care.* www.aihw.gov.au/mental-health/topic-areas/emergency-departments

15 Royal Commission. (2023). *Royal Commission into violence, abuse, neglect and exploitation of people with disability, criminal justice and people with disability.* https://disability.royalcommission.gov.au/system/files/2023-09/Final%20Report%20-%20Volume%208%2C%20Criminal%20justice%20and%20people%20with%20disability.pdf

16 Dowse, L., Rowe, S., Baldry, E., & Baker, M. (2021). Research report police responses to people with disability. *Royal Commission into violence, abuse, neglect and exploitation of people with disability.* https://disability.royalcommission.gov.au/publications/police-responses-people-disability

17 Bourke, E. M., Say, D. F., Carison, A., Hill, A., Craig, S., Hiscock, H., Babl, F. E., & O'Donnell, S. M. (2021). Emergency mental health presentations in children with autism spectrum disorder and attention deficit hyperactivity disorder. *Journal of Paediatrics and Child Health, 57*, 1572–9. https://doi.org/10.1111/jpc.15535

18 Shefer, G., Henderson, C., Howard, L. M., Murray, J., & Thornicroft, G. (2014). Diagnostic overshadowing and other challenges involved in the diagnostic process of patients with mental illness who present in emergency departments with physical symptoms–A qualitative study. *PLoS One. 9*(11), e111682. https://doi.org/10.1371/journal.pone.0111682. PMID: 25369130; PMCID: PMC4219761; Willis, T., Comartin, E., Victor, G., Kern, L., & Kubiak, S. (2021). Individuals with mental illness who have multiple encounters with law enforcement. *Journal of Offender Rehabilitation, 60.* https://doi.org/10.1080/10509674.2020.1863298.

19 WANADA, Women's Council for Domestic and Family Violence Services (WA), & Women's Community Health Network WA. (2022). *Towards an integrated response to domestic and family violence, alcohol and other drugs, and mental health: Project report.* Western Australian Network of Alcohol and other Drug Agencies. https://wanada.org.au/wp-content/uploads/wanada-wchn-wcfdvs-sfv-towards-integrated-response-to-dfv-aod-mh-project-report.pdf; Her Majesty's Inspectorate of Constabulary and Fire & Rescue Services (HMICFRS). (2018). *Policing and mental health: Picking up the pieces.* London: HMICFRS. www.justiceinspectorates.gov.uk/hmicfrs/publications/policing-and-mental-health-picking-up-the-pieces/

20 Slate, R. N., Frailing, K., Johnson, W. W., & Buffington, J. K. (2021). *The criminalization of mental illness: Crisis and opportunity for the justice system* (3rd ed.). Durham, NC: Carolina Academic Press; Siller, S. (2020). *Deinstitutionalization, mental health, and criminal populations: How the process of deinstitutionalization affected current incarceration rates of the mentally ill.* [PDF]. ResearchGate. www.researchgate.net/publication/342282257_Deinstitutionalization_Mental_Health_and_Criminal_Populations

21 Slate, R. N., Frailing, K., Johnson, W. W., & Buffington, J. K. (2021). *The criminalization of mental illness: Crisis and opportunity for the justice system* (3rd ed.). Durham, NC: Carolina Academic Press; Siller, S. (2020). *Deinstitutionalization, mental health, and criminal populations: How the process of deinstitutionalization affected current incarceration rates of the mentally ill.* [PDF]. ResearchGate. www.researchgate.net/publication/342282257_Deinstitutionalization_Mental_Health_and_Criminal_Populations

22 *American Journal of Psychiatry.* (2022). The psychiatric bed crisis in the United States: understanding the problem and moving toward solutions. *American Journal of Psychiatry, 179*(8), 586–88. https://doi.org/10.1176/appi.ajp.22179004; Statista. (2025). *Population of the United States from 1610 to 2020.* www.statista.com/statistics/1067138/population-united-states-historical/

23 Bourke, J. (2021). Historical perspectives on mental health and psychiatry. In G. Ikkos & N. Bouras (Eds.), *Mind, state and society: Social history of psychiatry and mental health in britain 1960–2010* (pp. 3–12). Cambridge: Cambridge University Press; Statista. (2025). *Estimated population of the United Kingdom from 1871 to 2023.* www.statista.com/statistics/281296/uk-population/; Australian Medical Association. (2025). *National overview public hospital capacity – Mental health care.* www.ama.com.au/clear-the-hospital-logjam/mhrc-national#:~:text=Measured%20by%20100%2C000%20population%2C%20a%20significant%20reduction%20in,of%20available%20mental%20health%20beds%20per%20100%2C000%20population.

24 Kyprianides, A., & Bradford, B. (2025). Policing and mental health: A rapid evidence assessment of the patterning of police activity. *The Police Journal.* https://doi.org/10.1177/0032258X251318210

25 Kyprianides, A., & Bradford, B. (2025). Policing and mental health: A rapid evidence assessment of the patterning of police activity. *The Police Journal.* https://doi.org/10.1177/0032258X251318210

26 Richard Lamb, H., & Weinberger, L. E. (2005). The shift of psychiatric inpatient care from hospitals to jails and prisons. *The Journal of the American Academy of Psychiatry and the Law, 33*(4), 529–34.

27 Australian Bureau of Statistics. (2021). *Prisoners in Australia.* www.abs.gov.au/statistics/people/crime-and-justice/prisoners-australia/latest-release.

US Department of Justice. (June 2021). *Indicators of mental health problems reported by prisoners.* Maruschak, Laura & Bronson, Jennifer Bureau of Justice Statistics. https://bjs.ojp.gov/sites/g/files/xyckuh236/files/media/document/imhprpspi16st.pdf; House of Commons. (2022). *Mental health in prison fifth report of session 2021-22.* https://committees.parliament.uk/publications/7455/documents/78054/default/.

28 Bower, C., Watkins, R. E., Mutch, R. C., et al. (2018). Foetal alcohol spectrum disorder and youth justice: a prevalence study among young people sentenced to detention in Western Australia. *BMJ Open, 8*, e019605. https://doi.org/10.1136/bmjopen-2017-019605.

29 Fazio, R., Pietz, C., & Denney, R. (2012). An estimate of the prevalence of autism-spectrum disorders in an incarcerated population. *Open Access Journal of Forensic Psychology*, *4*, 69–80.
30 San Francisco Government [sf.gov]. (2022). *Street crisis response team pilot final report.* www.sf.gov/sites/default/files/2022-06/SCRT%20Final%20Report_FINAL-%201%20year.pdf
31 Council State Governments. (2024). *Justice center law enforcement – Mental health learning sites.* Los Angeles Police Department. https://csgjusticecenter.org/wp-content/uploads/2020/04/MEU-Program-Outline-January-2020.pdf
32 Middleton, A., Woodward, A., Gunn, J., Bassilios, B., & Pirkis, J. (2017). How do frequent users of crisis helplines differ from other users regarding their reasons for calling? Results from a survey with callers to Lifeline, Australia's national crisis helpline service. *Health & Social Care in the Community*, *25*(3), 1041–49. https://doi.org/10.1111/hsc.12404
33 Andrews, G., & Baldry, E. (2013). Mental health frequent presenters: Key concerns, case management approaches, and policy and programme considerations for emergency services. In D. Chappell (Ed.), *Policing and the mentally ill: International perspectives* (1st edn; pp. 197–218). Boca Raton FL: CRC Press Taylor and Francis Group. www.crcpress.com/product/isbn/9781439881163; Henry, P., & Rajakaruna, N. (2018). *WA police force mental health co-response evaluation report.* www.parliament.wa.gov.au/publications.
34 Casey, M., Perera, D., Enticott, J., Vo, H., Cubra, S., Gravell, A., Waerea, M., & Habib, G. (2021). High utilisers of emergency departments: The profile and journey of patients with mental health issues. *International Journal of Psychiatry in Clinical Practice*, *25*(3), 316–24. https://doi.org/10.1080/13651501.2021.1904998.
35 Akins, S., Burkhardt, B. C., & Lanfear, C. (2015). Law enforcement response to "frequent fliers": An examination of high-frequency contacts between police and justice-involved persons with mental illness. *Criminal Justice Policy Review*. Advance online publication. https://doi.org/10.1177/0887403414559268; House, A. (2023). Serenity integrated mentoring and the high intensity network: A scheme that raises serious questions for practice and governance in UK psychiatry. *BJPsych Bulletin*, *47*(1), 1–4. https://doi.org/10.1192/bjb.2022.6.
36 Brown, C. P. (2019). *Reducing implicit bias errors in police decision making, particularly in time-sensitive incidents.* Winston Churchill Memorial Trust. www.churchilltrust.com.au/project/reducing-implicit-bias-errors-in-police-decision-making-particularly-in-time-sensitive-incidents/; Merino, Y., Adams, L., & Hall, W. J. (2018). Implicit bias and mental health professionals: Priorities and directions for research. *Psychiatric Services*, *69*(6), 723–25. https://doi.org/10.1176/appi.ps.201700294.
37 Akins, S., Burkhardt, B. C., & Lanfear, C. (2015). Law enforcement response to "frequent fliers": An examination of high-frequency contacts between police and justice-involved persons with mental illness. *Criminal Justice Policy Review*. Advance online publication. https://doi.org/10.1177/0887403414559268.

38 Baldry, E., & Dowse, L. (2013). Compounding mental and cognitive disability and disadvantage: Police as care managers. In D. Chappell (Ed.), *Policing and the Mentally ill: International perspectives* (pp. 219–34). CRC Press/Taylor & Francis Group.

39 Smith, N., & Trimboli, L. (2010). Comorbid substance and non-substance mental health disorders and re-offending among NSW prisoners. *Crime and Justice Bulletin*. NSW Bureau of Crime Statistics and Research. www.austlii.edu.au/au/journals/NSWCrimJustB/2010/2.pdf

40 Willis, T., Comartin, E., Victor, G., Kern, L., & Kubiak, S. (2021). Individuals with mental illness who have multiple encounters with law enforcement. *Journal of Offender Rehabilitation*, *60*(2), 117–37. https://10.1080/10509674.2020.1863298; Richard Lamb, H., & Weinberger, L. E. (2005). The shift of psychiatric inpatient care from hospitals to jails and prisons. *The Journal of the American Academy of Psychiatry and the Law*, *33*(4), 529–34.

41 Davis, M., Sheidow, A.J., & McCart, M.R. (2015). Reducing recidivism and symptoms in emerging adults with serious mental health conditions and justice system involvement. *Journal of Behavioral Health Services & Research, 42*(2), 172–90. https://doi.org/10.1007/s11414-014-9425-8

42 Building mental health into emergency responses. (2021) www.apa.org/monitor/2021/07/emergency-responses; Miles-Johnson, T., & Morgan, M. (2022). Operational response: Policing persons with mental illness in Australia. *Journal of Criminology*, *55*(2), 260–81. https://doi.org/10.1177/26338076221094385

43 Australian Institute of Health and Welfare [AIHW]. (2023). *Mental health services provided in emergency care*. www.aihw.gov.au/mental-health/topic-areas/emergency-departments; AIHW. (2024). *Ambulance attendances: Suicidal ideation, and suicidal and self-harm behaviours*. www.aihw.gov.au/suicide-self-harm-monitoring/data/ambulance-attendances/ambulance-attendances-for-suicidal-behaviours

44 Laragy, G. (2013). "A peculiar species of felony": Suicide, medicine, and the law in Victorian Britain and Ireland. *Journal of Social History, 46*(3), 732–43. https://doi.org/10.1093/jsh/shs123

45 UK Parliament. (2024). *Burying the dead*. UK Parliament. www.parliament.uk/about/living-heritage/transformingsociety/private-lives/death-dying/dying-and-death/burying/; Laragy, G. (2013). "A peculiar species of felony": Suicide, medicine, and the law in Victorian Britain and Ireland. *Journal of Social History*, *46*(3), 732–743. https://doi.org/10.1093/jsh/shs123; Bloch, S. (1987). The role of law in suicide prevention: Beyond civil commitment—A bystander duty to report suicide threats. *Stanford Law Review, 39*(4), 929–62. https://doi.org/10.2307/1228820.

46 Anderson, O. (1987) *Suicide in Victorian and Edwardian England*. Oxford [Oxfordshire]: Clarendon Press. https://archive.org/details/suicideinvictori0000ande/page/264/mode/2up.

47 In Vice Chancellor Wood's Court. Horne v. Anglo-Australian Insurance Company. (1861). *The American Law Register (1852–1891)*, *9*(8), 496–98. https://doi.org/10.2307/3302744.

48 Duncan, J. F. (1853). *Popular errors on the subject of insanity examined and exposed via internet archive*. https://archive.org/details/popularerrorson00duncgoog/page/n108/mode/2up
49 Millard, C. (2015). *A history of self-harm in Britain: A genealogy of cutting and overdosing*. Basingstoke (UK): Palgrave Macmillan. Chapter 3, Self-harm becomes epidemic: Mental Health (1959) and Suicide (1961) Acts. www.ncbi.nlm.nih.gov/books/NBK333527/.
50 Millard, C. (2015). *A history of self-harm in Britain: A genealogy of cutting and overdosing*. Basingstoke (UK): Palgrave Macmillan. Chapter 3, Self-harm becomes epidemic: Mental Health (1959) and Suicide (1961) Acts. www.ncbi.nlm.nih.gov/books/NBK333527/.
51 O'Neill, N., & Peisah, C. (2011). *Capacity to make a will*. https://classic.austlii.edu.au/au/journals/SydUPLawBk/2011/6.html#fnB65.
52 Arsenault-Lapierre, G., Kim, C., & Turecki, G. (2004). *Psychiatric diagnoses in 3275 suicide: A meta-analysis*. www.ncbi.nlm.nih.gov/pmc/articles/PMC534107/.
53 Strech, D., & Danis, M. (2023). When the cause of death does not exist: Time for the WHO to classify medical aid in dying. *EClinical Medicine, 62*, 102086. https://doi.org/10.1016/j.eclinm.2023.102086
54 End of Life Choices. (2024). https://endoflifechoicesca.org/; Oregon Health Authority. (2024). *Death With Dignity Act*. www.oregon.gov/oha/PH/PROVIDERPARTNERRESOURCES/EVALUATIONRESEARCH/DEATHWITHDIGNITYACT/Pages/index.aspx; Ministry of Health. (2024). *Assisted dying*. www.health.govt.nz/regulation-legislation/assisted-dying
55 Maydom, J. K., Blackwell, C., & O'Connor, D. B. (2024). Childhood trauma and suicide risk: Investigating the role of adult attachment. *Journal of Affective Disorders, 365*, 295–302. https://10.1016/j.jad.2024.08.005; Jannini, T. B., Longo, L., Rossi, R., Niolu, C., Siracusano, A., & Di Lorenzo, G. (2023). Complex post-traumatic stress disorder (cPTSD) and suicide risk: A multigroup mediation analysis exploring the role of post-traumatic symptomatology on hopelessness. *Journal of Psychiatric Research, 165*, 165–169. https://10.1016/j.jpsychires.2023.07.032; Burback, L., Dhaliwal, R., Reeson, M., Erick, T., Hartle, K., Chow, E., Vouronikos, G., Antunes, N., Marshall, T., Kennedy, M., Dennett, L., Greenshaw, A., Smith-MacDonald, L., & Winkler, O. (2023). Trauma focused psychotherapy in patients with suicidal ideation: A scoping review. *Current Research in Behavioral Sciences, 4*, 100102. https://10.1016/j.crbeha.2023.100102.
56 Brown, S., & Seals, J. (2019). Intimate partner problems and suicide: Are we missing the violence? *Journal of Injury and Violence Research, 11*(1), 53–64. https://doi.org/10.5249/jivr.v11i1.997.
57 Brown, S., & Seals, J. (2019). Intimate partner problems and suicide: Are we missing the violence? *Journal of Injury and Violence Research, 11*(1), 53–64. https://doi.org/10.5249/jivr.v11i1.997.
58 Fitzpatrick, S. J., Brew, B. K., Handley, T., & Perkins, D. (2022). Men, suicide, and family and interpersonal violence: A mixed methods exploratory study.

Sociology of Health & Illness, *44*(6), 991–1008. https://doi.org/10.1111/1467-9566.13476.

59 Legislation Victoria. (2024). *Family Violence Protection Act 2008.* https://content.legislation.vic.gov.au/sites/default/files/2020-10/08-52aa053%20authorised_0.pdf.

60 Legislation Victoria. (2024). *Family Violence Protection Act 2008.* https://content.legislation.vic.gov.au/sites/default/files/2020-10/08-52aa053%20authorised_0.pdf

61 Woolley, J. (2024). Policing perpetrator suicide threats in family violence cases: Competing priorities and contemporary challenges. *Policing and Society.* Advance online publication. https://doi.org/10.1080/10439463.2024.2357647.

62 The Lighthouse Project: C-SSRS. (2024). *Columbia-Suicide Severity Rating Scale (C-SSRS).* https://cssrs.columbia.edu/wp-content/uploads/C-SSRS-1-14-09-SinceLastVisit_AU5.1_eng-USori-1.pdf; Favril, L., Yu, R., Uyar, A., Sharpe, M., & Fazel, S. (2022). Risk factors for suicide in adults: Systematic review and meta-analysis of psychological autopsy studies. *Evidence-Based Mental Health, 25*(4), 148–55. https://doi.org/10.1136/ebmental-2022-300549; McMahon, E. M., Greiner, B. A., Corcoran, P., Larkin, C., Leitao, S., McCarthy, J., Cassidy, E., Bradley, C., McAuliffe, C., Griffin, E., Williamson, E., Foster, T., Gallagher, J., Perry, I. J., Kapur, N., & Arensman, E. (2022). Psychosocial and psychiatric factors preceding death by suicide: A case-control psychological autopsy study involving multiple data sources. *Suicide and Life-Threatening Behavior, 52*(5), 1037–47. https://doi.org/10.1111/sltb.12900.

63 High Court of Australia. (2024). *Stuart v Kirkland-Veenstra [2009] HCA 15.* https://eresources.hcourt.gov.au/showCase/2009/HCA/15.

64 High Court of Australia. (2024). *Stuart v Kirkland-Veenstra [2009] HCA 15.* https://eresources.hcourt.gov.au/showCase/2009/HCA/15.

65 California Court of Appeal, First District, Division 2. (1988). *ADAMS v. CITY OF FREMONT (1988) Nos. A074965, A075279.* https://caselaw.findlaw.com/court/ca-court-of-appeal/1288866.html

66 Blackwell, G (2023). *Reducing recidivism in behavioural health crisis cycles.* www.churchilltrust.com.au/project/the churchill-fellows-association-of-western-australia-churchill-fellowship-to-establish-diversionary-practices-for-mentally-and-intellectually-disabled-persons-engaging-police/.

67 Lopez, R. (2022). *'But we can't just leave!': How LAPD SWAT implemented a strategic disengagement policy.* www.police1.com/swat/articles/but-we-cant-just-leave-how-lapd-swat-implemented-a-strategic-disengagement-policy-lHT6VGQ1dTv9UN4f/.

68 Laragy, G. (2013). "A peculiar species of felony": Suicide, medicine, and the law in Victorian Britain and Ireland. *Journal of Social History, 46*(3), 732–43. https://doi.org/10.1093/jsh/shs123; Anderson, O. (1987). *Suicide in Victorian and Edwardian England.* Oxford [Oxfordshire] Clarendon Press. https://archive.org/details/suicideinvictori0000ande/page/264/mode/2up.

69 High Court of Australia. (2024). *Stuart v Kirkland-Veenstra [2009] HCA 15.* https://eresources.hcourt.gov.au/showCase/2009/HCA/15.

70 Lamb, H. R., Weinberger, L. E., & DeCuir, W. J. (2002). The police and mental health. *Psychiatric Services, 53*(10), 1266–71. https://doi.org/10.1176/appi.ps.53.10.1266.
71 Mendelson, D. (2014, October 10). Prevention of suicide: Police powers, parliamentary intent and judicial interpretation. *Journal of Law and Medicine, 16*(2009). Available at SSRN: https://ssrn.com/abstract=2508274.
72 Lamb, H. R., Weinberger, L. E., & DeCuir, W. J. (2002). The police and mental health. *Psychiatric Services, 53*(10), 1266–71. https://doi.org/10.1176/appi.ps.53.10.1266.

3 Community Crisis Response Systems

Introduction

This chapter explores the systems and structures designed to respond to behavioural health crises without involving police. These approaches – community-based, health-oriented, and often trauma-informed – offer critical support in moments of acute need. While managing individuals who cycle through repeated crises remains a long-term challenge, understanding these alternatives is vital to building a more responsive care system.

These non-police responses aren't designed to work in isolation. Each contributes to a larger, collaborative framework that supports people in crisis through various stages – immediate response, recovery, and ongoing care. Some models are short-term interventions; others remain involved along the road to stability.

Given the wide variety of approaches in use, this chapter organises them into three broad categories:

- **Crisis Call Lines** – How crisis calls are managed in the first instance.
- **Community Response Teams** – Non-police teams which respond on the ground, acknowledging the many variants in this field.
- **Crisis Stabilisation Centres** – Systems of inpatient care for individuals subject to apprehension or voluntary admissions, outside of Emergency Departments.

These systems play a vital role in protecting the dignity and wellbeing of individuals in crisis. They reduce reliance on police and reflect a more compassionate, effective way to respond to behavioural health needs.

Crisis Call Lines

Imagine picking up the phone in your darkest moment and finding someone on the other end who's just there to listen. No judgement, no rush – just a calm, steady voice. That kind of support didn't really exist until 1953, when

DOI: 10.4324/9781003749585-3

the world's first suicide prevention helpline was launched in London. It was a groundbreaking idea: giving people in crisis someone to talk to, anytime, day or night.[1]

The media at the time dubbed it the "Telephone Good Samaritan," a name that stuck – and for good reason.[2] This service quickly evolved into what we now know as the UK Samaritans, setting the standard for crisis response. Through the late 1950s and 1960s, similar helplines were appearing across the UK, and countries around the world began to adopt this model of crisis care, recognising the vital role these services play in suicide prevention.[3]

Crisis Lines: More Than Suicide

When most people think of crisis lines, their minds go straight to suicide prevention. It's an understandable assumption with many services originally developed to focus on suicide and the proclivity of publicity targeting suicidality. But that's only part of the story. Today, crisis lines are used for a much broader range of issues, often acting as a first point of contact for people in all kinds of crises.

The US national 988 Suicide & Crisis Lifeline provides a clear example, with data showing only about 34% of calls are directly related to suicidality. The rest? They cover everything from anxiety and depression to substance use, trauma, relationship breakdowns, and overwhelming life stressors. Similarly, a review of California's crisis lines found just 26% of calls were classified as explicitly suicide-related. Identifying nearly three-quarters of calls related to other serious emotional or psychological concerns, such as grief, loneliness, panic attacks, and trauma-based issues.[4]

Australian research highlights this as a global theme with one in four people preferring digital or phone-based support for broad mental health challenges. Lifeline Australia and Beyond Blue have reported call demand extends beyond suicidality, and service calls for a range of emotional support, particularly among younger people, rural populations, and those reluctant to seek face-to-face care.[5]

Evidence that demonstrates crisis lines now serve a broader behavioural health function than their suicide-prevention origins. Despite ongoing messaging centring on suicidality, these services routinely assist people experiencing a raft of behavioural health crises. This expanded role underscores their value as accessible, anonymous, and consistent support in the health system, challenging the misconception that their role is purely for imminent danger.[6]

Who Answers the Call? The Role of Not-for-Profit Providers

Crisis call lines have become an integral part of a broader continuum of care in behavioural health crisis systems, yet a critical question emerges: who's on the other end of the line? Increasingly, the answer isn't government agencies, it's not-for-profit and non-governmental organisations (NGOs). These organisations have assumed a central role in delivering crisis care, especially as demand for accessible and immediate support has grown globally. Many operate with a clear mandate to cater for specific communities, such as young people, veterans, LGBTQI+, regional populations, or heightened suicide risk, often tailoring their services to meet unique needs.[7]

This diversity can play a vital role in filling gaps that traditional systems sometimes overlook. However, operating crisis lines requires ongoing coordination, a well-trained workforce, and sustainable funding. Most not-for-profits rely on a mix of government grants, philanthropic contributions, and donations, but this model often leaves them vulnerable to resource constraints and at time longevity in service. Recent findings from the United Kingdom's Helpline Partnership report, "*Trends, Changes, and Developments in the Helpline Sector*" found that 90% of UK call lines are run by charitable organisations, yet only 8% provided overnight coverage, and fewer than half extended their services into the evening. On average, services operated for only 2,764 hours annually, less than one-third of the total hours in a year, leaving significant and critical gaps in service.[8]

These gaps in service highlight systemic challenges within the wider health service in terms of behavioural health crisis. Historically, the health service and policymakers have viewed crisis lines as supplementary, rather than essential, in crisis care systems.[9] Subsequently, this has contributed to the underfunded and competitive environment we see today. A point Mental Health Australia raised with the Australian Productivity Commission's *Inquiry into Mental Health* emphasising the current structures often pits different sectors against one another for limited resources, increasing division and reducing accessibility to support.[10] This division reinforces how crisis lines are frequently seen as supplementary to the broader health system.

Short-Term Relief v. Long-Term Impact

Further evidence of how crisis lines have been viewed as supplementary rather than part of the care continuum is how crisis lines have been framed as emergency support, only to be reached at a point of acute crisis, that is suicidality. Yet strategies, such as Australia's National Suicide Prevention Strategy, are starting to challenge this crisis-only role, recognising that call lines can deliver follow-up counselling and long-term connection.[11]

However, most research continues to focus on what happens *during* the call, such as whether callers report reduced stress at the end of engagement. While there has been a lack of attention to the *afterwards*, or longitudinal outcomes, whether individuals obtain ongoing care, recidivism rates of callers, or, in tragic cases, subsequently dies.[12] With research indicating more than half of suicidal callers have already made a plan, and nearly 1 in 10 have taken steps to self-harm prior to calling.[13] In the United States, approximately 3% of callers go on to attempt suicide within weeks of their call, while data from Northern Ireland suggest individuals who died by suicide after calling often had only brief or limited contact with the service.[14]

These findings highlighting the importance of coordinated follow-up to progress those short-term outcomes. With studies demonstrating longitudinal outcomes improve when people receive follow-up check-ins or referrals after the initial call.[15]

Together, the challenges of seeing call lines role as short-term emergency diversion combined with identified limitations in sustainability and service delivery it reveals a deeper systemic issue: crisis lines are failing to be embedded as an integral part of the broader health system. Reliance on not-for-profit providers has enabled a raft of service provision, yet left the sector fragmented, limited in capacity and susceptible to instability. At the same time creating inequity in care pathways and coordination of longitudinal follow-up and support. Addressing these concerns requires a shift in how crisis lines are perceived in federal health systems.

A Return to Government-Led Models

As demand grows for access to crisis call line services, and the need for integration into broader health systems, some governments are realising there is a need to reclaim ownership to ensure sustainability, reliability, and validate crisis call lines role in the care continuum. A key shift has been the rollout of national, easy-to-remember three-digit crisis numbers, designed to improve accessibility and integrate call lines into the wider health system.

The United States exemplifies this shift launching the 988 Suicide & Crisis Lifeline, in July 2022. Developed by the Substance Abuse and Mental Health Services Administration (SAMHSA), the goal was simple but powerful:

> To save lives by serving anyone, at any time, from anywhere across the nation, and in a manner that promotes linkages to ongoing local supports.[16]

In its first year, *988* received nearly 5 million contacts, a 150% increase compared to the previous year when operating under a full 10-digit number.[17]

Similar reform had already been implemented in the United Kingdom. In 2016, the National Health Service (NHS) introduced *NHS111 First Response for Mental Health*, a health-led service managed by NHS Trusts.

Outcomes of this change resulted in less than 3% of callers requiring emergency department admission, and fewer than 2% of calls leading to police involvement.[18] Outcomes nearly identical to the US 988 experience where only 2% or less calls required police intervention, demonstrating when health services take the lead, crisis response can become sustainable, safer, and more appropriate.[19]

Such initiatives have expanded globally, such as Canada 988 and Netherlands 113, demonstrating the trend towards government-led three-digit crisis call lines being intergrade within formal health systems.[20] Another innovative example of systems-based thinking in terms of crisis call management comes from Austin, Texas, when in 2021, the city introduced Mental Health as a distinct category in its 911 emergency call system alongside police, ambulance, and fire. This reform altered how call-takers now assessed and managed behavioural health crisis calls from the outset allowing connection directly to behavioural health professionals or mobilising community response teams, providing individuals a more appropriate pathway to care.[21]

These examples demonstrate how government-led embedding of crisis lines into the wider health system can transform behavioural health crisis response. It also exhibits how through a systems thinking lens crisis lines become not only more sustainably accessible, but also through coordination outcomes align within a systemwide continuum of care, which is more consumer centric.

Recidivist Callers and Crisis Cycling

Embedding crisis call lines into a government-led health-based continuum of care also addresses the phenomenon of recidivism. Just as overt models of behavioural health crisis systems have individuals who are subject to chronic crisis cycling so too do crisis call lines. A Swedish study found many callers return to the same helpline repeatedly, not because they're unable to progress, but because they value the sense of familiarity and control a service provides. While this autonomy may be beneficial to the user, it puts pressure on already-stretched services presently not designed for long-term care.[22] Similarly, Australian data revealed just 3% of callers to *Lifeline* accounted for 60% of all calls a pattern of crisis cycling mirroring other areas within the field of behavioural health crisis.[23]

Implications of this recidivism have been raised by the United Kingdom Samaritans, who identified recurring callers as problematic, sometimes labelling callers as "dependent" or "manipulative". Such terminology indicates sectoral pressures aligning to the broader behavioural health crisis system, where identified chronic crisis cycling individuals may be endemic of a system unable to meet their deeper needs in the first place.[24].

Ultimately chronic crisis cycling calls demonstrate both the benefits and limitations crisis call lines have in a wider health system. They provide a sense of immediate support and connection for those in crisis or are vulnerable in the community. However, without complete integration into the wider health sector they risk developing an embedded cohort of individuals locked in crisis cycling patterns – another factor which highlights and supports the need for integrating crisis call lines into a government-led health system.

Barriers to Trust and Engagement

While crisis call lines have evolved and become essential to crisis intervention there still remains some limitations in how those who use them perceive their role, which in turn may affect service delivery. One of the biggest barriers is trust, especially around confidentiality. The US 988 Suicide & Crisis Lifeline found some young callers, especially teenagers, fail to disclose or downplay their suicidal thoughts because they're worried their parents or guardians may be contacted. A concern which was also identified when engaging with first-responders and military personnel, who often stayed silent to protect their careers.[25]

Australian research provides some insight, noting when the initial question to a caller is "Are you going to kill yourself?" the engagement can feel jarring, especially prior to conversation or rapport building. When such statements are coupled with disclosure that emergency services might be contacted, the exchange feels more like a warning than a reassurance.[26] For someone already feeling distressed, such interactions can feel clinical, rushed, or even threatening, with call-takers focusing on their own liability, rather than caring and supportive.

Conclusion: Rethinking the Role of Crisis Call Lines

There is a need to challenge the view that crisis call lines are supplementary services on the periphery of the broader health system, or as a tool designed only to act upon immediate harm such as suicidality. Evidence demonstrates they provide support to individuals facing a wide range of challenges, from anxiety and trauma to substance use and social isolation. Over time they have come to evolve into essential gateways into the broader health system, offering immediate support and, in some cases, linking callers to long-term care.

Despite this expanding role, crisis lines face their own set of challenges. Many operate with limited financial security, restricted hours of service, overly-narrow demographics, and lack of integration into broader health system. These pressures can be impacted by demands of chronic crisis cycling callers and the competitive landscape, which often reflects models of business practices rather than coordinated healthcare systems.

The answer lies in reimagining crisis call lines as integral components of a systems approach to behavioural health crisis management. Rather than retaining an outsourced adjunct to the health system, they should be returned into mainstream government-led health services. In this way crisis lines will be seen as key players in a larger, more integrated health system that is flexible and user-centric.

Community Response Teams

The ongoing demand to reduce the reliance on police in behavioural health crises (BHC) has led to the development of an array of non-police approaches to crisis response, such as Community Responder Teams (CRTs), Paramedic Response Teams (PRTs), Peer Support Teams (PST), and other formats. Some of these teams such as CRT are similar to police Co-Responder programs, but without a police presence, whilst some are a collection of community members. These approaches aim to offer specialised, non-police, on-scene resolutions, avoiding involuntary care, and diversion from judicial settings.

Variations in Program Design

Although this chapter will primarily focus on Community Responder Teams, it is important to acknowledge that not all community response teams operate under the paramedic and clinician framework. Several variations exist in terms of team composition, all of which fall within the broader realm of CRTs for the purposes of this discussion. A broad description of these models include:

- **Clinician / Crisis Workers**: Staffed by professionals in behavioural health and/or professional crisis workers. Examples of this model is Toronto Community Crisis Service (TCCS), Canada, where teams of two mental health professionals respond to behavioural health crisis, similarly Atlanta's Policing Alternatives & Diversion Initiative or PADI.[27]
- **Peer Support**: In this model, peer workers – individuals with lived experience – work alongside clinicians or crisis workers. Examples of this model are Salt Lake, USA's Mobile Crisis Outreach Teams (MCOT) operating from the Huntsman Mental Health Institute that pairs a trained clinician with a peer support specialist to respond in the community, similarly San Diego's Mobile Crisis Response Teams (MCRT) teams a peer support with a clinician and case manager.[28]

Mobile Community Mental Health Teams

Mobile Community Mental Health Teams (MCMHTs) are worth noting as their own category, and for the purpose of this discussion, such mobile teams are those established directly in the healthcare system to provide community outreach. MCMHTs likewise operate to stabilise individuals in the community, yet hold the power to initiate involuntary care orders. Canadian research has demonstrated that MCMHTs, when appropriately staffed, are capable of managing complex, high-risk patients and play a crucial role in reducing service reliance and improving long-term outcomes.[29] MCMHTs are particularly important expediting care for individuals following the onset of psychotic conditions, where delays can hinder recovery prospects and long-term prognosis becomes less favourable.[30]
Examples of such programs include:

- **Psychiatric Mobile Response Teams (PMRT) Los Angeles, USA**[31]
  Part of the Los Angeles County Department of Mental Health, PMRT, provides in-field evaluations of individuals experiencing crises, aiming to prevent unnecessary hospitalisation or incarceration while maintaining the capacity for involuntary detention when required.
- **Mobile Crisis De-Escalation Team (MoDe) Vancouver Canada**[32]
  MoDe provides same-day outreach to individuals in crisis. However, its services are limited to pre-identified referral partners from housing/shelter and community service providers, excluding individuals at immediate risk of suicide or posing a safety threat to others.
- **Crisis Assessment and Treatment Teams (CATT) Australia**[33]
  Known by various names across states, CATTs deliver mobile clinical support to individuals in crisis, offering services that range from 12-hour to 24/7 responses.

History of Community Response

Community-based response is not a new practice. In Eugene, Oregon, the *Crisis Assistance Helping Out On The Streets* (CAHOOTS) program was launched in 1989, as a collaboration between the Eugene Police Department and White Bird Clinic. Teams composed of a paramedic and a crisis worker provide non-police responses to low-risk calls involving mental illness and homelessness. Incidents which had an element of criminal activity, violence, or life-threatening emergencies, remained the responsibility of police.[34]

Since its inception, academics and advocates alike hold CAHOOTS as a successful diversion model, leading to the development of approximately one hundred similar programs across North America.[35] Examples include:

- **Support Team Assisted Response (STAR), Denver, Colorado**[36] – Paramedics and clinicians operate from 6:00 a.m. to 10:00 p.m., delivering low-risk crisis services in the community.
- **Street Crisis Response Team (SCRT), San Francisco, California**[37] – Operating citywide 24/7, staffed by two paramedics and a clinician utilising a modified ambulance.
- **Behavioral Health Emergency Assistance Response Division (B-HEARD), New York City**[38] – Paramedics and a mental health professional operate across four boroughs, seven days a week, for 16 hours each day.

Beyond North America, it is estimated that over 200 similar programs have emerged globally[39]:

- **Psykiatriambulans (PAM), Stockholm, Sweden**[40] – Psychiatric nurses and paramedic provide emergency response 11:00 a.m. to 3:00 a.m. daily.
- **Mental Health Joint Response Car, London, England**[41] – A paramedic and a mental health nurse responding to low-risk behavioural health crises from 11:00 a.m. to 11:00 p.m. daily.
- **Mental Health Co-Responder (MH-CoRe), Queensland, Australia**[42] – A paramedic and senior mental health clinician jointly address active behavioural health crisis, piloted in 2019.

These programs represent a significant shift in collaborative, non-police community responses to behavioural health crisis. While similarly designed to reduce police involvement, their operational models vary widely making it difficult to universally evaluate their success. With available data often incomplete, insufficient, or open to self-reporting bias, for example, Stockholm's Psykiatriambulans noted, "There are no pretrial data collected, and no control group available to compare with. The data presented are purely descriptive." Yet despite these limitations, it concluded the program provided high-quality prehospital service and reduced the workload for both police and hospital services.[43]

Self-reporting remains the dominant mode of evaluation reported. Yet, when taken as a collective, it is possible to identify recurring themes, most commonly outcomes include[44]:

- Police Attendance (including Use-of-Force and Arrest rates)
- Emergency Department presentations
- Cost-Effectiveness

Though more rigorous research is necessary in this rapidly evolving field, the existing evidence highlights the importance in examining how CRTs influence response and management of active behavioural health calls for service in terms of the wider health system.

Reducing Police Engagement and Involuntary Care

Establishing CRTs is often predicated on reducing reliance upon police in BHCFS, with success commonly reported on these metrics. The CAHOOTS program, for example, reportedly diverts 8–17% of 911 calls away from police. While New York's B-HEARD program reported in 2024 they responded to 14,591 incidents, representing a 29% diversion rate.[45] Not all studies directly report diversion rates, however, but rather used activity levels as success indicators. Denver's STAR program reported responding to approximately 400 calls a month, with San Francisco's SCRT handling around 1,200, and London's MHJRC addresses around 450.[46]

This diversion from police attendance is further demonstrated when CRTs are engaged. CAHOOTS reported that only 1% of calls they attend require police assistance, and a 2022 global study of CRTS revealed less than 5% of incidents resulted in calls for police backup.[47] Although these figures do not represent complete police diversion, they do nonetheless demonstrate a significant shift towards engaging individuals in crisis without police and the possibility of negative outcomes.

Beyond reducing police engagement, CRTs have been shown to reduce the frequency of involuntary hospitalisation. London's MHJRC conveys only 18% of individuals to emergency departments, whilst San Francisco's SCRT, places only 7% of engagements on a mental health hold, citing 72% were due to a presentation of danger.[48] Additionally, Canadian research noted CRTs reduced hospital admissions rates compared to police-only response, while a Dutch study found if a CRT consultation occurred with a juvenile in their home emergency hospital admission rates were similarly reduced.[49]

Positive Consumer Engagement

Consumer satisfaction following engagement with community responder teams consistently identifies non-police CRT models, closely followed by Co-Responder models, as the preferred crisis response programs.[50] Improved patient care also demonstrates longitudinal benefits: individuals manage by CRT retain positive view of the experience up to 20 months after the crisis, in contrast to other interventions.[51] Supported by evidence from New York, where individuals engaged by CRTs for suicidal thoughts, or behaviours showed higher rates of follow-up re-engagement post emergency department discharge, rising from 30% to 70% when compared standard outpatient psychiatric clinics.[52]

Beyond improved clinical outcomes, CRTs offer broader societal advantages. Denver's STAR program purported a 34% reduction in recorded low-level offences commonly associated with behavioural health crisis situations, such as drug use, trespassing, and disorderly behaviour. Research suggests two likely reasons behind this phenomenon: either non-police responders did not record such offences, or there was a genuine reduction in criminal behaviour. Regardless of the reason, what is clear is, by departing from traditional policing responses to a health-focused care model increases the likelihood individuals are managed in a health rather than judicial setting.[53]

Financial Benefits

A Swedish study uniquely explored the societal benefit deploying CRTs in terms of human capital savings when reviewing Stockholm's Psykiatriambulans. Human capital calculates the potential life value of individuals saved, when looking at measures such as productivity and future earnings. With the study estimating PAM's human-value savings were up to SEK82 million over the course of two years.[54] While specific to Stockholm, this model of calculating savings could be applied more broadly to other behavioural health crisis interventions, including those delivered by community mental health teams, police, or other services.

More direct financial savings have been recorded across several CRTs with CAHOOTS recording savings between $2.2 million to $8.5 million per year attributed to reduced police interventions.[55] Similarly, London's MHJRC program initial 2013 projections estimated total cost of emergency department attendances would decrease from £921,536 to £510,099, representing a potential 44.6% annual saving.[56] Savings supported by a systematic review of CRTs finding 69% of patients managed by CRTs were not admitted to hospitals, leading to substantial savings in terms of inpatient care for individuals in crisis.[57]

Barriers to Success

However, while these results demonstrate benefits of community responder teams, a European study identified many CRTs operated without sufficient post-transport treatment options. Particularly a lack of adequate crisis stabilisation centres resulting in continued use of emergency departments.[58] Highlighting a need for comprehensive systems of care beyond immediate crisis response.

However, the biggest threat to non-police response teams comes from policymakers. As previously explored with crisis lines many community responder teams are still seen as supplementary services and not integral health service provision. Accordingly, these programs can be disbanded as quickly as they are implemented. A critical example of this is after decades of service delivery and held as a world leader by a raft of academics and practitioners, even in this text, Eugene's CAHOOTS program had its funding ceased in April 2025.[59] Highlighting a critical vulnerability such programs operate within.

Conclusion

Current research on community responder teams (CRTs), although limited and often based on self-reported data, underscores the significant benefits these teams can offer at various levels of behavioural health crisis intervention. These programs have shown reductions in emergency department transports, cost savings, possible reduction in low-level crime and a growing preference for their services from patients and families over traditional police-only responses.

However, questions persist regarding the full effectiveness of CRTs. Most teams continue to operate under limited timeframes, and typically activated for low-risk behavioural health crisis calls that do not present significant safety concerns. Further some successful CRTs find themselves let down when there is a lack of supporting systems. Such as alternative places of care to emergency departments or political stability, as evidenced by the cancellation of the highly successful CAHOOTS program.

Despite these challenges, every successful intervention carried out by a CRT represents a measurable reduction in the involvement of police and the judicial system. This reinforces the crucial role CRTs play within a broader health system.

Crisis Stabilisation Centres

A critical element in managing behavioural health crisis (BHC), particularly those at risk, is the provision of safe and secure clinical settings. These spaces can support both voluntary presentations and those requiring urgent involuntary care due to risk. Historically, hospital emergency departments have been the default. However, despite the physical safety they may provide, EDs are not always conducive to fostering emotional and psychological wellbeing during a crisis.

Research by Navas et al. (2022) revealed the majority of crisis patients reported their experience in emergency departments to be negative. While healthcare providers reported they found it challenging to care for crisis patients in these settings and particularly difficult when communicating with frequent users with co-occurring mental health and substance use disorders, borderline personality disorder, or suicidal behaviours and ideation.[60] These complexities can be exacerbated by prolonged waiting times. For example, in Australia BHC patients wait seven hours, compared to a four-hour median for non-BHC patients, with similar differences in wait times in the USA where patients in BHC spend 42% more time in EDs than non-psychiatric presentations.[61]

Moving from Emergency Departments

Globally there is a shift to implement systematic changes in urgent care settings, with the Substance Abuse and Mental Health Services Administration (SAMHSA) in the United States, asserting that individuals in crisis require "A Safe Place for Help" as part of an integrated crisis care system.[62] This shift in crisis care has seen the establishment of Behavioural Health Crisis Stabilisation Centres (CSC). These centres, going by various names including Certified Community Behavioural Health Clinics, Crisis Cafes, and Urgent Crisis Care Units, are designed as safe places for crisis stabilisation, providing on-demand crisis care, de-escalation, and emotional wellbeing in less stimulating environments than emergency departments, inpatient psychiatric units, and police cells.[63]

Most crisis stabilisation centres began as local initiatives and community collaborations. Examples of early initiatives include the *Psychiatric Emergency Services* in Houston, Texas, and the *Spokane Regional Stabilisation Center* in Spokane, Washington. Centres which accommodate both voluntary "walk-ins" and referrals from emergency services or police for individuals requiring involuntary care. Typically, they provide up to 23 hours of observation and stabilisation care for individuals in acute crisis. With strong support for these alternative crisis systems, the early 2000s, particularly in the US, saw an expansion of CSCs and reshaping of the broader system of crisis care.[64]

A clear indicator of change was marked in 2024 when the US Congress introduced legislation endorsing Certified Community Behavioural Health Clinics (CCBHC) to be supported by Medicaid.[65] This federal initiative aims to provide a 24/7 urgent crisis care service for mental health and substance use to anyone who seeks it, regardless of their age, residence, and without financial restrictions.

To attain certification, clinics must provide nine core services, either directly or through formal partnerships. These services include[66]:

1 Crisis Services
2 Outpatient Mental Health and Substance Use Services
3 Person- and Family-Centred Treatment Planning
4 Community-Based Mental Health Care for Veterans
5 Peer Family Support and Counsellor Services

6 Targeted Care Management
7 Outpatient Primary Care Screening and Monitoring
8 Psychiatric Rehabilitation Services
9 Screening, Diagnosis, and Risk Assessment

Crisis stabilisation is not unique to the USA with models being established across the globe. Canada has various crisis stabilisation centres operating under models similar to those in the US offering 24/7 support to walk-in patients and individuals referred from police and emergency services, enhancing flexibility in addressing individuals in crisis.[67] Whilst in the United Kingdom the National Health Service has established an array of alternatives to emergency department or psychiatric inpatient supports, through a national rollout of crisis cafes, safe havens, and crisis houses.[68]

In Australia, the federal government launched Medicare Mental Health Centres, as free, walk-in services.[69] Although free and accessible they operate with limited hours of service and do not accept involuntary patients from emergency services or the police. However, in 2021 the Urgent Mental Health Care Centre in Adelaide, South Australia, was launched providing a 24/7 service for individuals who either walk-in or are apprehended by police, an initiative which may act as a precursor for change across the broader Australian healthcare sector.

Emergency Department Diversion

Initially designed to act as alternatives to emergency departments, it makes sense research has focused on this outcome. Studies have identified when a walk-in CSC facility opens, ED presentations for behavioural health dropped on average by 3%.[70] A rate which may not seem dramatic but scale is important. In Australia during the 2023/24 financial year, the *Australian Institute of Health and Welfare* reported around 310,000 mental health ED presentations. A 3% reduction in ED presentations would represent around 9,300 people in crisis a year receiving care in more supportive and therapeutic settings.[71]

Evidence suggests this diversion rate for ED is not just a short-term phenomenon with a recorded 8.3% decrease in 30-day and a 13.5% decrease in 1-year re-presentation rates of those individuals whose initial crisis was managed in a crisis stabilisation centre.[72] This may be associated to findings that patients treated at CSCs experience a 60% increase in attendance at scheduled follow-up mental health appointments within 30 days of discharge.[73]

Further research shows traditional EDs have a proclivity for prematurely discharging patients presenting for behavioural health, where CSCs singular focus results in provision of comprehensive and specific care, seeing individuals being appropriately stabilised before discharge.[74] These findings highlight how delivering a person-centred care model, within a comfortable, non-judgemental, and compassionate environment prevents crises from escalating.

Suicidality and Crisis Stabilisation Centres

Research from Illinois, USA, showed crisis stabilisation centres are effective in addressing the distress experienced by individuals in acute crisis, thereby improving suicide prevention services.[75] Outcomes reinforced by a Midwest USA study that recorded a significant decrease in inpatient psychiatric admissions of suicidal patients, from 57% to 27% after the implementation of a new crisis stabilisation centre.[76] Extending beyond suicidality though, research shows CSCs therapeutic model consistently reduces the likelihood that any individual presenting in crisis will be admitted as inpatients.[77] Outcomes which are enhanced when undertaken away from overstimulating surroundings and delivered in a timely manner, two aspects often lacking in emergency departments.[78]

Conclusion

Emerging research highlights the significant benefits Crisis Stabilisation Centres achieve in a broader behavioural health crisis system. Not only do these centres improve patient care and outcomes, but studies suggest that when local healthcare systems adopt 23-hour crisis stabilisation centres, overall healthcare costs tend to decrease.[79]

Crisis stabilisation centres have also been proven to improve longitudinal outcomes. Likely due to the specificity of role and enhanced follow-up care post crisis intervention, reducing the need for repeated emergency care or inpatient admissions.[80] However, as with many supplementary alternative care models there are recommendations for expansion of operating hours and increased capacity to meet the growing demand for services.

Moving forward, improving places for individuals to be housed when in crisis fits logically into improving the wider behavioural health crisis system. Thereby, alleviating pressure on emergency departments, police, and frontline responders, who find themselves already overstretched while also providing more client focused care to individuals in crisis.

Observational Summary

There is a growing societal demand for a reduction of the role police play in behavioural health crises. For this shift to be meaningful and successful, it is crucial that communities establish non-police services capable of matching the 24/7 mobility and capacity police currently provide. Globally, an array of different models of non-police crisis systems have emerged. While, none of these programs demonstrated a capability to address all aspects of behavioural health crises, together they form a systems-based approach, fitting the Substance Abuse and Mental Health Services Administration (SAMHSA) framework, which divides crisis management into three key stages[81]:

1. Someone to Contact – Crisis Call Lines
2. Someone to Respond – Community Responder Teams
3. A Safe Place for Help – Crisis Stabilisation Centres

Using this framework, we can explore the interplay between these systems.

1. **Someone to Contact: Crisis Call Lines**
   are a critical component of non-police response systems, providing immediate, accessible support to individuals in crisis. These lines often function as a circuit breaker, offering de-escalation without the need for on-site intervention. Historically, crisis call lines have operated in a decentralised and self-regulated manner, which has sometimes limited their effectiveness. However, recent governance changes, such as the introduction of 988 in the United States, 111 in England, and 988 in Canada, have introduced more clinical and structured approaches to crisis intervention, promising to enhance the quality and reach of these services.
2. **Someone to Respond: Community Responder Teams**
   The "someone to respond" stage can be divided into two categories: Mobile Community Mental Health Teams (MCMHT) providing community-based clinical approaches and imminent reactive Community Responder Teams (CRTs). MCMHTs are in-built into traditional mental healthcare systems. Providing crisis intervention with professionals who are familiar with or have access to an individual's medical history and treatment plan. While this familiarity can improve the response quality, MCMHTs often struggle with slower response times, making them less effective in urgent situations.
   In contrast, Community Responder Teams (CRTs) offer more rapid responses and can provide clinical care beyond that typically available through police-only interventions. CRTs are also better integrated with emergency health services and can often access health service systems facilitating smoother transitions to care. Although in most cases lacking 24/7 service, their partnership with emergency medical services represents a more agile response to crisis.

3 **A Safe Place for Help: Crisis Stabilisation Centres** provide essential care for individuals in crisis in environments that are more therapeutic and suited to their needs than traditional emergency department settings. Improving access to ongoing clinical care and overall cost savings they have demonstrated value in the healthcare system. Although to be effective, they must be available around the clock for both "walk-in" and involuntary patients, enabling equity of care for individuals in crisis.

The growing demand for non-police crisis response systems reflects broader societal perspectives towards policing. This demand has successfully resulted in some world leading programs to support vulnerable individuals in crisis. Improving access to support outside of traditional policing dependence, showing overall benefits for communities as a whole.

However, despite the progress there are limits. In situations involving serious danger, such as active violence, weapons being present, or an imminent threat to others, policing involvement becomes unavoidable. Many of these programs also face operational challenges: limited hours, mobility, resourcing, and critically capacity to deliver a 24/7 service. A likely product of these systems often being seen as supplementary rather than a critical component of traditional healthcare systems. This leaves them vulnerable to political and financial pressures, as extraordinarily exampled by the recent closure of CAHOOTS in Eugene, Oregon. Despite decades of acclaim as a leading model of non-police community response, the program failed to retain support of policymakers.

These limitations do not mean non-police systems are failing. Taking a sporting analogy: "*it's all about the one-percenters*". Even small demand diversions, say 10% at each stage, can compound into a significant success in reducing police involvement. The exact maths isn't the point here, but showing how incremental wins add up.

Future discussions should build on these successes. The challenge is how to embed frontline non-police crisis systems into the broader crisis care continuum, whilst simultaneously evolving police practices and culture to work alongside these health-based models. This topic will be explored in the next chapter.

Notes

1 Samaritans. (2025). *Our history*. www.samaritans.org/about-samaritans/our-history/.

2 Samaritans. (2025). *Our history*. www.samaritans.org/about-samaritans/our-history/.

3 Draper, J., & McKeon, R. T. (2024). The journey toward 988: A historical perspective on crisis hotlines in the United States. *Psychiatric Clinics of North America, 47*(3), 473–90. https://doi.org/10.1016/j.psc.2024.04.003; Lifeline. (March 2023). *Lifeline marks 60 years of being just a call away for Aussies in distress.* https://lifelinedirect.org.au/hunter/news/lifeline-celebrates-60-years-of-supporting-australians-through-every-challenge.
4 Ramchand, R., Jaycox, L., Ebener, P., Gilbert, M. L., Barnes-Proby, D., & Goutam, P. (2017). Characteristics and proximal outcomes of calls made to suicide crisis hotlines in California. *Crisis, 38*(1), 26–35. https://doi.org/10.1027/0227-5910/a000410.
5 Mental Health Association. (2021). *Submission to Productivity Commission into mental health.* Productivity Commission. www.pc.gov.au/__data/assets/pdf_file/0012/243111/sub538-mental-health.pdf.
6 SAMHSA. (2023). *(1) Suicide & crisis lifeline.* www.samhsa.gov/find-help/988; Ramchand, R., Jaycox, L., Ebener, P., Gilbert, M. L., Barnes-Proby, D., & Goutam, P. (2017). Characteristics and proximal outcomes of calls made to suicide crisis hotlines in California. *Crisis, 38*(1), 26–35. https://doi.org/10.1027/0227-5910/a000410.
7 Roth, K. B., & Szlyk, H. S. (2021). Hotline use in the United States: Results from the collaborative psychiatric epidemiology surveys. *Administration and Policy in Mental Health, 48*, 564–78. https://doi.org/10.1007/s10488-020-01089-0
8 Helplines. (2019). *Helplines partnership – Trends, changes and developments in the helpline sector 2017–2019.* https://helplines.contentfiles.net/media/documents/Helpline_Insight_Research_Report_2017-2019.pdf
9 Draper, J., & McKeon, R. T. (2024). The journey toward 988: A historical perspective on crisis hotlines in the United States. *Psychiatric Clinics of North America, 47*(3), 473–90. https://10.1016/j.psc.2024.04.003.
10 Mental Health Association. (2021). *Submission to Productivity Commission into mental health.* www.pc.gov.au/__data/assets/pdf_file/0012/243111/sub538-mental-health.pdf.
11 Australian Government. (2020). *National suicide prevention strategy for Australia's health system: 2020–2023.* www.health.gov.au/resources/publications/national-suicide-prevention-strategy-for-australias-health-system-2020-2023?language=en.
12 Hoffberg, A.S., Stearns-Yoder, K.A., & Brenner, L.A. (2020). The effectiveness of crisis line services: A systematic review. *Frontiers in Public Health, 7*, 399. https://doi.org/10.3389/fpubh.2019.00399.
13 Chan, C., Wong, H., & Yip, P. S. (2018). Exploring the use of telephone helpline pertaining to older adult suicide prevention: A Hong Kong experience. *Journal of Affective Disorders, 236*, 75–79. https://10.1016/j.jad.2018.04.093; Gould, M. S., Kalafat, J., Harrismunfakh, J. L., & Kleinman, M. (2007). An evaluation of crisis hotline outcomes part 2: Suicidal callers. *Suicide and Life-Threatening Behavior, 37*, 338–52. https://doi.org/10.1521/suli.2007.37.3.338.

14 Ramsey, C., Ennis, E., & O'Neill, S. (2019). Characteristics of lifeline crisis line service users who have died by suicide. *Suicide and Life-Threatening Behavior, 49*(1), 293–302. https://doi.org/10.1111/sltb.12476.
15 Ramsey, C., Ennis, E., & O'Neill, S. (2019). Characteristics of lifeline crisis line service users who have died by suicide. *Suicide and Life-Threatening Behavior, 49*(1), 293–302. https://doi.org/10.1111/sltb.12476.
16 Substance Abuse and Mental Health Services Administration. (April 2024). *Saving lives in America: 988 quality and services plan.* www.samhsa.gov/sites/default/files/saving-lives-american-988-quality-service-plan.pdf
17 SAMHSA. (2023). *Suicide & crisis lifeline.* www.samhsa.gov/find-help/988.
18 NHS England. (2023). *New mental health 111 services reduces A&E visits by a third.* www.england.nhs.uk/integratedcare/resources/case-studies/new-mental-health-111-service-reduces-ae-visits-by-a-third/.
19 988 Suicide Crisis Helpline. (2025). https://988.ca/; Scoop. (2019). *Make the call: Dial 145 to seek mental health help Talian Harapan 145 is aimed at providing crisis support.* https://thescoop.co/2019/02/13/make-the-call-dial-145-to-seek-mental-health-help/.
20 9-8-8 Suicide Crisis Helpline. (2025). *Get help.* https://988.ca; 113 Suicide Prevention. (2025). *English.* www.113.nl/english.
21 Austin Texas. (2021). *Mental health option added to 9-1-1.* www.austintexas.gov/blog/mental-health-option-added-9-1-1
22 Iversen, C., & Westerlund, M. (2024). Users' perspectives on crisis helplines in relation to professional mental health services. *Crisis, 45*(3), 173–79. https://doi.org/10.1027/0227-5910/a000876.
23 Spittal, M. J., Fedyszyn, I., Middleton, A., et al. (2015). Frequent callers to crisis helplines: Who are they and why do they call? *Australian & New Zealand Journal of Psychiatry, 49*(1), 54–64. https://doi.org/10.1177/0004867414541154
24 Pollock, K., Armstrong, S., Coveney, C., & Moore, J. (2010). *An evaluation of Samaritans telephone and email emotional support service.* National Institute for Health Research, University of Nottingham.
25 Zabelski, S., Kaniuka, A. R., Robertson, R. A., & Cramer, R. J. (2023). Crisis lines: Current status and recommendations for research and policy. *Psychiatric Services, 74*(5), 505–12. https://doi.org/10.1176/appi.ps.20220294.
26 Roennfeldt, H., Hill, N., Byrne, L., & Hamilton, B. (2024). Exploring the lived experience of receiving mental health crisis care at emergency departments, crisis phone lines and crisis care alternatives. *Health Expectations, 27,* e14045. https://doi.org/10.1111/hex.14045.
27 City of Toronto. (2025). *Toronto community crisis service: Who we are.* www.toronto.ca/community-people/public-safety-alerts/community-safety-wellbeing-programs/toronto-community-crisis-service/tccs-who-we-are/; Policing Alternatives & Diversion Initiative. (2025). *Policing Alternatives & Diversion Initiative.* www.atlantapad.org/
28 Utah – Mobile Crisis Outreach Teams (MCOT): University of Utah Health. (2025). *Crisis diversion: Mobile Crisis Outreach Teams (MCOT).* Huntsman

Mental Health Institute. https://healthcare.utah.edu/hmhi/programs/crisis-diversion#mobilecrisisoutreachteamsmcot; San Diego – Mobile Crisis Response Teams (MCRT): County of San Diego Health & Human Services Agency. (2025). *Mobile Crisis Response Teams (MCRT)*. www.sandiegocounty.gov/content/sdc/hhsa/programs/bhs/BHS_MCRT.html
29 Sunderji, N., de Bibiana, J.T., & Stergiopoulos, V. (2015). Urgent psychiatric services: A scoping review. *Canadian Journal of Psychiatry, 60*(9), 393–402. https://doi.org/10.1177/070674371506000904.
30 Thornicroft, G., & Tansella, M. (2004). Components of a modern mental health service: A pragmatic balance of community and hospital care: Overview of systematic evidence. *British Journal of Psychiatry, 185*(4), 283–90. https://doi.org/10.1192/bjp.185.4.283.
31 Department of Mental Health. (2025). *Psychiatric Mobile Response Teams (PMRT)*. https://dmh.lacounty.gov/our-services/countywide-services/eotd/pmrt/
32 Vancouver Coastal Health. (2025). *Vancouver Mobile Crisis De-Escalation Team* (MoDe). www.vch.ca/en/service/vancouver-mobile-crisis-de-escalation-team-mode#short-description--21946.
33 Suicide Call Back Service. (2025). *Help for suicide emergency – Crisis assessment and treatment teams*. www.suicidecallbackservice.org.au/feeling-suicidal/help-for-suicide-emergency-crisis-assessment-and-treatment-teams/; Canberra Health Services. (2025). *Home Assessment and Acute Response Team (HART)*. www.canberrahealthservices.act.gov.au/services-and-clinics/services/home-assessment-and-acute-response-team-haart; Government Western Australia. (2025). *East Metropolitan Health Service, Assessment and Treatment Team*. www.emhs.health.wa.gov.au/Hospitals-and-Services/Mental-Health-Alcohol-and-Other-Drugs/Community-Services/CECMHS
34 Eugene. (2025). *CAHOOTS*. www.eugene-or.gov/5129/CAHOOTS; White Bird Clinic. (2025). *CAHOOTS (Crisis Assistance Helping Out on the Streets)*. https://whitebirdclinic.org/cahoots/.
35 International Crisis Response Association. (2025). *Directory*. https://icraconnect.org/directory/; Just Mental Health. (2025). *Programs*. https://justmentalhealth.ca/programs
36 Denver Gov. (2025). *Support Team Assisted Response (STAR) Program*. www.denvergov.org/Government/Agencies-Departments-Offices/Agencies-Departments-Offices-Directory/Public-Health-Environment/Community-Behavioral-Health/Behavioral-Health-Strategies/Support-Team-Assisted-Response-STAR-Program.
37 San Francisco Government [sf.gov]. (2022). *Street Crisis Response Team Pilot final report*. www.sf.gov/sites/default/files/2022-06/SCRT%20Final%20Report_FINAL-%201%20year.pdf.
38 The Mayor's Office of Community Mental Health. (2025). B-*HEARD*. https://mentalhealth.cityofnewyork.us/b-heard
39 Just Mental Health. (2025). *Programs*. https://justmentalhealth.ca/programs.
40 AISAB. (2025). *Psykiatriambulans (PAM)*. www.aisab.nu/sv-se/ambulanssjukvard/vara-ambulanser-och-fordon/psykiatriambulans-pam.

41 Trainer, M. (2020). *Mental Health Joint Response Car Pilot – Evaluation summary report.* https://aace.org.uk/wp-content/uploads/2020/08/MHJRC-Summary-Report-Final-11082020.pdf; London Ambulance Service. (2025). *Mental health care.* www.londonambulance.nhs.uk/calling-us/mental-health-care/
42 Queensland Government. (2021). *Enhanced frontline care for patients experiencing mental health crisis.* https://statements.qld.gov.au/statements/91932.
43 Bouveng, O., Bengtsson, F. A., & Carlborg, A. (2017). First-year follow-up of the Psychiatric Emergency Response Team (PAM) in Stockholm County, Sweden: A descriptive study. *International Journal of Mental Health, 46*(2), 65–73. https://doi.org/10.1080/00207411.2016.1264040.
44 Marcus, N., & Stergiopoulos, V. (2022). Re-examining mental health crisis intervention: A rapid review comparing outcomes across police, co-responder and non-police models. *Health & Social Care in the Community, 30*, 1665–79. https://doi.org/10.1111/hsc.13731.
45 Eugene. (2025). *CAHOOTS.* www.eugene-or.gov/5129/CAHOOTS; White Bird Clinic. (2020). *Crisis assistance helping out on The Streets Media Guide 2020.* https://whitebirdclinic.org/wp-content/uploads/2020/07/CAHOOTS-Media.pdf#:~:text=The%20most%20common%20types%20of%20calls%20diverted%20to,crisis%20responses%20involve%20more%20than%20one%20call%20type; City of New York. (2025). *Re-imagining New York City's mental health emergency response, Data overview, B-HEARD.* https://mentalhealth.cityofnewyork.us/bheard-data
46 Gillespie, S., Curran-Groome, W., & Rogin, A. (2024). *Evaluating alternative crisis response in Denver's Support Team Assisted Response (STAR) Program: Interim findings.* www.denvergov.org/files/assets/public/v/1/public-health-and-environment/documents/cbh/star/evaluating_alternative_crisis_response_in_denvers_support_team_assisted_response_program-interim_findings.pdf; SF.Gov. (2025). *Street Crisis Response Team, street crisis monthly updates.* www.sf.gov/street-crisis-response-team; London Ambulance Service. (2025). *London Ambulance Service celebrates a decade of specialist care for mental health patients.* www.londonambulance.nhs.uk/2025/02/21/london-ambulance-service-celebrates-a-decade-of-specialist-care-for-mental-health-patients/.
47 Eugene. (2025). *CAHOOTS.* www.eugene-or.gov/5129/CAHOOTS; White Bird Clinic. (2020). *Crisis assistance helping out on The Streets Media Guide 2020.* https://whitebirdclinic.org/wp-content/uploads/2020/07/CAHOOTS-Media.pdf#:~:text=The%20most%20common%20types%20of%20calls%20diverted%20to,crisis%20responses%20involve%20more%20than%20one%20call%20type; Marcus, N., & Stergiopoulos, V. (2022). Re-examining mental health crisis intervention: A rapid review comparing outcomes across police, co-responder and non-police models. *Health & Social Care in the Community, 30*, 1665–79. https://doi.org/10.1111/hsc.13731.
48 London Ambulance Service. (2025). *London Ambulance Service celebrates a decade of specialist care for mental health patients.* www.londonambulance.nhs.uk/2025/02/21/london-ambulance-service-celebrates-a-decade-of-specialist-care-for-mental-health-patients/; San Francisco Government [sf.gov]. (2022).

Street Crisis Response Team Pilot final report. www.sf.gov/sites/default/files/2022-06/SCRT%20Final%20Report_FINAL-%201%20year.pdf.

49 Marcus, N., & Stergiopoulos, V. (2022). Re-examining mental health crisis intervention: A rapid review comparing outcomes across police, co-responder and non-police models. *Health & Social Care in the Community, 30*, 1665–79. https://doi.org/10.1111/hsc.13731; So, P., Wierdsma, A. I., Kasius, M. C., Cornelis, J., Lommerse, M., Vermeiren, R. R. J. M., & Mulder, C. L. (2021). Predictors of voluntary and compulsory admissions after psychiatric emergency consultation in youth. *European Child & Adolescent Psychiatry, 30*(5), 747–56. https://doi.org/10.1007/s00787-020-01558-9.

50 Pope, L. G., Patel, A., Fu, E., Zingman, M., Warnock, A., Ellis, S., & Compton, M. T. (2023). Crisis response model preferences of mental health care clients with prior misdemeanor arrests and of their family and friends. *Psychiatric Services, 74*(11), 1163–70. https://doi.org/10.1176/appi.ps.20220363.

51 Marcus, N., & Stergiopoulos, V. (2022). Re-examining mental health crisis intervention: A rapid review comparing outcomes across police, co-responder and non-police models. *Health & Social Care in the Community, 30*, 1665–79. https://doi.org/10.1111/hsc.13731.

52 Currier, G.W., Fisher, S.G., & Caine, E.D. (2010). Mobile crisis team intervention to enhance linkage of discharged suicidal emergency department patients to outpatient psychiatric services: A randomized controlled trial. *Academic Emergency Medicine, 17*(1), 36–43. https://doi.org/10.1111/j.1553-2712.2009.00619.x.

53 Dee, T.S., & Pyne, J. (2022). A community response approach to mental health and substance abuse crises reduced crime. *Science Advances, 8*(eabm2106). https://doi.org/10.1126/sciadv.abm2106.

54 Carlborg, A., Sibbel, R., & Helgesson, M. (2020). *Health economic evaluation of the psychiatric emergency response team (PAM) in Stockholm County.* Research Square. https://doi.org/10.21203/rs.3.rs-106323/v1

55 White Bird Clinic. (2020). *CAHOOTS & the police departments.* https://whitebirdclinic.org/what-is-cahoots/; National League of Cities. (2024). *Eugene, OR: Community response model.* www.nlc.org/resource/reimagining-public-safety-impact-updates/eugene-or-community-response-model/

56 Trainer, M. (2020). *Mental Health Joint Response Car Pilot – Evaluation summary report.* https://aace.org.uk/wp-content/uploads/2020/08/MHJRC-Summary-Report-Final-11082020.pdf

57 Carpenter, R. A., Falkenburg, J., White, T. P., & Tracy, D. K. (2013). Crisis teams: Systematic review of their effectiveness in practice. *The Psychiatrist, 37*(7), 232–237. https://doi.org/10.1192/pb.bp.112.039933.

58 de Jong, I. C., van der Ham, L. A. J., & Waltz, M. M. (2022). Responding to persons in mental health crisis: A cross-country comparative study of professionals' perspectives on psychiatric ambulance and street triage models. *Journal of Community Safety and Well-Being, 7*(Suppl 1), S36–S44. https://doi.org/10.35502/jcswb.250

59 White Bird Clinic. (n.d.). *CAHOOTS: Crisis Assistance Helping Out On The Streets.* White Bird Clinic. Retrieved December 1, 2025, from https://whitebirdclinic.org/cahoots/; Oregon Public Broadcasting. (2025, June 4).

Eugene after CAHOOTS: The end of the crisis response program and the efforts to bring it back. OPB. www.opb.org/article/2025/06/04/eugene-after-cahoots-the-end-of-the-crisis-response-program-and-the-efforts-to-bring-it-back/

60 Navas, C., Wells, L., Bartels, S.A., & Walker, M. (2022). Patient and provider perspectives on emergency department care experiences among people with mental health concerns. *Healthcare, 10*(7), 1297. https://doi.org/10.3390/healthcare10071297

61 Australian Medical Association. (October 2024). *2024 Public hospital report card – Mental health edition.* www.ama.com.au/sites/default/files/2024-10/2024-ama-public-hospital-report-card-mental-health-edition.pdf; ustralian Institute of Health and Welfare. (2024). *Emergency department care access.* www.aihw.gov.au/reports-data/myhospitals/intersection/access/ed; Nordstrom, K., Berlin, J. S., Nash, S. S., Shah, S. B., Schmelzer, N. A., & Worley, L. L. M. (2023). Boarding of mentally ill patients in emergency departments: American Psychiatric Association Resource Document. *Focus, 21*(1), 74–79. https://doi.org/10.1176/appi.focus.23022001.

62 Substance Abuse and Mental Health Services Administration. (2025). *Model definitions for behavioral health emergency, crisis, and crisis-related services* (HHS Publication No. SMA XX–xxxx [or PEPXX-XX-XX XXX]). U.S. Department of Health and Human Services, Substance Abuse and Mental Health Services Administration.

63 Balfour, M. E., & Zeller, S. L. (2023). Community-based crisis services, specialized crisis facilities, and partnerships with law enforcement. *Focus, 21*(1), 18–27. https://doi.org/10.1176/appi.focus.20220074.

64 The Harris Center. (2025). *The Harris Center for Mental Health and IDD – Crisis services.* www.theharriscenter.org/services/crisis-services; Spokane County. (2025). *Spokane Regional Stabilization Center.* www.spokanecounty.org/5717/Spokane-Regional-Stabilization-Center.

65 Medicaid. (2025). *CCBHC demonstration background.* www.medicaid.gov/medicaid/financial-management/certified-community-behavioral-health-clinic-ccbhc-demonstration/ccbhc-demonstration-background.

66 SAMHSA. (2023). *Certified Community Behavioral Health Clinics (CCBHCs).* www.samhsa.gov/communities/certified-community-behavioral-health-clinics

67 Canada Mental Health Association. (2025). *Crisis stabilization.* https://cmhatv.ca/find-help/crisis-access-services/crisis-stabilization/

68 NHS England. (2025). *Crisis and acute mental health care.* www.england.nhs.uk/mental-health/adults/crisis-and-acute-care/

69 Australian Government. (2024). *Department of Health and Aged Care – Medicare Mental Health Centres.* www.health.gov.au/our-work/medicare-mental-health-centres; Australian Government. (2025). *About Medicare Mental Health.* www.medicarementalhealth.gov.au/about-us.

70 Burns, A., Vest, J. R., Menachemi, N., et al. (2025). Availability of behavioral health crisis care and associated changes in emergency department utilization. *Health Services Research, 60*(2), e14368. https://doi.org/10.1111/1475-6773.14368.

71 Australian Institute of Health and Welfare. (2025). *State and territory emergency department data: Mental health services.* Australian Government. www.aihw.gov.au/mental-health/topic-areas/hospital-based-services/emergency-departments/state-and-territory-data.

72 Schwartz, S., Michel, J., Brown, E., et al. (2025). Assessing the impact of an innovate behavioral health clinic: A retrospective cohort study. *BMC Psychiatry, 25*, 250. https://doi.org/10.1186/s12888-025-06669-8.

73 Kim, A.K., Vakkalanka, J.P., Van Heukelom, P., Tate, J., & Lee, S. (2022). Emergency psychiatric assessment, treatment, and healing (EmPATH) unit decreases hospital admission for patients presenting with suicidal ideation in rural America. *Academic Emergency Medicine, 29*(2), 142–49. https://doi.org/10.1111/acem.14374

74 Anderson, K., Goldsmith, L.P., Lomani, J., Ali, Z., Clarke, G., Crowe, C., & Gillard, S. (2022). Short-stay crisis units for mental health patients on crisis care pathways: Systematic review and meta-analysis. *BJPsych Open, 8*(4), e144. https://doi.org/10.1192/bjo.2022.534.

75 Saxon, V., Mukherjee, D., & Thomas, D. (2018). Behavioural health crisis stabilization centers: A new normal. *Journal of Mental Health and Clinical Psychology.* www.mentalhealthjournal.org/articles/behavioral-health-crisis-stabilization-centers-a-new-normal.pdf.

76 Kim, A. K., Vakkalanka, J. P., Van Heukelom, P., Tate, J., & Lee, S. (2022). Emergency psychiatric assessment, treatment, and healing (EmPATH) unit decreases hospital admission for patients presenting with suicidal ideation in rural America. *Academic Emergency Medicine, 29*(2), 142–49. https://doi.org/10.1111/acem.14374.

77 Anderson, K., Goldsmith, L. P., Lomani, J., Ali, Z., Clarke, G., Crowe, C., & Gillard, S. (2022). Short-stay crisis units for mental health patients on crisis care pathways: Systematic review and meta-analysis. *BJPsych Open, 8*(4), e144. https://doi.org/10.1192/bjo.2022.534.

78 Postorivo, D., Parker, S., Whiteford, H., et al. (2025). Person-centred crisis support services as alternatives to emergency departments: A systematic scoping review. *Social Psychiatry and Psychiatric Epidemiology, 60*, 25–37. https://doi.org/10.1007/s00127-024-02776-1.

79 Postorivo, D., Parker, S., Whiteford, H., et al. (2025). Person-centred crisis support services as alternatives to emergency departments: A systematic scoping review. *Social Psychiatry and Psychiatric Epidemiology, 60*, 25–37. https://doi.org/10.1007/s00127-024-02776-1; Saxon, V., Mukherjee, D., & Thomas, D., (2018) Behavioural health crisis stabilization centers: A new normal. *Journal of Mental Health and Clinical Psychology.* www.mentalhealthjournal.org/articles/behavioral-health-crisis-stabilization-centers-a-new-normal.pdf.

80 Balfour, M. E., & Zeller, S. L. (2023). Community-based crisis services, specialized crisis facilities, and partnerships with law enforcement. *Focus, 21*(1), 18–27. https://doi.org/10.1176/appi.focus.20220074.

81 Substance Abuse and Mental Health Services Administration. (2025). *Model definitions for behavioral health emergency, crisis, and crisis-related services* (HHS Publication No. PEP24-01-037). U.S. Department of Health and Human Services. https://988crisissystemshelp.samhsa.gov/sites/default/files/2025-08/SAMHSA_Model_Definitions_508_080525.pdf.

4 Police Crisis Response Systems

Introduction

Policing is often associated with responding to, managing, and investigating crime. Yet, in reality, a significant portion of police work extends into the social safety, with police officers managing relationships, neighbourhood disputes, and behavioural health crisis.[1] The challenge is police officers are largely untrained in many social issues such as relationship counselling, mental illness, neurodiversity, or substance use disorder.[2]

This gap in skills ignites debate on whether police should be involved in behavioural health crises at all. Critics focus on criminalisation and use-of-force; while policing itself raises similar concern arguing they should be the "last resort".[3] The challenge arises in finding alternative services for those difficult, troublesome, and dangerous situations beyond the capacity of social services.[4]

As Lord Adebowale emphasised to the UK Parliament: police have a duty to protect life, which includes responding to people in crisis.[5] However, particularly in the United States, this duty has been brought into question in terms of whether police do hold a legal "special relationship" with individuals in crisis after several court rulings.[6]

Policing has always had a broad role, with many non-crime aspects willingly accepted by society and policing alike, such as missing persons, disaster response, and family violence. In this chapter, we'll explore how different jurisdictions have approached the contentious social welfare issue of behavioural health crisis – sometimes successfully, sometimes not as much.

Co-Responder

The Co-Responder model is a progressive approach in responding to crisis, by combining a police officer and healthcare professionals, such as Authorised Mental Health Practitioners (AMHPs), to jointly respond to active behavioural health crisis calls for service. The idea is to provide rapid,

DOI: 10.4324/9781003749585-4

on-scene clinical support, with better skills in de-escalation, access to care, reducing criminal outcomes or involuntary hospitalisation. Co-responder programs aim to provide individuals in crisis a more humanistic, compassionate, and health-focused response. Yet its progressive character lies not in terms of age, with version having existed in some jurisdictions for decades, but in its challenge to traditional default police-only response.

Origins and Early Expansion

Canada was a leading pioneer in Co-Responder programs in 1978 in Vancouver. Launching "Car 87" as a collaboration between Vancouver Coastal Health and Vancouver Police Department, it allowed a police officer and clinician to deliver on-scene assessments and interventions for mental health calls.[7] A simple idea of sharing resources to address a shared demand.

The United States followed suit in 1993, when Los Angeles Police Department and the Los Angeles County Department of Mental Health collaborated to establish the Systemwide Mental Assessment Response Team (SMART), which remains the largest co-responder program in the US.[8]

The success of these early initiatives spurred a growth of co-responder programs across North America. Hamilton, Canada, introduced its Crisis Outreach and Support Team (COAST) in 1997, followed by Houston, Texas, launching its Crisis Intervention Response Team (CIRT) in 2008.[9] By 2024, a survey of US policing agencies found that over 40% had implemented some form of co-responder program, with approximately 45% of these initiatives launched since 2020. Growth which indicates co-responder programs are no longer seen as experiments but a vital component of North American policing and community behavioural health systems.[10]

Co-responder programs are not unique to North America gaining traction globally. Australia's first program launched in 2007, with Victoria's Police Ambulance Clinical Early Response (PACER). PACER operated as a secondary response model, requiring an initial police presence to secure the scene before its arrival[11] – with Western Australia following suit in 2016 with the Mental Health Co-Response (MHCR) program.[12] However, MHCR innovation was staffing each vehicle with a clinician and two trained police officers, removing the requirement of untrained police officers to attend first when no serious threat was present.[13]

Meanwhile, the UK in 2013 launched Street Triage schemes in Cleveland and Leicestershire recording early success in reducing involuntary apprehensions.[14] Encouraged by these results, the UK Government encouraged expansion of Street Triage saying it would "help keep people out of custodial settings and reduce the demands on valuable police time."[15] By 2023, approximately 70% of National Health Service (NHS) catchments operated a Street Triage program, integrating clinicians into police vehicles, control rooms, and custody areas.[16]

New Zealand's 2020 launch of the Co-Response Team (CRT) saw another variation adopting a tri-agency model teaming a paramedic, clinician, and police officer.[17] A police-funded review praised CRT as "game-changing" and recommended its broader adoption, echoing similar findings from an independent review of Western Australia's MHCR.[18] These initial successes saw co-responder programs expand across Australia and New Zealand just as they had in the northern hemisphere.[19]

Limitations of Service Capacity

Despite initial success and expansion, concerns were raised regarding co-responder effectiveness, with many programs operating within limited hours or catchment areas, seeing an inability to meet all demand. Often these issues were attributed to conflicts in resourcing between partnering agencies.[20]

Operational processes also caused inefficiencies across programs: such as secondary response creating longer waits at scene for clinicians, unclear triaging of calls, inequitable funding, inconsistent policies between partner agencies, and differing expectations of co-responder teams. These factors all contributed to underutilisation of services.[21]

Research in Indianapolis, USA, compared co-responder programs with standard police responses finding no significant improvement in outcomes. However, researchers acknowledged limitations, undertaking the study in 2021 during the COVID-19 pandemic and with an agency where all personnel were trained in behavioural health interventions.[22] Furthermore, its measure of success – whether individuals experienced further arrests, outpatient encounters, or emergency department visits within 12 months – was a high threshold, arguably even for clinical services.[23]

What this study does highlight is the difficulty of conducting comprehensive evaluations of co-responder effectiveness. Several factors contribute to this challenge. Firstly, there are significant variations in program designs – staffing, service availability, operational structures, and jurisdictional legislation. Secondly, lack of independent pre/post-implementation evaluations or randomised control trials undermines the robustness of findings. Finally, local differences in police and health data recording practices introduce additional complexities in analysis.[24]

Another issue is the reliance on police-reported data which has the potential to be biased depending on organisational perspectives of co-responder programs value, can skew findings, and impact the credibility of assessments.[25]

Benefits of Co-Responder Programs

Overall, research on co-responder programs tend to find improvements in response to crisis, with studies highlighting the following impacts:

- **Use-of-Force** – Co-responder models generally reduce the use-of-force with Canadian research finding a drop from 12.1% of encounters involving regular patrols, compared to 4.2% when a co-responder model was employed.[26] Similarly, in Western Australia, research showed a reduction in force from 14% to 6% when MHCR was engaged compared to police-only.[27] Findings suggest co-responder teams with their clinical aspect can contribute to de-escalation and reduction of force.
- **Involuntary Apprehension** – Evidence from recent studies also show reductions in involuntary care apprehensions. With a 2024 controlled trial in Virginia, USA, finding co-responder models demonstrated what researchers described as "a significant effect on reducing subsequent hospitalisation."[28] Supporting this, a 2024 study from San Mateo County, USA, reported a 16% reduction in involuntary detentions and a 17% overall decrease in 911 mental health-related calls after establishing a co-responder program.[29]

These findings align with international evidence. In England, Street Triage programs contributed to reductions in involuntary transportation by rates ranging from 56% to 78%. Australian data support this trend, showing a drop in involuntary apprehensions from 71% to 27% when co-responders were activated compared to police-only approaches.[30]

These reductions are frequently attributed to the inclusion of a clinician in the team who can enable assessment and support at scene, reducing transportation and sustained benefits, such as reduced readmissions following the crisis event.[31]

- **Consumer Experience** – Service users consistently express a preference for co-responder programs over police-only interventions.[32] An Australian survey of consumers even found co-responder services were preferred over standalone clinical responses, due to benefits such as faster response times, enhanced de-escalation, greater empathy, and improved treatment outcomes.[33]

Additionally, co-responder programs are reported as significantly less traumatic than police-as-usual responses, with experiences more likely to be addressed in a compassionate, medical context, reducing feelings of criminalisation and fostering a supportive environment for recovery.[34]

- **Cost** – Financial benefits of co-responder programs have regularly been reported. In Georgia, USA, a study identified a 23% reduction in response attendance costs, with further savings in reduced hospital expenditure with a 55% to 28% diversion rate between co-responder to police-only responses.[35] This research underscores the on-flowing economic advantages of co-responder programs beyond scene attendance, such as reducing demand on hospitals, courts, custody settings to name a few.

The Future of Co-Response

Despite academic debates on the efficacy of co-responder programs, their widespread endorsement by communities, legislative bodies, coronial inquiries, and consumers provides a compelling indicator of their success. Underscored by their rapid expansion, reflecting their perceived value in addressing behavioural health crises.[36] This expansion and success has resulted in international unification under the International Co-Responder Alliance (ICRA) established in 2021, facilitating monthly online forums, an annual conference, and a platform to advertise employment opportunities, effectively connecting crisis professionals globally.[37]

Importantly, evidence continues to support the positive impact of the model. A 2020 study of police forces across several USA states showed that when there were adequate health resources available to support police officers at BHCFS, there were higher rates of diversion from the criminal justice system.[38] Simply bringing a clinician to the scene in a co-responder format effectively achieves this, enabling a rapid accountability shift from policing to health services. A shift which can only function efficiently if there is a full collaboration between the systems.

As calls grow for more integrated crisis response systems, co-responder programs are the practical embodiment of that ideology. Combining resources to effectively respond to, de-escalate, and integrate health-based outcomes on-scene at crisis calls. Their continued expansion and sustainability highlight the value communities place on co-responder programs as a key component of a systems-based approach to crisis intervention.

Conclusion

The evidence is clear: no single sector is able to address the complexity of behavioural health crisis alone. A systems-based approach which addresses shared responsibilities, common goals, mutual understanding, and collaboration of resources is the ideal model communities are seeking. The co-responder model is essentially a first step in this broader systems-based approach to crisis. One that can only foster a culture which seeks to priorities safety, dignity, and human centric responses to crisis.

Serenity Integrated Mentoring

Serenity Integrated Mentoring (SIM), also known as the High-Intensity Network (HIN), was a collaborative "model of care" implemented in the United Kingdom between 2016 and 2021. The initiative brought together health services and police forces to address the needs of "High-Intensity Users" (HIUs) of public services, particularly those frequently detained under Section 136 of the Mental Health Act (MHA).[39] [40]

SIM originated on the Isle of Wight, directed by the Hampshire and Isle of Wight Constabulary and spearheaded by Police Sergeant Paul Jennings. The program was conceived as an innovative mental health workforce transformation model, aiming to improve support and outcomes for individuals who were disproportionately engaging emergency and crisis services.[41]

The initial pilot, known as the "Isle of Wight Integrated Recovery Programme," focused on a subset of HIUs who accounted for approximately 11.5% of those engaging with Hampshire Police's Street Triage team.[42]

The pilot program reported remarkable success in addressing high-intensity users through a proactive and collaborative approach with National Health Service (NHS) partners to crisis response. Within the first year, it achieved a 66% reduction in police-initiated crisis detentions, culminating in a complete 100% reduction within 18 months.[43]

This achievement was made possible by embedding a police officer directly into the care pathways of individuals who frequently accessed emergency services. Working alongside mental health professionals, the integrated team delivered more coordinated and comprehensive support tailored to the needs of these individuals.[44]

The success of this collaborative approach in breaking the cycle of mental health crises earned the pilot team several prestigious national awards, including[45]:

- October 2016: Nursing Times Awards:
  - Winner – HRH Prince of Wales Award for Integrated Approaches to Care
- October 2016: National Health Service Innovation Accelerator (NIA):
  - Sgt Paul Jennings – SIM Innovator – awarded NIA Fellowship to accelerate spread and support adoption of innovation at pace across England

- May 2017: Health Services Journal Value in Healthcare Awards Categories:
  - Winner – Clinical Support Services
  - Winner – Mental Health
  - Highly Commended – Workforce Efficiency

The most prestigious recognition for the initiative was the NHS Innovation Accelerator Fellowship, which aims to create "the conditions and cultural change necessary for proven innovations to be adopted faster and more systematically through the NHS, and to deliver examples into practice for demonstrable patient and population benefit".[46]

The rollout of SIM across the UK had a significant impact on the National Health Service. In June 2017, NHS England highlighted SIM in a news article showcasing "ground-breaking patient care innovations." The initiative was prominently featured as a leading example ahead of the 2017 NHS Innovation Accelerator awards.[47] In the article, Sergeant Paul Jennings, representing SIM, shared his perspective on the program's expansion:

> The NHS Innovation Accelerator is supporting me to expand this local project across the country so that we can save as many lives as possible. It has enabled me, as a police officer, to have a voice in the NHS, by providing knowledge, expertise, and senior strategic-level support.[48]

The strategic impact of SIM on healthcare was further underscored in 2017 when the Royal College of Emergency Medicine referenced the initiative in their *Frequent Attenders in the Emergency Department Best Practice Guideline*. The guideline emphasised the importance of longitudinal HIUs management, highlighting SIM as a model example, stating:

> A good example of this is the SIM project in the Isle of Wight...This project embedded a police mental health specialist within a community mental health team. A combination of compassion, discipline, perseverance and assertiveness reduced both ED attendance in individuals and overall, 136 suite usage over 3 years.[49]

Supported by the NIA Accelerator Fellowship and dedicated funding, along with strategic backing from health circles, SIM rapidly expanded across police jurisdictions and NHS Trusts throughout the United Kingdom.[50] It gained widespread recognition in both health and police sectors as a progressive approach to managing "High-Intensity Users." By the time of its rollout, SIM had been established in at least 23 NHS Trusts and their associated police forces, with the Metropolitan Police – one of the UK's most prominent policing agencies – deploying 21 dedicated SIM officers.[51]

As part of the NHS Accelerator funding initiative, Paul Jennings transitioned from policing to formally establish the High-Intensity Network (HIN). Assuming the role of National Programme Manager, he spearheaded the nationwide rollout of SIM.[52] HIN delivered a comprehensive three-day training course for NHS Trusts and police forces across England involved in SIM, providing detailed guidance on its operational implementation and reporting requirements.[53]

However, concerns arose regarding the SIM model's perceived punitive and police-led approach to managing High-Intensity Users. Critics questioned the therapeutic benefits for individuals treated within this framework, citing a lack of robust evidence to demonstrate positive outcomes. Further criticism centred on the rapid expansion of SIM across the UK, despite being piloted in only one jurisdiction and relying largely on self-reported data to validate its claims of effective patient management.

Although NHS Health Innovator supported the expansion nationally of SIM within two years of the award Professor Tim Kendall, National Clinical Director for Mental Health, asked NHS Mental Health Trusts to review their models of care, particularly those involving SIM or SIM like approaches for managing service users.[54] Alongside individual Trust reviews, the *Health Innovator Network* commissioned an independent evaluation led by Mike Farrar. A key question raised in the published report was why the "initial evidence base for SIM, based on a small number of individuals," did not prompt more rigorous scrutiny during the selection process. The report suggested that a comprehensive evaluation at the outset might have led to SIM being excluded from the Health Innovator program or warranted a more cautious approach to rolling SIM out.[55]

Although concerns about SIM's rapid expansion became prominent in 2021, early signs of potential issues were evident as far back as 2018. Greater attention to ongoing research at the time might have encouraged a more cautious approach to its rollout. A research team inclusive of Paul Jennings and the Department of Clinical, Educational, and Health Psychology at University College London conducted a study examining the implementation of SIM in London. Their findings were published in the paper, *"A Feasibility Assessment of Serenity Integrated Mentoring (SIM) Implementation in London, England."*[56] Notably, the paper's abstract itself reveals early concerns, including the following conclusion:

> We recommend a Phase I trial with a pre-post design and follow-up, which will require further work to standardise data on emergency service use, and consideration of the limitations this study encountered in obtaining meaningful self-report information. Despite the challenges, we

> recommend that this unique service be urgently evaluated if it is to be widely used within the NHS.[57]

An intriguing aspect of evaluating SIM's impact on the UK's approach to policing behavioural health crises is the surprising scarcity of open-source literature accessible to the public. This is particularly unexpected given the program's past widespread praise and promotion across various government sectors. It appears references to SIM within health and police domains have either been erased or minimise, contributing to a troubling lack of transparency regarding its implementation and outcomes.

Although SIM has been discontinued as a nationwide initiative, its core principles of proactive collaboration between service providers, including police, persist in some UK jurisdictions. For example, Devon and Cornwall Police have adopted a localised High-Intensity Program (HIP) modelled on SIM, whilst Merseyside Police developed their High Demand Action Plan program.[58]

These programs highlight the value of proactive collaboration in addressing the cyclical nature of behavioural health crises. Effectively supporting individuals trapped in patterns of recidivist crisis cycling necessitates the continued involvement of policing as a key component of this collaborative framework. The broader implications and potential benefits of such proactive, collaborative approaches will be examined in greater detail later in this book.

Right Care, Right Person

The "Right Care, Right Person" (RCRP) policy is a significant shift in how police services across the United Kingdom manage and respond to behavioural health calls for service. RCRP was developed in 2021 by Humberside Police who sought to realign responsibilities for BHCFS away from police, advocating professionals, such as clinicians or social workers, are more suited to manage crisis.

RCRP was endorsed by the National Police Chiefs Council seeing the policy expand across the UK and influence international jurisdictions alike. However, despite the ambitious intentions to realign crisis care response, serious concerns have emerged regarding its implementation, especially in relation to pace of rollout, inter-agency coordination, training, and patient safety.

Implementation and National Rollout

Chief Constable Paul Anderson of Humberside Police launched *Right Care, Right Person (RCRP)* under a central tenet that police resources should focus their core duties on detecting crime, keeping the king's peace, and protecting life and property.[59] This initiative introduced a more rigorous triaging system for BHCFS, resulting in the denial of police intervention for certain incidents that previously warranted a response.[60]

This model was informed by both legal and operational principles. Firstly, under common law, police do not owe a general duty of care to protect individuals from harm caused by themselves or others.[61] Secondly, under *Article 2 of the Human Rights Act 1998*, the police's duty of care is triggered only when there is a specific and identifiable threat of death; a risk of serious injury alone does not activate this duty.[62]

The premise is to ensure "the right person, with the right skills, training, and experience to best meet their needs" responds to BHCFS. In some cases, this means redirecting certain calls to health services rather than the police.[63] A principle echoing criticisms of an over-reliance on police, who lack the expertise, to handle BHCFS, can result in inappropriate actions, increased tensions, or even tragic outcomes.[64]

Key to Humberside Police's RCRP rollout Chief Constable Anderson underscored the importance of collaboration when addressing the UK House of Commons, stating that it took "just in excess of three years" to develop and emphasised that "it was not something we did to health; we did it with health."[65] With Humberside Police reporting RCRP success in substantially reducing the number of BHCFS incidents requiring police deployment from 78% in 2019 to just 25% by mid-2022.[66]

Following Humberside Polices' reported success the Metropolitan Police, one of the UK's most prominent policing agencies, announced plans to adopt RCRP citing "we are failing them [individuals in crisis] first by sending police officers, not medical professionals" and "failing Londoners a second time by taking large amounts of officer time away from preventing and solving crime as well as dealing properly with victims, in order to fill gaps for others".[67]

However, despite sharing the same principles Humberside Police and the Metropolitan Police adopted markedly different approaches to implementing the Right Care, Right Person policy. Humberside Police took a collaborative approach, working with stakeholders over a three-year period. In contrast, the Metropolitan Police's implementation was seen as more adversarial. Commissioner Sir Mark Rowley announced on the 24th of May 2023 that RCRP would commence in August 2023, later to be revised to November 2023, giving stakeholders only six months' notice.[68] Secondly, where Humberside Police explicitly described RCRP development as a collaborative process, the Metropolitan Police's approach was perceived by some stakeholders as more unilateral, at times appearing an ultimatum rather than collaborative reform.[69]

Nevertheless, Humberside's reported success and the high-profile implementation by the Metropolitan Police contributed to momentum for national adoption. In early 2023, the UK Home Secretary, Suella Braverman, expressed her support in a letter to all Police Chief Constables, encouraging a "consensus to work together to develop a National Partnership Agreement incorporating the principles of the Right Care, Right Person operating model."[70]

An ambitious timeline for the national rollout included[71]:

- A review of the Humberside model by March 2023,
- The development of National Police Chiefs' Council (NPCC) toolkits by June 2023, and
- Guidance for Mental Health Trusts by July 2023.

Remarkably, within less than a year, RCRP became the UK's standard policing approach to Behavioural Health Calls for Service. The College of Policing released RCRP toolkits and policy papers, solidifying this model as the new national standard.[72]

International Adaptation

The influence of the Right Care, Right Person (RCRP) model has extended well beyond its UK origins, gaining momentum within several international jurisdictions. Within a year of the Metropolitan Police adopting RCRP, the New South Wales Police Force in Australia directly cited RCRP as a key driver of systems reform in its *Review of the NSW Police Force Response to Mental Health Incidents in the Community*.[73] Western Australia Police have followed a similar direction, updating its public guidance on welfare checks to read *"If you are concerned about someone's welfare, they need the right care from the right person."*[74]

New Zealand Police announced a shift in their approach to crisis, indicating an intention to scale back involvement in BHCFS on the principle that a response is provided by "the right person at the right time."[75] A rationale that echoes the Right Care, Right Person messaging of the United Kingdom.

The speed of international policing's uptake of Right Care, Right Person is unsurprising. In July 2023, Deputy Chief Constable Rachel Bacon, the UK's National Police Chiefs' Council (NPCC) lead for RCRP, indicated the approach could save as many as one million officer hours annually.[76]

A message reinforced by the Metropolitan Police who reported that "Met officers spend well over 10,000 hours each month responding to mental health concerns", which they hoped to redirect through RCRP.[77]

Meanwhile the UK College of Policing highlighted that Humberside Police reduced officer responses to BHCFS from 78% in January 2019 to just 25% by May 2022, under the model demonstrating the scale of police resourcing benefits.[78] Understandably, such projections resonate with policing leadership seeking to address operational demand pressures.

Implementation Challenges and Stakeholder Criticisms

Despite the UK national rollout obtaining recognition and a swift following amongst international policing leadership, RCRP's expansion has attracted broad criticism within the United Kingdom. Advocacy groups, professional associations, local health authorities, and political leaders have all questioned the pace, objectives, and process of implementation.

While the NPCC emphasised that "police forces roll out RCRP with partners rather than imposing it on them", the Local Government Association (LGA), together with the Association of Directors of Adults Social Services and the Association of Directors of Children's Services, wrote to Ministers highlighting several risks, such as[79]:

- RCRP being rolled out too quickly with inadequate local engagement
- Police forces introducing RCRP without agreed processes or shared understanding of the implications for LGA
- The possibility that police may cease to engage in cases where their involvement remains appropriate

National charity *Mental Health Matters* echoed these concerns during a UK Parliament Committee Session, questioning police obligations under the Mental Health Act, increased reliance on ambulance services, the capacity for health services to adequately respond, and the implications for staff and patient safety.[80]

RCRP was again raised in the UK Parliament on the 14th November 2023, when the Health and Social Care Committee questioned the Secretary of State about funding and support for the program.[81] Scrutiny which rose as police forces were rapidly rolling out the model, even though National Health Service trusts were expressing difficulty in preparing for the rollout. Committee Chair Steve Brine MP emphasised the importance of patient outcomes, stating, "*It's not enough to know that the changes will save police officer hours; they must also demonstrably serve the interests of patients who rely on mental health services in their hour of need.*"[82]

This emphasis on patient wellbeing echoes concerns that were raised by Bird et al., (2024) who questioned whether RCRP genuinely was prioritising appropriate care.[83] They observed that a key measure of the Humberside pilot, and national rollout, would have been to track the mental health outcomes of individuals previously subject to police interventions. However, as this was not done, the full impact of the model and the claim that patient wellbeing is its central focus remains unproven.[84]

Concerns reflected in the December 2024 *Rapid Review* conducted by the UK Home Office and the Department of Health and Social Care.[85] The review identified several implementation challenges:

- Health and social care staff reported feeling excluded from decision-making
- Resourcing barriers to managing incidents previously managed by police
- Gaps and unclear responsibilities for responding to crisis calls
- Ambulance services questioning whether they were the appropriate, or right person, for BHCFS
- Safety concerns among staff who lack police powers and training in use-of-force

Risk Identified in Coronial Inquests

Several recent inquests of the *UK Chief Coroner's Office* have raised concerns on how aspects of the RCRP rollout have contributed to service failures. These findings, published via *Preventing Future Deaths (PFD)* reports, point to a series of emerging themes, some of which are examined below.[86]

Lack of Training

The 2024 inquest into the death of Ryan Ouslem highlighted the inadequate training provided to frontline police officers and serious deficiencies in police training under the new RCRP protocols with the coroner stating:

> I am concerned because this new approach under the 'Right Care, Right Person' policy will still need police officers to understand mental health issues in order to know when to pass matters on for mental health services to deal and what information to provide.[87]

Lack of Ownership and Responsibility

A major concern raised in multiple inquests relates to the lack of clear responsibility for when responding to BHCFS. This issue was evident in the 2023 inquest into the death of Heather Findlay where the coroner observed:

> From the evidence I heard, the police / health trust partnership working allows each agency to regard such a situation as the other's responsibility,

> whilst nobody is on the ground attempting to retrieve a seriously ill patient who is meant to be inside a locked ward for their own safety.[88]

With the 2025 case of Paul Alexander, reinforcing how RCRP establishes gaps in protocols and responsibility being passed between services, where the coroner found:

> The evidence from the RCRP lead at the ambulance service indicated the scenario that arose with Paul was not an isolated example. As such there appears to be a lacuna in how emergency services will respond to such a situation when it was accepted this was a call expressing concern for Paul's welfare.[89]

Inconsistent Risk Assessment Practices

However, the most concerning theme exposes how police risk assessments under RCRP often dismissed clinical judgements. Officers treated calls from clinicians similarly to those from the public. Highlighted in the 2024 case of Tcherno Bari where the coroner raised these matters citing:

> RCRP and [College of Policing: Missing Person Authorised Professional Practice] APP do not require attending constables to have particular regard to the expertise of mental health clinicians and hesitate or be extra vigilant before rejecting their opinion on risk category. RCRP and APP appear to regard reports from mental health clinicians no differently to those from members of the public, and family and friends of the missing person.[90]

Similar issues were identified in the 2025 case of Sophie Cotton, where police did not to attend despite four separate calls for assistance, two of which came from Sophie's clinical team, who were physically present at her address and repeatedly expressed serious concerns for her safety. The coroner found that the "Right Care, Right Person" assessment led police to refuse to attend and identified several specific failings:

- *No decision was made for police to attend, even after a third call and a second being from a professional*
- *"Right Care, Right Person" advice to redirect the matter to mental health services ignored the fact that mental health teams or crisis teams lack any power to enter locked premises without police assistance*
- *Supervisory reviews of negative decisions under RCRP causes additional delay in circumstances when attendance could be extremely time-sensitive.*[91]

Similar concerns have emerged in other jurisdictions adopting RCRP-inspired models. In April 2024, in Fremantle Western Australia, a tragic incident occurred when police declined to attend a call from ambulance officers who believed a man required urgent mental health care. The man was displaying severe paranoia, and his mother was subsequently killed by him.[92] When questioned by the media, the Western Australia Police Force Commissioner stated that "it was the right care, the right people involved" noting that ambulance officers had advised at the time the man was not committing an offence or being aggressive.[93]

These cases illustrate the potential risks of applying RCRP principles rigidly, without sufficient nuance or consideration of situational complexity. They also highlight broader concerns in terms of risk when only one sector within a crisis response model fully adopts or is prepared for the operational and cultural shift in service delivery, as required by RCRP.

Lessons from Past Policy

The UK's rapid embrace of Right Care, Right Person draws comparisons to the earlier *Serenity Integrated Mentoring (SIM)* model, which, as previously discussed, was eventually dismantled following grassroots campaigns such as *Stop SIM*. RCRP expansion similarly originates from a single policing jurisdiction and is based largely on self-reported police resourcing data. Yet, to date there has been no independent evaluation of Right Care, Right Person to measure broader impacts.[94] Not only on policing but also the health sector, other emergency responders, and those people in crisis. This lack of oversight mirrors concerns raised about SIM's rapid expansion from the Isle of Wight, where initial reports lacked independence and transparency.

Ironically the Metropolitan Police, now a leading proponent of RCRP, was once a major user of SIM, at one time having 21 dedicated SIM officers.[95] As the *Met* now states on its website: *"SIM was stopped fully in May 2021 following the 'Stop SIM' campaign. We can confirm none of our MH teams still use the scheme."*[96]

This precedent raises important questions about the validity, and sustainability of police-led mental health intervention models, particularly when implemented quickly and without adequate oversight, collaboration from service providers or meaningful involvement of individuals with lived experience.

New Operational Reality

Right Care, Right Person represents a critical juncture in the evolution of behavioural health crisis response. Offering the potential to reduce stigma and trauma associated with inappropriate police responses to BHCFS.[97] And while the transition has predominately been driven by policing priorities, it has gradually gained support by many in the social and health services sector, who are positioned to shoulder those calls police shall withdraw from.

A 2025 poll of over 1700 UK social workers found that while only 13% fully endorsed RCRP in its present form, a further 46% expressed conditional support. Commentary from the survey suggests many social workers viewed police involvement in crisis calls was outside their remit and a symptom of broad gaps in mental health resourcing. At the same time, survey participants expressed concern about the rapid pace at which RCRP was being implemented.[98]

At its core, RCRP represents societies call for the right professional to respond to BHCFS. However, the success of such reform depends more than reducing police resourcing. It requires effective inter-sector collaboration, coordination, training, and sustainable funding for all services in the crisis response system. Without a foundation of collaboration, there is a risk that policing simply shifts a burden rather than contributing to meaningful systems change.

As the UK and other jurisdictions continue adopting RCRP-like models, amid political advocacy, public scrutiny, and ongoing debate, the true effectiveness of these changes remains to be fully measured. This is particularly important when considered when viewed through the experiences of those with lived experience, and the impact such reform has on their emotional and physical wellbeing.

Ultimately, RCRP signals a broader evolution in how intervention and management of behavioural health calls for service are understood, triaged, and managed. How this model matures over time will offer valuable insights into the future of crisis response and the systems required to support it.

Crisis Intervention Teams

In September 1987, in Memphis Tennessee, police fatally shot a man after his mother called 911 to lodge a Behavioural Health Call for Service. The man was reported to be self-harming and threatening people with a knife. Responding officers claimed he lunged at them resulting in the use of deadly force.[99] This tragic event resulted in widespread outcry from civil rights and mental health advocates, who citied it highlighted the failings of policing's approach to BHCFS. Whilst exposing inadequacies of police training and a health system which relied on police to act as first responders.

The Origins of the Memphis Model

In response, the National Alliance on Mental Illness (NAMI), Memphis Police Department, University of Memphis, and University of Tennessee collaborated to create an alternative approach called the Memphis Police Crisis Intervention Team (PCIT), also known as the Memphis Model. It launched with two goals[100]:

- Improve Officer and Consumer Safety
- Divert Individuals with Mental Illness from the criminal system to appropriate health care services

The Memphis Model was built on three community pillars:

Police – Development of a cohort of volunteer officers who obtained specialised mental health, de-escalation, and local service pathway training. These officers would become responsible for responding to active BHCFS citywide. They would assess risks, criminality and connect individuals with care.[101]

Advocacy Groups – Persons with lived experience, families, and mental health advocates provide vital feedback on police training programs, mental health receiving facilities, and policies for crisis management.[102]

Mental Health Professionals – Provide pivotal support in training, crisis care delivery, and transition to post-crisis treatment. Additionally, enabling "no wrong door" policies for urgent access to crisis care.[103]

The premise of the original Memphis Model was effective crisis intervention was not reliant on training police alone. Rather BHCFS are a community challenge necessitating a community coordinated response.[104] With early evaluations showing reductions in injuries and arrest rates the Memphis Model swiftly expanded into 2,700 jurisdictions across the United States.[105]

CIT International Arrives

The success of the Memphis Model led to the creation of *Crisis Intervention Team International* (CITI) in 2008, by Dr. Randy Dupont and Major Sam Cochran (Ret.), both instrumental figures in developing the original Memphis CIT program.[106] In 2019, CITI published the *Crisis Intervention Team (CIT) Programs: A Best Practice Guide for Transforming Community Responses to Mental Health Crises* for communities seeking to implement a CIT program. The guide introduced an expansion to four goals:

1 Improve safety during police encounters with people in crisis.
2 Increase timely access to mental health services.
3 Limit police involvement to threats of violence or criminal concern, whilst increasing the role of health professionals and peer support.
4 Reduce trauma during crisis to support long term.[107]

The new CIT Guide purported itself as a flexible resource rather than a prescriptive template. Allowing communities to adapt CIT to their specific needs. Although, this adaptability has seen CIT programs differ significantly between communities.[108]

Variation in Implementation and Systemic Limitations

Research points to this flexibility resulting in diverse perspectives on the program's primary focus: for some, CIT is perceived as a community safety strategy; for others CIT is as an officer safety initiative; for others, it serves as in-service training for police education whilst others see it as a mechanism for jail diversion, among other interpretations.[109]

Frequently, policing agencies are the primary drivers of communities implementing a CIT program, seeing an emphasis on officer training and formation of specialised response teams. Possibly explaining the predominance of research consistently prioritising evaluation of CIT effectiveness by focusing on police officer change in knowledge and attitudes to measure a program's success, rather than systemwide impacts such as hospitalisation linkage of community care continuity. Leading some researchers to argue that CIT's community-level potential remains underdeveloped.[110]

Regularly evidenced challenges in CIT practice which hamper attainment of the CIT ideal are as follows:

- **Lack of Crisis Care Access**: surveys of police agencies operating CIT programs indicate only 18% of agencies have access to 24/7 psychiatric facilities, and only 31% reported formal agreements with them.[111]
- **Fragmentation of Emergency Systems**: competing priorities of stakeholders often results in disorganisation and breakdowns in response execution.[112] A cohesion which as a critical element remains inadequately addressed in many jurisdictions.[113]
- **Training Disparities**: CITI discourages widespread and mandatory training of police officers citing "*training officers who do not have the specific interest, personal motivation, or skills to be CIT officers is not encouraged*"[114] Yet critiques argue this stance has two downsides:
  - Officers who lack motivation to undertake CIT training, due to biases or lack of knowledge, are arguably those most in need of such training.[115]
  - By only having a small cohort of trained officers (i.e., 20–25%) means a significant percentage of calls remain handled by untrained responders thereby undermining the effectiveness of CIT.[116]

These limitations and variations in CIT practice raise concerns about whether CIT has an ability to meet its core objectives across all jurisdictions globally as desired.

The Co-Responder Debate

CITI has taken a clear position against the implementation of police-led co-responder programs, where clinicians are embedded in police patrol vehicles. In a paper published in July 2021, CITI argued:

> most people experiencing a mental health crisis are not violent nor are they engaged in criminal behavior. They report that having police involved is stigmatizing and increases trauma at a time when they feel extremely frightened and vulnerable. Furthermore, the negative impact of police involvement is disproportionately experienced in communities of color, who are demanding alternatives to law enforcement response. Simply putting a clinician in a police car does not address these concerns.[117]

Despite this position, many jurisdictions operating CIT programs also adopt police-led co-responder models. Cities such as Los Angeles, Houston, New York City, and Portland have integrated police/health co-response approaches into their CIT frameworks.[118]

These models, in theory, could bridge the gap between CIT-trained officers and emergency departments while supporting the broader CIT goal of building community systems-based response models. However, the adoption of co-response in CIT jurisdictions highlights discrepancies between CITI's philosophical stance and the practical realities of jurisdictions seeking to expand intervention options.

Discrepancies in CIT Efficacy

The efficacy of CIT is further questioned considering its stated goals, particularly in reducing injuries during encounters and achieving de-escalation outcomes.[119] A systematic review conducted by Taheri (2016) found inconclusive evidence regarding CIT's ability to meet these objectives. Taheri observed:

> Unfortunately, there is insufficient evidence to conclude if these models reduce officer injury during encounters between police officers and persons with mental illness. At this time, however, there appears to be some evidence that CIT has no effect on outcomes of arrest, nor on officer use of force. [120]

This evidence points to an ongoing tension between the aspirational goals of CIT and its practical implementation, raising concerns about its capacity to reliably achieve the outcomes it was designed to address.

Despite systemic criticisms of Crisis Intervention Team programs efficacy, significant research has demonstrated meaningful benefits at the individual officer level. A study of 586 police officers across six police agencies in Georgia, USA found CIT training enhanced an array of officer aspects[121]:

- Knowledge: Greater understanding of mental illnesses.
- Attitudes: More empathy, diverse and open attitudes towards individuals in crisis.
- Self-Efficacy: Improved confidence in handling crisis or suicidality.
- Reduced Stigma: Greater willingness to engage with individuals in crisis.
- De-Escalation: Enhanced abilities to defuse potentially volatile situations.
- Referral Decisions: More appropriate referrals to services rather than use of the criminal justice system.

This evidence suggests that while systemic challenges remain, the training itself delivers meaningful improvements in areas critical to improving a police officers' ability to respond to behavioural health calls for service.

Working towards Systemic Change

CIT International continues to promote CIT as being more than a program for improving policing response, but for improving mental health systems, particularly in terms of crisis response.[122] Yet, evidence supporting these broader systemic improvements remains limited. Scholars like Compton and Watson emphasise the need for evaluation of community-level effect citing research should examine CITs "effectiveness not only for improving officer and call-level outcomes, but also for system-level outcomes related to reducing the role of police in a mental health crisis response system."[123]

Despite the dearth of robust evidence regarding such systemic impacts, the scope of CIT has clearly expanded beyond its original focus on policing. Supported by the National Alliance on Mental Illness (NAMI), which has promoted the integration of CIT training into diverse fields, including prisons, schools, universities, and municipal agencies. With CITI's annual US-based conference now attracting thousands of attendees, offering a platform for interdisciplinary engagement through workshops, presentations, and exhibitions.[124]

Conclusion

Originating as a response to a devastating tragedy, the Crisis Intervention Teams program has since expanded as a nationally recognised model across the United States, with influence extending internationally. It is widely purported by Crisis Intervention Teams International to be a collaborative approach to managing behavioural health crises, with a focus towards first responders directly linking to health providers.

There is further research which has evidenced clear benefits in CIT programs improving police officer's preparedness and attitudes towards behavioural health crisis. However, beyond improving police officer efficacy CIT's broader systemic change remains uneven and often inoperable. As Curry et al. (2023) observe as follows:

> Although the CIT model was well intended and conceived ..., in a majority of localities it has been reduced to the one component of training of police officers, with no clear reduction in adverse population outcomes.[125]

This observation with other researchers' similar findings highlights the key challenge for CITI's objective. Whilst police officer training is an integral part of improving crisis response it in itself is not sufficient. If CITI intends to build fully integrated, systems-based response, then there needs to be a focus towards prioritising health professional training at the same rate as police. A shift which falls in line with the goals of the original Memphis Model in creating a health led community care system.

Observational Summary

This chapter has examined four primary modalities employed globally by policing jurisdictions to address police involvement in managing Behavioural Health Crises, which is a key aspect of community safety. It is important to note that this list is by no means exhaustive of all possible approaches. Rather, the discussion of each modality serves to highlight the underlying motivational ideologies that have shaped their development.

These ideologies can be summarised as follows:

1 **Distancing – Right Care, Right Person (RCRP)**
RCRP is grounded in the principle that health-related matters should be addressed by health professionals, a premise that garners broad support across the policing and health sectors. This model advocates for rigorous vetting of behavioural health service requests to assess the appropriateness of police involvement and ensure that the "Right Person" is deployed to

the scene. However, concerns have been raised regarding the true effectiveness of RCRP, particularly when it appears to focus more on reducing police engagement rather than improving service delivery. Criticism from community leaders highlights that RCRP metrics tend to emphasise police hours saved rather than assessing effectiveness of addressing consumers core needs. Moreover, as the UK Independent Office for Police Conduct has pointed out, there are circumstances in which police may still have a duty of care in a 'health only' case, especially in situations where failure to intervene could result in serious harm or even death.[126]

2 **Collaboration – Co-Responder**
The Co-Responder model represents a highly integrated approach, with both police officers and health professionals working side by side at the scene of a crisis. The strength of this model lies in the opportunity for shared learning, increased access to information, improved de-escalation, and a more responsive approach to the needs of individuals in crisis. However, the Co-Responder model differs from others in that police are consistently involved in every intervention, which may limit efforts to reduce police presence in non-criminal behavioural health incidents. Nevertheless, feedback from both practitioners and communities suggests that the collaborative nature of Co-Responder programs is widely appreciated, indicating that there is a strong desire for joint responses to crises.

3 **Preventative – Serenity Integrated Mentoring (SIM)**
SIM was developed to target individuals who cycle through behavioural health crises repeatedly. The aim is to reduce the overall demand on emergency services by focusing on this smaller, high-frequency group. Although SIM is not designed to address the broader spectrum of crisis response to BHCFS, its preventive approach seeks to reduce recidivism by providing tailored intervention. Thereby ultimately reducing BHCFS demand and such need for response systems. A key critique of SIM, however, is its reliance on the police to escalate some individuals into judicial settings, which runs counter to the general aim of moving individuals into a fully health-managed setting, as preferred by most advocacy groups.

4 **Systems-Based – Crisis Intervention Teams (CIT)**
CIT is a comprehensive approach aimed at fostering community-based responses to BHC. The core ideology of CIT is to enhance police understanding through specialised training, while also creating non-police response systems and appropriate care facilities. However, despite its claims to a broader community-based approach, CIT remains heavily centred on police involvement, particularly with a predominate focus on police training. An issue highlighted in CITI's own promotional catch phrase "*CIT is more than just training...it's a community program.*"[127]

Subsequently the emphasis on police training and the use of this training as a key measure in the discourse of the model's effectiveness by policymakers, advocacy, and academics alike may restrict the model's broader potential for fostering non-police-driven solutions, thus limiting the full realisation of its community-based aspirations.

A Perspective:

While each of these models employs a distinct methodology, they share a common goal: to improve the outcomes of police engagement with individuals in behavioural health crises. Despite their varying operational challenges, these approaches have considerable potential if considered together. A hybrid model that integrates the principles of distancing, collaboration, prevention, and systems-based approaches – with enhanced call vetting, improved police training, collaborative on-scene responses, and proactive community partnerships – would likely provide a more holistic and effective solution. Such an integrated approach would not only improve the overall response to behavioural health crises but also foster a more supportive, community-centred system.

Notes

1 Quattlebaum, M., & Tyler, T. (2020). Beyond the law: An agenda for policing reform. *Boston University Law Review*, *100*(3), 1017; Edwards, C. J. (2011). *Changing policing theories for 21st century societies* (3rd ed.). Federation Press.
2 El-Sabawi, T., & Carroll, J. J. (2020). A model for defunding: An evidence-based statute for behavioral health crisis response. *Elon University Law Studies*. https://papers.ssrn.com/sol3/papers.cfm?abstract_id=3683432.
3 Billingham, Z. (2018). *Policing and mental health: Picking up the pieces*. Her Majesty's Inspectorate of Constabulary and Fire & Rescue Services, www.justiceinspectorates.gov.uk/hmicfrs/publications/policing-and-mental-health-picking-up-the-pieces/.
4 Quattlebaum, M., & Tyler, T. (2020). Beyond the law: An agenda for policing reform. *Boston University Law Review*, *100*(3), 1017.
5 Adebowale, V. (2013). *Independent report commission on mental health and policing*. www.basw.co.uk/system/files/resources/basw_22916-3_0.pdf.
6 DeShaney v. Winnebago County Department of Social Services, 489 U.S. 189 (1989). Open-access source: https://supreme.justia.com/cases/federal/us/489/189/; Town of Castle Rock v. Gonzales, 545 U.S. 748 (2005). Open-access source: https://supreme.justia.com/cases/federal/us/545/748/.
7 Vancouver Police Department. (2024). *1978: Car 87 program begins*. https://vpd.ca/news/1978/06/18/1978-car-87-program-begins/
8 Council State Governments. (2024). *Justice Center law enforcement – Mental health learning sites*. Los Angeles Police Department. https://csgjusticecenter.org/wp-content/uploads/2020/04/MEU-Program-Outline-January-2020.pdf.

9 Ghelani, A. (2022). Knowledge and skills for social workers on mobile crisis intervention teams. *Clinical Social Work Journal*, *50*(4), 414–25. https://doi.org/10.1007/s10615-021-00823-x; Houston Police Department. (2024). *Mental Health Division CIRT.* www.houstoncit.org/cirt/.

10 Uding, C. V., Moon, H. R., & Lum, C. (2024). The status of co-responders in law enforcement: Findings from a national survey of law enforcement agencies. *Policing: An International Journal.*. https://doi.org/10.1108/PIJPSM-04-2024-0062.

11 Henry, P., & Rajakaruna N. (2018). *Western Australia Police Force mental health co-response evaluation report.* www.parliament.wa.gov.au/publications.

12 Henry, P., & Rajakaruna, N. (2018). *Western Australia Police Force mental health co-response evaluation report.* www.parliament.wa.gov.au/publications.

13 Henry, P., & Rajakaruna, N. (2018). *Western Australia Police Force mental health co-response evaluation report.* www.parliament.wa.gov.au/publications.

14 Parliament UK. (2015). *Policing and Mental Health Services, Police and Health services collaboration.* (https://publications.parliament.uk/pa/cm201415/cmselect/cmhaff/202/20206.htm

15 Gov.UK. (20 August 2013). *Press release – Extending the street triage scheme: New patrols with nurses and the police.* www.gov.uk/government/news/extending-the-street-triage-scheme-new-patrols-with-nurses-and-the-police

16 Kirubarajan, A., Puntis, S., Perfect, D., Tarbit, M., Buckman, M., & Molodynski, A. (2018). Street triage services in England: Service models, national provision and the opinions of police. *BJPsych Bulletin*, *42*, 1–5. doi:10.1192/bjb.2018.62.; Gov.UK. (20 August 2013). *Press release – Extending the street triage scheme: New patrols with nurses and the police.* www.gov.uk/government/news/extending-the-street-triage-scheme-new-patrols-with-nurses-and-the-police.

17 New Zealand Police. (17 October 2022). *Better outcomes for mental health.* www.police.govt.nz/news/ten-one-magazine/better-outcomes-mental-health.

18 Kuehl, S., Cooper, L., & Every-Palmer, S. (2024). "Able to stop things from escalating" – Stakeholders' perspectives of police, ambulance and mental health co-response to 911-mental health calls. *The Police Journal.* https://doi.org/10.1177/0032258X241253965; Henry, P., & Rajakaruna N. (2018). *Western Australia Police Force mental health co-response evaluation report.* www.parliament.wa.gov.au/publications.

19 Parliament WA. (24 February 2022). *Police — Mental health co-response program.* www.parliament.wa.gov.au/hansard/hansard.nsf/16ab30a0303e54f448256bf7002049e8/e2308818ee9e7c33482588bd00220b5e/$FILE/A41%20S1%2020220224%20p694d-695a.pdf; New Zealand Police. (17 October 2022). *Better outcomes for mental health.* www.police.govt.nz/news/ten-one-magazine/better-outcomes-mental-health.

20 Kuehl, S., Cooper, L., & Every-Palmer, S. (2024). "Able to stop things from escalating" – Stakeholders' perspectives of police, ambulance and mental health

co-response to 911-mental health calls. *The Police Journal.* https://doi.org/10.1177/0032258X241253965; Horspool, K., Drabble, S. J., & O'Cathain, A. (2016). Implementing street triage: A qualitative study of collaboration between police and mental health services. *BMC Psychiatry, 16*(1), 313. https://doi.org/10.1186/s12888-016-1026-z

21 Bailey, K., Paquet, S. R., Ray, B. R., Grommon, E., Lowder, E. M., & Sightes, E. (2018). Barriers and facilitators to implementing an urban co-responding police-mental health team. *Health & Justice, 6*(1), 21. https://doi.org/10.1186/s40352-018-0079-0; Lamanna, D., Shapiro, G. K., Kirst, M., Matheson, F. I., Nakhost, A., & Stergiopoulos, V. (2018), Co-responding police–mental health programmes: Service user experiences and outcomes in a large urban centre. *International Journal of Mental Health Nursing, 27*, 891–900. https://doi.org/10.1111/inm.12384.

22 Lowder, E. M., Grommon, E., Bailey, K., & Ray, B. (2024). Police-mental health co-response versus police-as-usual response to behavioral health emergencies: A pragmatic randomized effectiveness trial. *Social Science & Medicine, 345*, 116723. https://10.1016/j.socscimed.2024.116723.

23 Lowder, E. M., Grommon, E., Bailey, K., & Ray, B. (2024). Police-mental health co-response versus police-as-usual response to behavioral health emergencies: A pragmatic randomized effectiveness trial. *Social Science & Medicine, 345*, 116723. https://10.1016/j.socscimed.2024.116723.

24 Office of Justice Programs. (2021). *Assessing the impact of co-responder team programs: A review of research* (NCJ 305544). U.S. Department of Justice, Bureau of Justice Assistance. www.ojp.gov/library/publications/assessing-impact-co-responder-team-programs-review-research.

25 Marcus, N., & Stergiopoulos, V. (2022). Re-examining mental health crisis intervention: A rapid review comparing outcomes across police, co-responder and non-police models. *Health & Social Care in the Community, 30*, 1665–1679. https://doi.org/10.1111/hsc.13731; Fisher, O., Donahoo, C., Bosley, E., Cloux, R., Garner, S., Powell, S., Pickard, J., Grevis-James, N., & Wyder, M. (2024). Barriers and enablers to implementing police mental health co-responder programs: A qualitative study using the Consolidated Framework for Implementation Research. *Implementation Research and Practice, 5*. https://doi.org/10.1177/26334895231220259

26 Blais, E., Landry, M., & Elazhary, N., et al. (2022). Assessing the capability of a co-responding police-mental health program to connect emotionally disturbed people with community resources and decrease police use-of-force. *Journal of Experimental Criminology, 18*, 41–65. https://doi.org/10.1007/s11292-020-09434-x

27 Henry, P., & Rajakaruna N. (2018). *Western Australia Police Force mental health co-response evaluation report.* www.parliament.wa.gov.au/publications

28 Yang, S.-M., & Lu, Y.-F. (2024). Evaluating the effects of co-response teams in reducing subsequent hospitalization: A place-based randomized controlled trial. *Policing: A Journal of Policy and Practice, 18.* https://doi.org/10.1093/police/paad080.

29 Dee, T. Geiser, K. Gerstein, A. Pyne, J., & Woo, C. (2024). *Impact Report San Mateo County, California Community Wellness and Crisis Response Team Pilot Program: December 2021 through June 2024.* https://gardnercenter.stanford.edu/sites/g/files/sbiybj24036/files/media/file/impactreport_2024-10-15.pdf.
30 Keown, P., French, J., Gibson, G., Newton, E., Cull, S., Brown, P., Parry, J., Lyons, D., & McKinnon, I. (2016). Too much detention? Street Triage and detentions under Section 136 Mental Health Act in the North-East of England: A descriptive study of the effects of a Street Triage intervention. *BMJ Open, 6*(11), e011837. https://doi.org/10.1136/bmjopen-2016-011837; Henry, P., & Rajakaruna N. (2018). *Western Australia Police Force mental health co-response evaluation report.* www.parliament.wa.gov.au/publications.
31 Meehan, T., Brack, J., Mansfield, Y., & Stedman, T. (2019). Do police–mental health co-responder programmes reduce emergency department presentations or simply delay the inevitable? *Australasian Psychiatry, 27*(1), 18–20. https://doi.org/10.1177/1039856218797424.
32 Lamanna, D., Shapiro, G. K., Kirst, M., Matheson, F. I., Nakhost, A., & Stergiopoulos, V. (2018). Co-responding police–mental health programmes: Service user experiences and outcomes in a large urban centre. *International Journal of Mental Health Nursing, 27*, 891–900. https://doi.org/10.1111/inm.12384
33 Evangelista, E., Lee, S., Gallagher, A., Peterson, V., James, J., Warren, N., Henderson, K., Keppich-Arnold, S., Cornelius, L., & Deveny, E. (2016). Crisis averted: How consumers experienced a police and clinical early response (PACER) unit responding to a mental health crisis. *International Journal of Mental Health Nursing, 25*, 367–76. https://doi.org/10.1111/inm.12218.
34 Puntis, S., Perfect, D., Kirubarajan, A., et al. (2018). A systematic review of co-responder models of police mental health 'street' triage. *BMC Psychiatry, 18*, 256. https://doi.org/10.1186/s12888-018-1836-2.
35 Scott, R. L. (2000). Evaluation of a mobile crisis program: Effectiveness, efficiency, and consumer satisfaction. *Psychiatric Services, 51*(9), 1153–1156. https://doi.org/10.1176/appi.ps.51.9.1153.
36 Uding, C. V., Moon, H. R., & Lum, C. (2024). The status of co-responders in law enforcement: Findings from a national survey of law enforcement agencies. *Policing: An International Journal, 48*(1), 69–97. https://doi.org/10.1108/PIJPSM-04-2024-0062.
37 International Co-Responder Alliance. (2024). www.coresponderalliance.org/.
38 Jachimowski, K. G., Smathers, C. J., Smathers, L. N., & Lemmon, R. J. (2021). The impact of mental health resources on police officer action. *Journal of Police and Criminal Psychology, 36*(2), 193–203. https://doi.org/10.1007/s11896-020-09395-x.
39 House, A. (2023). Serenity Integrated Mentoring and the High Intensity Network: A scheme that raises serious questions for practice and governance in UK psychiatry. *BJPsych Bulletin, 47*(1), 1–4. https://doi.org/10.1192/bjb.2022.6; Jennings, P., & Matheson-Monnet, C. B. (2017). Multi-agency

mentoring pilot intervention for high intensity service users of emergency public services: The Isle of Wight Integrated Recovery Programme. *Journal of Criminological Research, Policy and Practice, 3*(2), 105–18. https://doi.org/10.1108/JCRPP-01-2017-0007
40 Health Innovation Network South London. (2020). *SIM London: Support for a better life, April 2018 – May 2020.* https://healthinnovationnetwork.com/wp-content/uploads/2020/10/SIM-London-End-of-Year-Report-2020FINAL.pdf.
41 Health Innovation Network South London. (2020). *SIM London: Support for a better life, April 2018 – May 2020.* https://healthinnovationnetwork.com/wp-content/uploads/2020/10/SIM-London-End-of-Year-Report-2020FINAL.pdf.
42 Jennings, P., & Matheson-Monnet, C. B. (2017). Multi-agency mentoring pilot intervention for high intensity service users of emergency public services: The Isle of Wight Integrated Recovery Programme. *Journal of Criminological Research, Policy and Practice, 3*(2), 105–18. https://doi.org/10.1108/JCRPP-01-2017-0007
43 Jennings, P., & Matheson-Monnet, C. B. (2017). Multi-agency mentoring pilot intervention for high intensity service users of emergency public services: The Isle of Wight Integrated Recovery Programme. *Journal of Criminological Research, Policy and Practice, 3*(2), 105–18. https://doi.org/10.1108/JCRPP-01-2017-0007.
44 Matheson-Monnet, C. B., & Jennings, P. (2017). A review of quality improvement (QI) specialised interventions in the USA and England to reduce the number of police mental health crisis detentions and provide support to high intensity utilisers (HIUs). *Open Medicine Journal, 4*(1).
45 HSJ Solutions. (2017). *Trust in Collaboration introduces a project aiming to help people with high intensive patterns of behaviour, eliminating the need for crisis calls and reducing hospital admissions.* https://solutions.hsj.co.uk/story.aspx?storyCode=7016754.
46 NHS Innovation Accelerator [NIA]. (2024). https://nhsaccelerator.com/about-us/our-history-and-impact/.
47 NHS England. (23 June 2017). *News NHS England kicks off international search for ground-breaking patient-care innovations.* www.england.nhs.uk/2017/06/international-search-for-ground-breaking-patient-care-innovations/.
48 NHS England. (23 June 2017). *News NHS England kicks off international search for ground-breaking patient-care innovations.* www.england.nhs.uk/2017/06/international-search-for-ground-breaking-patient-care-innovations/.
49 Royal College of Emergency Medicine. (2017). *Best practice guide: Frequent attenders in the emergency department.* https://res.cloudinary.com/studio-republic/images/v1635411714/Frequent_Attenders_in_the_ED_Aug2017/Frequent_Attenders_in_the_ED_Aug2017.pdf?_i=AA.
50 Aves, W. (2023). *Serenity integrated mentoring: Past, present and future.* www.psychiatryisdrivingmemad.co.uk/post/sim-past-present-and-future.

51 Mayor of London. (2021, May 27). *Metropolitan police service involvement in serenity integrated mentoring (2).* www.london.gov.uk/who-we-are/what-london-assembly-does/questions-mayor/find-an-answer/metropolitan-police-service-involvement-serenity-integrated-mentoring-2?__cf_chl_tk=btY0Mr5njZu4CMSMcWE6WXTcpWaVJdeUBr_Uu7xYw4I-1718524704-0.0.1.1-7743.
52 GOV.UK. (2024). *Companies house – High Intensity Network LTD.* Retrieved February 5, 2026, from https://find-and-update.company-information.service.gov.uk/company/11699463; BMJ Group. (2018). *International Forum on Quality & Safety in Healthcare – Paul Jennings.* Retrieved February 5, 2026, from https://internationalforum.bmj.com/amsterdam/2017/10/18/paul-jennings/.
53 Open Forum Events. (2024). *Speaker – Paul Jennings.* Retrieved February 5, 2026, from www.openforumevents.co.uk/speakers/paul-jennings/; Jennings, P. (2019, June 19). *Serenity integrated mentoring (SIM) and the high intensity network workshop* [PowerPoint slides]. SlideShare. www.slideshare.net/slideshow/paul-jennings-serenity-integrated-mentoring-sim-and-the-high-intensity-network-workshop/150610887#55.
54 Farrar, M. (2021). *Independent review of AHSN network involvement in support to mental health trusts and police forces for the adoption of the serenity integrated mentoring (SIM) model or equivalent.* https://thehealthinnovationnetwork.co.uk/wp-content/uploads/2023/05/Independent-Review-into-AHSN-role-in-SIM-Mike-Farrar-FINAL-V1.pdf.
55 Farrar, M. (2021) *Independent review of AHSN network involvement in support to mental health trusts and police forces for the adoption of the serenity integrated mentoring (SIM) model or equivalent.* https://thehealthinnovationnetwork.co.uk/wp-content/uploads/2023/05/Independent-Review-into-AHSN-role-in-SIM-Mike-Farrar-FINAL-V1.pdf.
56 Anokhina, A., Martin, P., Pizzo, E., Barbosa, E. C., Nagularaj, L., Sinclair, C., Urbonaite, K., Podmore, B., Morris, S., Jennings, P., & Fonagy, P. (2018). *A feasibility assessment of serenity integrated mentoring (SIM) implementation in London, England.* www.arc-nt.nihr.ac.uk/media/ggzgif43/sim_feasibility_assessment_30-09-19.pdf.
57 Anokhina, A., Martin, P., Pizzo, E., Barbosa, E. C., Nagularaj, L., Sinclair, C., Urbonaite, K., Podmore, B., Morris, S., Jennings, P., & Fonagy, P. (2018). *A feasibility assessment of serenity integrated mentoring (SIM) implementation in London, England.* www.arc-nt.nihr.ac.uk/media/ggzgif43/sim_feasibility_assessment_30-09-19.pdf
58 Blackwell, G. (2023). *Reducing recidivism in behavioural health crisis cycles.* The Churchill Fellows Association of Western Australia Churchill Fellowship to establish diversionary practices for mentally and intellectually disabled persons engaging police. www.churchilltrust.com.au/project/the-churchill-fellows-association-of-western-australia-churchill-fellowship-to-establish-diversionary-practices-for-mentally-and-intellectually-disabled-persons-engaging-police/

59 College of Policing. (2023, October). *Right Care, Right Person – Humberside Police.* Retrieved February 5, 2026, from www.college.police.uk/support-forces/practices/smarter-practice/right-care-right-person.

60 Home Office (UK). (2024). *Policy paper National Partnership Agreement: Right Care, Right Person (RCRP).* www.gov.uk/government/publications/national-partnership-agreement-right-care-right-person/national-partnership-agreement-right-care-right-person-rcrp.

61 College of Policing. (2024). *Legal overview for RCRP.* www.college.police.uk/guidance/right-care-right-person-toolkit/legal-overview-rcrp.

62 College of Policing. (2024). *Legal overview for RCRP.* www.college.police.uk/guidance/right-care-right-person-toolkit/legal-overview-rcrp.

63 Home Office (UK). (2024). *Policy paper National Partnership Agreement: Right Care, Right Person (RCRP).* www.gov.uk/government/publications/national-partnership-agreement-right-care-right-person/national-partnership-agreement-right-care-right-person-rcrp.

64 Watson, A. C., Pope, L. G., & Compton, M. T. (2021). Police reform from the perspective of mental health services and professionals: Our role in social change. *Psychiatric Services, 72*(9), 1085–1087. https://doi.org/10.1176/appi.ps.202000572; Miles-Johnson, T., & Morgan, M. (2022). Operational response: Policing persons with mental illness in Australia. *Journal of Criminology, 55*(2), 260–281. https://doi.org/10.1177/26338076221094385.

65 House of Commons. (2023). *Health and Social Care Committee oral evidence: Mental health: Right Care, Right Person, HC 1836.* https://committees.parliament.uk/oralevidence/13663/pdf/

66 College of Policing. (2023, October). *Right Care, Right Person – Humberside Police.* www.college.police.uk/support-forces/practices/smarter-practice/right-care-right-person.

67 Metropolitan Police. (2024). *Introduction of Right Care, Right Person model.* www.met.police.uk/notices/met/introduction-right-care-right-person-model/.

68 Metropolitan Police. (2024). *Introduction of Right Care, Right Person model.* www.met.police.uk/notices/met/introduction-right-care-right-person-model/.

69 The Guardian. (20 May 2023). *The Guardian view on the Met's mental health ultimatum: a deadline is not a solution.* www.theguardian.com/commentisfree/2023/may/29/the-guardian-view-on-the-mets-mental-health-ultimatum-a-deadline-is-not-a-solution; Metropolitan Police. (2024). *Introduction of Right Care, Right Person model.* www.met.police.uk/notices/met/introduction-right-care-right-person-model/.

70 Braverman, S. (2023, February 23). *Home Office correspondence letter to chief constables and police and crime commissioners (accessible).* www.gov.uk/government/publications/mental-health-and-policing-letter-from-the-home-secretary/letter-to-chief-constables-and-police-and-crime-commissioners-accessible.

71 Braverman, S. (2023, February 23). *Home Office correspondence letter to chief constables and police and crime commissioners (accessible).* www.gov.uk/government/publications/mental-health-and-policing-letter-from-the-home-secretary/letter-to-chief-constables-and-police-and-crime-commissioners-accessible.

72 College of Policing. (2023, October). *Right Care, Right Person – Humberside Police.* www.college.police.uk/support-forces/practices/smarter-practice/right-care-right-person; GOV.UK. (2024, April 17). *Police paper National Partnership Agreement: Right Care, Right Person.* www.gov.uk/government/publications/national-partnership-agreement-right-care-right-person/national-partnership-agreement-right-care-right-person-rcrp.

73 New South Wales Police Force. (2024). *Review of the NSW Police Force response to mental health incidents in the community.* www.police.nsw.gov.au/__data/assets/pdf_file/0004/884974/Review_of_the_NSW_Police_Force_response_to_mental_health_incidents_in_the_community.pdf.

74 Government of Western Australia. (2025, May). *Western Australia Police Force, Police welfare checks.* www.wa.gov.au/organisation/western-australia-police-force/police-welfare-checks.

75 New Zealand Police. (2024, August 30). *Police announce phased plan to reduce service to mental health demand.* www.police.govt.nz/news/release/police-announce-phased-plan-reduce-service-mental-health-demand.

76 National Police Chiefs Council. (2023, July 16). *1M officer hours saved with new approach to mental health.* https://news.npcc.police.uk/releases/police-to-save-1-million-officer-hours-as-forces-adopt-new-model-to-ensure-specialist-care-for-health-incidents.

77 Metropolitan Police. (2023). *Introduction of Right Care, Right Person model.* www.met.police.uk/notices/met/introduction-right-care-right-person-model/.

78 College of Policing. (2023, October). *Right Care, Right Person – Humberside Police.* www.college.police.uk/support-forces/practices/smarter-practice/right-care-right-person.

79 Local Government Association. (2023). *Right Care, Right Person: Policing and mental health and welfare checks.* Retrieved February 5, 2026, from www.local.gov.uk/topics/social-care-health-and-integration/right-care-right-person-policing-and-mental-health-and#:~:text=Right%20Care%2C%20Right%20Person%20%28RCRP%29%20is%20a%20partnership,to%20calls%20to%20Police%20regarding%20concerns%20about%20welfare.

80 UK Parliament. (2023). *Committee Mental Health: Right Care, Right Person Non-inquiry session.* https://committees.parliament.uk/writtenevidence/125358/pdf/

81 UK Parliament. (2023). *Urgent answers needed on funding for 'Right Care, Right Person' mental health strategy.* https://committees.parliament.uk/committee/81/health-and-social-care-committee/news/198473/urgent-answers-needed-on-funding-for-right-care-right-person-mental-health-strategy/

82 UK Parliament. (2023). *Urgent answers needed on funding for 'Right Care, Right Person' mental health strategy.* https://committees.parliament.uk/committee/81/health-and-social-care-committee/news/198473/urgent-answers-needed-on-funding-for-right-care-right-person-mental-health-strategy/

83 Bird, H., Bryant, L., & Kadiri, H. (2024). Defunding the police is good for our mental health. *The Political Quarterly*, *95*, 474–79. https://doi.org/10.1111/1467-923X.13449.
84 Bird, H., Bryant, L., & Kadiri, H. (2024). Defunding the police is good for our mental health. *The Political Quarterly*, *95*, 474–79. https://doi.org/10.1111/1467-923X.13449.
85 Government UK. (2024, December 3). *Home Office | Department of Health & Social Care | Research and Analysis Right Care, Right Person.* www.gov.uk/government/publications/evaluating-the-implementation-of-right-care-right-person/right-care-right-person#annex-a.
86 Courts and Tribunals Judiciary. (2024). *Prevention of future death reports.* www.judiciary.uk/prevention-of-future-death-reports/.
87 Courts and Tribunals Judiciary. (2024, September). *Ryan Ouslem: Prevention of future deaths report.* www.judiciary.uk/prevention-of-future-death-reports/ryan-ouslem-prevention-of-future-deaths-report/.
88 Courts and Tribunals Judiciary. (2023, June). *Heather Findlay: Prevention of future deaths report.* www.judiciary.uk/prevention-of-future-death-reports/heather-findlay-prevention-of-future-deaths-report/.
89 Courts and Tribunals Judiciary. (2025, May). *Paul Alexander: Prevention of future deaths report.* www.judiciary.uk/prevention-of-future-death-reports/paul-alexander-prevention-of-future-deaths-report/.
90 Courts and Tribunals Judiciary. (2024, June). *Tcherno Bari: Prevention of future deaths report.* www.judiciary.uk/prevention-of-future-death-reports/tcherno-bari-prevention-of-future-deaths-report/.
91 Courts and Tribunals Judiciary. (2025, May). *Sophie Cotton: Prevention of future deaths report.* www.judiciary.uk/prevention-of-future-death-reports/sophie-cotton-prevention-of-future-deaths-report/.
92 WAToday. (2024, May 3). *WA's top cop denies police ignored alleged murder victim's triple-zero calls in days before her death.* www.watoday.com.au/national/western-australia/wa-s-top-cop-denies-police-ignored-alleged-murder-victim-s-triple-zero-calls-in-days-before-her-death-20240503-p5fopt.html.
93 WAToday. (2024, May 3). *WA's top cop denies police ignored alleged murder victim's triple-zero calls in days before her death.* www.watoday.com.au/national/western-australia/wa-s-top-cop-denies-police-ignored-alleged-murder-victim-s-triple-zero-calls-in-days-before-her-death-20240503-p5fopt.html.
94 Wondemaghen, M. (2024). Policing psychiatric illness: An organisational paradox for Health & Law. *International Journal of Law and Psychiatry*, *97*, 102017. https://10.1016/j.ijlp.2024.102017.
95 Mayor of London. (2021, May). *Metropolitan police service involvement in serenity integrated mentoring.* www.london.gov.uk/who-we-are/what-london-assembly-does/questions-mayor/find-an-answer/metropolitan-police-service-involvement-serenity-integrated-mentoring-2; Metropolitan Police. (n.d). *Serenity Integrated Mentoring (SIM) teams based in NHS Mental Health Trusts.* www.met.police.uk/foi-ai/metropolitan-police/d/august-2022/serenity-integrated-mentoring-sim-teams-based-in-nhs-mental-health-trusts/.

96 Mayor of London. (2021, May). *Metropolitan police service involvement in serenity integrated mentoring.* www.london.gov.uk/who-we-are/what-london-assembly-does/questions-mayor/find-an-answer/metropolitan-police-service-involvement-serenity-integrated-mentoring-2; Metropolitan Police. (n.d). *Serenity Integrated Mentoring (SIM) teams based in NHS Mental Health Trusts.* www.met.police.uk/foi-ai/metropolitan-police/d/august-2022/serenity-integrated-mentoring-sim-teams-based-in-nhs-mental-health-trusts/.

97 O'Reilly, C. (2025). Editorial: Right Care, Right Person? Changing police responses to mental health crises. *Journal of Mental Health, 34*(2), 125–27. https://doi.org/10.1080/09638237.2025.2478373.

98 Koutsounia, A. (2025, January 7). *Social work opinion split over police involvement in mental health incidents, poll finds.* Community Care. www.communitycare.co.uk/2025/01/07/social-work-police-mental-health-incidents-readers-take/.

99 Rogers, M., McNiel, D., & Binder, R. (2019). Effectiveness of police crisis intervention training programs. *The Journal of the American Academy of Psychiatry and the Law, 47*(4), 414–21. https://doi.org/10.29158/JAAPL.003863-19. Retrieved from https://escholarship.org/uc/item/3670c01r.

100 CIT Center. (n.d.). *About CIT.* The University of Memphis. www.cit.memphis.edu/aboutCIT.php; Usher, L., Watson, A., Bruno, R., Andriukaitis, S., Kamin, D., Speed, C., & Taylor, S. (2019). *Crisis Intervention Team (CIT) programs: A best practice guide for transforming community responses to mental health crises.* Memphis: CIT International; Dupont, R., Cochran, S., Pillsbury, S., (2007). *Crisis Intervention Team core elements.* The University of Memphis. www.cit.memphis.edu/information_files/CoreElements.pdf.

101 Dupont, R., Cochran, S., & Pillsbury, S., (2007). *Crisis Intervention Team core elements.* The University of Memphis. www.cit.memphis.edu/information_files/CoreElements.pdf.

102 Dupont, R., Cochran, S., & Pillsbury, S., (2007). *Crisis Intervention Team core elements.* The University of Memphis. www.cit.memphis.edu/information_files/CoreElements.pdf.

103 Dupont, R., Cochran, S., & Pillsbury, S., (2007). *Crisis Intervention Team core elements.* The University of Memphis. www.cit.memphis.edu/information_files/CoreElements.pdf

104 Compton, M., Bahora, M., Watson, A., & Oliva, J., (2008). A comprehensive review of Extant Research on Crisis Intervention Team (CIT) Programs. *Journal of the American Academy of Psychiatry and the Law.* Online Mar 2008, *36*(1), 47–55.

105 Steadman, H. J., Deane, M. W., Borum, R., & Morrissey, J. P. (2000). Comparing outcomes of major models of police responses to mental health emergencies. *Psychiatric Services, 51*(5), 645–49. https://doi.org/10.1176/appi.ps.51.5.645; Dupont, R., & Cochran, S., (2000). Police response to mental health emergencies – Barriers to change. *Journal of the American Academy of Psychiatry and the Law.* Online Sep 2000, *28*(3), 338–344; NAMI (National Alliance on Mental Illness. (n.d.). *Crisis Intervention Team (CIT)*

Programs. www.nami.org/advocacy/crisis-intervention/crisis-intervention-team-cit-programs/.
106 CIT International. (n.d.). *What is CIT?* www.citinternational.org/What-is-CIT.
107 Usher, L., Watson, A., Bruno, R., Andriukaitis, S., Kamin, D., Speed, C., & Taylor, S. (2019). *Crisis Intervention Team (CIT) Programs: A best practice guide for transforming community responses to mental health crises.* Memphis: CIT International.
108 Compton, M., Bahora, M., Watson, A., & Oliva, J., (2008). A comprehensive review of Extant Research on Crisis Intervention Team (CIT) Programs. *Journal of the American Academy of Psychiatry and the Law.* Online Mar 2008, *36*(1), 47–55.
109 Compton, M., Bahora, M., Watson, A., & Oliva, J., (2008). A comprehensive review of Extant Research on Crisis Intervention Team (CIT) Programs. *Journal of the American Academy of Psychiatry and the Law.* Online Mar 2008, *36*(1), 47–55.
110 Compton, M. T., Broussard, B., Hankerson-Dyson, D., Krishan, S., Stewart, T., Oliva, J. R., & Watson, A. C. (2010). System- and policy-level challenges to full implementation of the Crisis Intervention Team (CIT) model. *Journal of Police Crisis Negotiations, 10*(1–2), 72–85. https://doi.org/10.1080/15332581003757347.

Office of Justice Programs. (2021, March). *Assessing the impact of co-responder team programs: A review of research* (NCJ 305544). U.S. Department of Justice, Bureau of Justice Assistance. www.ojp.gov/library/publications/assessing-impact-co-responder-team-programs-review-research.
111 Compton, M. T., Broussard, B., Hankerson-Dyson, D., Krishan, S., Stewart, T., Oliva, J. R., & Watson, A. C. (2010). System- and policy-level challenges to full implementation of the Crisis Intervention Team (CIT) model. *Journal of Police Crisis Negotiations, 10*(1–2), 72–85. https://doi.org/10.1080/15332581003757347.
112 Forshee, D. (2020). Crisis Intervention Team. In M. J. Fitz-Gerald & J. Takeshita (Eds.), *Models of emergency psychiatric services that work. Integrating psychiatry and primary care.* Cham: Springer. https://doi.org/10.1007/978-3-030-50808-1_6.
113 Compton, M. T., Broussard, B., Hankerson-Dyson, D., Krishan, S., Stewart, T., Oliva, J. R., & Watson, A. C. (2010). System- and policy-level challenges to full implementation of the Crisis Intervention Team (CIT) model. *Journal of Police Crisis Negotiations, 10*(1–2), 72–85. https://doi.org/10.1080/15332581003757347
114 Usher, L., Watson, A., Bruno, R., Andriukaitis, S., Kamin, D., Speed, C., & Taylor, S. (2019). *Crisis Intervention Team (CIT) Programs: A best practice guide for transforming community responses to mental health crises.* Memphis: CIT International.
115 Campbell, A. (2019). Failure on the front line: How the Americans with disabilities act should be interpreted to better protect persons in mental health crisis

from fatal police shootings. *Columbia Human Rights Law Review*. http://hrlr.law.columbia.edu/hrlr/failure-on-the-front-line-how-the-americans-with-disabilities-act-should-be-interpreted-to-better-protect-persons-in-mental-health-crisis-from-fatal-police-shootings/.

116 Rogers, M., McNiel, D., & Binder, R. (2019). Effectiveness of police crisis intervention training programs. *The Journal of the American Academy of Psychiatry and the Law*, *47*(4), 414–21. http://dx.doi.org/10.29158/jaapl.003863-19. Retrieved from https://escholarship.org/uc/item/3670c01r; Watson, A., & Compton, M. (2019). What research on crisis intervention teams tells us and what we need to ask. *Journal of the American Academy of Psychiatry and the Law* Online November 2019, JAAPL.003894-19; https://doi.org/10.29158/JAAPL.003894-19.

117 CIT International. (2021, July 6). *Why doesn't CIT International promote the embedded co-responder model?* Retrieved February 5, 2026, from https://cdn.wildapricot.com/212987/resources/Documents/Position%20Papers/CIT%20Int%20Embedded%20Co-response%20Position%20Paper.pdf.

118 Los Angeles Police Department. (2025). *Mental evaluation unit*. www.lapdonline.org/detective_bureau/content_basic_view/51704; City of Houston. (2025). *Houston Police Department Mental Health Division*. www.houstontx.gov/police/divisions/mental_health/index190528;htm#:~:text=The%20department%2C%20in%20collaboration%20with%20community%20mental%20health,possible%20to%20individuals%20in%20serious%20mental%20health%20crises; New York City Police Department. (2025). *Collaborative Policing*. www.nyc.gov/site/nypd/bureaus/administrative/collaborative-policing.page.

119 Watson, A., & Compton, M. (2019). What research on crisis intervention teams tells us and what we need to ask. *Journal of the American Academy of Psychiatry and the Law* Online November 2019, JAAPL.003894-19; https://doi.org/10.29158/JAAPL.003894-19.

120 Taheri, S. A. (2016). Do crisis intervention teams reduce arrests and improve officer safety? A systematic review and meta-analysis. *Criminal Justice Policy Review*, *27*(1), 76–96. https://doi.org/10.1177/0887403414556289.

121 Compton, M. T., Bakeman, R., Broussard, B., Hankerson-Dyson, D., Husbands, L., Krishan, S., … Watson, A. C. (2014). The police-based Crisis Intervention Team (CIT) Model: I. Effects on officers' knowledge, attitudes, and skills. *Psychiatric Services*, *65*(4), 517–22. https://doi.org/10.1176/appi.ps.201300107.

122 Watson, A., & Compton, M. (2019). What research on crisis intervention teams tells us and what we need to ask. *Journal of the American Academy of Psychiatry and the Law* Online November 2019, JAAPL.003894-19; https://doi.org/10.29158/JAAPL.003894-19.

123 Watson, A., & Compton, M. (2019). What research on crisis intervention teams tells us and what we need to ask. *Journal of the American Academy of Psychiatry and the Law* Online November 2019, JAAPL.003894-19; https://doi.org/10.29158/JAAPL.003894-19.

124 CIT International. (n.d.). *CIT Conference 2024.* www.citinternational.org/Conference

125 Curry, J., Sloan, L., Rush, W. K., & Gulrajani, C. (2023). The changing landscape of mental health crisis response in the United States. *Journal of the American Academy of Psychiatry and the Law, 51*(1), 6–12. https://doi.org/10.29158/JAAPL.220111-22.

126 Independent Office for Police Conduct. (2024). *Right Care, Right Person position statement – March 2024.* www.policeconduct.gov.uk/publications/right-care-right-person-position-statement-march-2024.

127 CIT International. (n.d.). *CIT what is it?* www.citinternational.org/What-is-CIT

5 Non-Clinical Outcomes to Crisis

Introduction

This chapter will look at those moments where police involvement in behavioural health crisis is unavoidable. While behavioural health challenges are best managed in clinical settings, there are often times when circumstances dictate that police and criminal justice systems must act. Times which escalate beyond the capacity of community services to safely respond. However, both police and justice systems overtime have worked to better understand behavioural health crisis and respond more appropriately.

It is important to acknowledge police generally want the same outcomes as clinicians, advocates, and consumers: safe, non-judicial, and health-led resolution. However, just as important, there is a need to acknowledge society also demands police prevent harm, reduce threats, and respond to those circumstances no other service is able or willing to attend. In these times, when police are left without clinical options, officers are often required to use non-clinical outcomes to resolve a call for service. We must accept in these times it is not always a failure of individual officers but an indication of how all systems will have a limit in managing behavioural health calls clinically.

This chapter will examine three key areas: *tactical disengagement, judicial management*, and *tactical resolution* (or use-of-force). Some of the following material may be challenging, but the aim is not to shock. Instead, it is intended to foster an honest and robust discussion on when police are left as the only option in crisis, how systems can improve their non-clinical resolution options for behavioural health calls.

Tactical Disengagement

Police have arrived on scene to an incident where a person is alone in their home, distressed, likely having made suicidal inferences, possibly armed, and refusing to engage with services. No crime has been committed. No

DOI: 10.4324/9781003749585-5

one else is at risk. Yet, a behavioural health call for service was initiated and police responded as requested. Should they go in?

These kinds of situations are becoming an increasingly common demand on policing. Police officers are often tasked with responding to behavioural health crises, even when no criminal act has taken place or third party is at risk. This creates complex legal, ethical, and tactical challenges, especially when the person in crisis is barricaded, non-compliant, or threatening self-harm. The dilemma: when to intervene, and when to back off?

The Operational Paradox

Police officers are trained to use de-escalation techniques – tools meant to reduce harm and resolve situations peacefully.[1] But these techniques rely heavily on communication, which doesn't always work. In cases where someone is experiencing severe psychological distress or is determined to follow their own course of action, even the most skilled officer may struggle to de-escalate.[2]

This brings us to what the author calls an *Operational Paradox*, the difficult balancing act officers face between the legal limits of their authority and their personal or professional desire to help. Sometimes, officers feel morally compelled to step in, especially when someone appears to be a danger to themselves. A concept tied to *parens patriae*, a legal principle asserting the state has a role in protecting individuals who can't protect themselves.[3]

But here's the problem: just because an officer wants to act doesn't mean the law supports it. In fact, the courts have made it clear that the authority to intervene has strict boundaries. In this environment, officers who do act run the risk of finding themselves facing complaints and legal liability.

Judicial Directions

In the United States, courts have increasingly scrutinised police conduct in these very situations resulting in several landmark cases. These highlight the evolving societal and legal expectations.

In *Adams v. City of Fremont* (1998), the California Court of Appeal established police officers have no legal duty under tort law to prevent a suicide during a mental health crisis. And further their failure to prevent a suicide didn't create legal liability, as cited:

> Police officers responding to a crisis involving a person threatening suicide with a loaded firearm have no legal duty under tort law that would expose them to liability if their conduct fails to prevent the threatened suicide from being carried out. [4]

This direction has been solidified by the following rulings:

- *Drummond v. City of Anaheim* (2003): The Ninth Circuit ruled that excessive force, regardless of mental illness, can be considered a constitutional violation. This emphasised the need for proportional, justified responses.[5]
- *Scott v. Smith* (2024): In a Las Vegas case, the court found deadly force was excessive where the person was mentally ill, unarmed, and not a danger to others or officers. The ruling confirmed that mental illness alone does not justify force.[6]

Scott v Smith is also interesting when considering the notion of *parens patriae* in a police officer's role with the court directly stating the following:

> Because Scott was mentally ill, was not suspected of a crime, and did not present a risk to officers or others, the *government's interest in applying force was limited*.[7]

This legal caution isn't limited to the US; around the world, similar cases are raising concerns about how police should respond to mental health crises.

An Australian inquest into the fatal police shooting of Mr. Fackender, a man with a known history of paranoia towards police, found the officers' decision to forcibly enter his home to enforce a Community Treatment Order was described as follows:

> premature, unnecessary and created a dangerous situation.... The police officers had, effectively, contained the scene.[8]

Comments echoed in the inquest of Todd McKenzie where, tactical officers, aware of McKenzie's deteriorating mental health, breached his residence to affect a mental health apprehension. The coroner ruled as follows:

> Serious physical confrontation was almost assured... The breach and hold should not have occurred when it did and probably should not have occurred at all.[9]

These rulings collectively illustrate the legal tightrope officers must walk. Feeling morally compelled to react and help someone who appears in distress, but also mindful that their authority to act isn't unlimited, even if they believe the subjects life is at risk.

Instead, police and first-responders now have to consider the following options:

- Is the person a threat to others?
- Is there a need to intervene to prevent the perceived risk?
- Is force going to be needed to take this person into protective custody?
- Could leaving the subject to manage their own distress be a better option?

This balancing act of a moral obligation opposed to legal limits of support creates the Operational Paradox officers must navigate.

Suicide by Cop: Expanding the Operational Paradox

Another relevant consideration is the phenomenon commonly referred to as Suicide by Cop. This term describes incidents where a person deliberately behaves in a threatening or confrontational way, to provoke officers to use deadly force. In essence, the individual utilises police as the tool to end their life.[10]

The *US District Court for the Southern District of Florida* has addressed this ruling citing when an individual's actions are intended to result in their death at the hands of police, the incident may legally be classified as a suicide.[11] This infers the individual, not the officer, is viewed as having caused the fatal outcome.

However, this legal classification does not automatically protect officers from legal scrutiny or eliminate a need to assess whether their use of fatal force was lawful and reasonable. In Florida, in a case involving the death of Paul Palmquist, it was reported they had expressed to acquaintances their desire to be killed by police in the days leading up to the incident. Subsequently, at the incident, Palmquist's behaviour was aggressive towards police and prompted them to shoot.

It was argued in court as Palmquist had expressed suicidal intentions by this very means, the officers' actions should be mitigated; however, the court disagreed stating as follows:

> Sergeant Selvik did not know Palmquist's motivation and intent when he shot him, the magistrate judge reasoned, and thus the evidence had no bearing on whether Selvik acted reasonably... Knowledge of facts and circumstances gained after the fact has no place in the jury's post-hoc analysis of the reasonableness of the actor's judgment.
>
> (US District Court, Palmquist Case)[12]

Consequently, while the suicidal intent of the subject may provide context for understanding the broader situation, it does not legally influence the assessment of the officer's conduct at the time of the use-of-force.

From these recurring themes, two central questions emerge for policymakers and police agencies trying to navigate this Operational Paradox:

- **Is suicidal ideation alone enough to justify police intervention?**
- **If an individual poses no imminent threat beyond themselves, is the use-of-force justified?**

Evolution of Tactical Disengagement

Such changing public attitudes, court decisions, and internal questions within police agencies have all contributed to a major shift in how policing responds to mental health crises. Particularly prominent in this shift is the use of tactical disengagement in the United States. A strategy where police will choose not to engage with a person in crisis under certain conditions.

In 2019, the Los Angeles Police Department (LAPD) implemented a landmark policy known as *Tactical Disengagement*.[13] Designed to assist officers responding to behavioural health calls for service, especially those involving suicidal ideation.

The LAPD's policy directs officers to *tactically disengage* from an incident if the following applies[14]:

- No crime has been committed.
- No third party is in danger.
- The individual is not compliant, but also not presenting a clear and immediate threat to themselves or others.

Tactical Disengagement advocates officers consider leaving, delaying contact, delaying custody or plan to make contact at a different time when a more appropriate mental health response can be coordinated, inclusive of individuals making suicidal comments.[15] The idea is it seeks to preserve life, respect individual autonomy, and minimise harm, recognising police officers are not always the appropriate response.

Importantly, this policy also reflects a current legal reality: police officers are not always required to enforce mental health laws, especially when no crime has occurred and there is no active threat.

Since LAPDs *tactical disengagement* inception, several police agencies across the US have developed similar policies encouraging officers to disengage when safe to do so, with notable examples:

- **Boston Police Department**:
  Officers can call off a response if there are concerns about harm to officers or civilians, even if a Section 12 (a Massachusetts law permitting

involuntary psychiatric evaluation) is in place. This approach includes a "cooling off" period to facilitate de-escalation.[16]

- **San Francisco Police Department**:
  It emphasises the safeguarding of life, dignity, and liberty of all persons. By clearly stating just because there is legal authority to take a person into custody, it does not override law enforcement discretion to pursue a safer course of action whenever feasible, before resorting to force.[17]
- **Kansas City Police Department**:
  Officers are required to attend training that includes segments on "tactical disengagement and redeployment," teaching them how to back off and reassess situations to avoid violent confrontations.[18]

International Perspectives on Disengagement in Behavioural Health Crises

While the concept of complete tactical disengagement is gaining traction in the United States, similar principles have yet to be as widely discussed or adopted as a response to mental health crises around the world.

In Australia, tactical disengagement refers more to creating space from the threat and setting a cordon to contain whilst evaluating and considering other appropriate tactics.[19]

Whilst in the UK the College of Policing stresses a focus towards tactical communication and containment techniques to manage conflict situations, without using physical force, through the use of the mnemonic BUGEE. BUGEE stands for[20]

- **B**e prepared to back off,
- **U**se of effective cover,
- **G**ive space and time if possible,
- **E**arly negotiation,
- **E**vacuate immediate area.

But neither of these ideologies support officers to consider a complete disengagement from the incident scene by delaying contact, delaying custody, or planning contact at a different time when a more appropriate mental health response can be coordinated.

Some Incidents Preclude Disengagement

Disengagement policies are designed to remove police from creating potentially life-threatening encounters through tactical resolution of incidents. However, it must also be clearly understood tactical resolution, that is use-of-force, will remain the primary outcome of those incidents where the subject of a behavioural health crisis call poses a real and imminent threat of harm to third parties.[21]

Conclusion

The movement toward ***tactical disengagement*** reflects a broader shift in how communities view the role of police in mental health crises. As legal cases, coronial inquests, and new policies have shown, the expectation that officers resolve every behavioural health incident, especially when no crime has occurred and no third party is at risk, can lead to unintended, often tragic, consequences.

By stepping back in carefully assessed situations, police can avoid escalating crises while considering their duty of care to all who may be impacted beyond the subject of the incident and respecting individual autonomy. This approach does not signal indifference but rather a recognition of appropriate boundaries and societal expectations. Increasingly, it's understood that not all crises require a police response and that sometimes, ***doing less can actually safely resolve more.***

Judicial Management

Sometimes when police respond to Behavioural Health Calls for Service (BHCFS), they encounter situations where criminal offending has occurred. In such cases, police officers are required to switch from crisis responder back to their role as criminal investigators, which can result in criminal proceedings. This is where the those living with neurodiversity, substance use disorders and mental illness challenges can find themselves becoming caught at the intersection of the criminal justice and health care systems.[22]

This raises the question: ***how should police and judicial systems respond to defendants whose complex cognitive or psychiatric needs impact on both their behaviour and their culpability, particularly when their alleged offending involves violence or victims.*** These situations can create a real social dilemma. On one hand, when victims are involved, there is strong public expectations to uphold justice through accountability. On the other hand, there is increasing recognition that untreated cognitive or psychiatric conditions may contribute to repeated offending behaviour.

This section explores how judicial systems attempt to navigate this dilemma by balancing punitive accountability with therapeutic rehabilitation, focusing on the growth and role of Mental Health Courts.

But before this this discussion commences, the author wishes to highlight two distinct points. Firstly, people with cognitive or psychiatric disorders who interact with police are significantly more likely to be the victims of crime rather than the perpetrator.[23] Secondly, this discussion is not about attributing blame to those living with behavioural health challenges. Rather, it is about looking at how the justice system can provide improved outcomes for both victims and offenders when offending occurs.

Mental Illness, Cognitive Disorders, and Criminal Responsibility

It is tempting to presume all persons living with a mental, cognitive or substance use impairment who commits a crime should be automatically exempt from legal responsibility. However, both legal and clinical perspectives emphasis that the mere presence of a cognitive or psychiatric condition does not, on its own, negate an individual's capacity to distinguish right from wrong. The question of criminal responsibility in these situations is far more complex requiring carefully assessed and individualised approaches.

This position is reflected in international human rights articles, within the United Nations Convention on the Rights of Persons with Disabilities (CRPD). Article 12 – *Equal Recognition Before the Law* affirms as follows:

> *Parties shall recognize that persons with disabilities enjoy legal capacity on an equal basis with others in all aspects of life.*[24]

This article reinforces that individuals with disabilities, including those with mental or cognitive impairment, should be presumed to possess legal capacity and autonomy. It challenges assumptions of inherently diminished capacity and underscores a need for individualised assessment.

Internationally, this concept has been broadly written into legislation. Examples include UK's Criminal Procedure (Insanity and Unfitness to Plead) Act 1991, California's Penal Codes Chapter 6 Competence of the Defendant, Western Australia's Criminal Law (Mental Impairment) Act 2023, and New South Wales's Mental Health and Cognitive Impairment Forensic Provisions Act 2020.[25] While these frameworks may differ in local jurisdictional contexts, they share the idea of assessing and managing culpability whilst preserving core legal principles of fairness, justice, and public safety.

It is essential to distinguish between individuals whose actions are genuinely beyond their control due to a cognitive or psychiatric condition, and those who, despite such a diagnosis, hold sufficient understanding of the wrongfulness or unlawfulness of their conduct.

The *International Commission of Jurists* (2022) adds an important perspective to this debate on culpability. They argue the CRPD's rejection of the traditional medical model of disability supports the notion that excluding individuals from full participation in criminal proceedings solely on the basis of mental disability effectively denies their legal capacity.[26] As such, long held concepts of fitness to plea and insanity clauses are in themselves a form of disability discrimination, and call for a reimaging of how criminal responsibility is framed, assessed, accommodated, and enacted in contemporary justice systems

A Therapeutic Approach to Court

In response to this complex intersection of judicial and healthcare systems when addressing crime, Mental Health Courts have evolved in many parts of the world. These courts are designed as problem-solving courts that aim to address underlying issues which may instigate criminal behaviours. They typically operate in a collaborative, multi-disciplinary approach. Where judges, prosecutors, defence lawyers, and clinical professionals work together to support individuals with cognitive or behavioural conditions progressing unnecessarily in the justice system.[27]

What makes Mental Health Courts unique to traditional courts is the adoption of the therapeutic jurisprudence concept. This approach acknowledges that the legal process and those professionals involved can work together to not only uphold the law but also promote the emotional, psychological, and social wellbeing of participants. Therefore, by prioritising support over punishment, therapeutic courts are likely to achieve longer-lasting and more positive outcomes for participants.[28]

Therapeutic Jurisprudence courts, work with a range of individuals living with behavioural health challenges, inclusive of mental illness, substance use, or neurodivergent conditions (i.e., ADHD or Autism).[29] In this text, the term "Mental Health Courts" will be used broadly to refer to any court that supports individuals across the behavioural health spectrum and not just solely mental illness.

Research has shown the therapeutic approach used by Mental Health Courts can produce tangible benefits. For example, a 2024 meta-analysis of more than a dozen studies found a 42% reduction in recidivism among participants who participated in treatment programs established in a therapeutic court setting.[30] Additionally studies have found those managed in a therapeutic mental health court system had lower rates of violent reoffending compared to those who were not.[31] Outcomes which highlight the effectiveness of a multi-disciplinary, humanistic approach in supporting individuals often in crisis and reducing crisis cycling.

Global Expansion of Mental Health Courts

The original concept of therapeutic courts commenced in the United States to address substance use. The humanistic and support-based principles soon expanded to other areas including offender profiles within family violence, Mental Health Courts, and intellectual developmental disability.

This success has led to their adoption in jurisdictions around the world, including Canada, Europe, the United Kingdom, and Australia.[32]

With this expansion though, there is significant variations between jurisdictions in how these courts are structured and operate. These differences see variations in the types of courts established, and the legal processes and support services offered before, during, and after court proceedings.

For instance, in the United Kingdom, some therapeutic concepts are intertwined in the criminal justice system rather than being specific specialist courts. The Mental Health Treatment Requirement (MHTR) is a national program allowing general courts to mandate clinical support as part of sentencing. Through MHTR, individuals receive personalised one-to-one psychological interventions with the program open to those with mental illness and neurodevelopmental/neurodivergence disorders.[33]

In contrast in Western Australia the judicial system takes a more segmented approach. Therapeutic courts are delineated to focus on specific diagnostic profile and function independently including Drug Court, Intellectual Disability Diversion Program Court, and Mental Health (START) Court.[34]

Meanwhile, Houston, Texas has taken an innovative approach to therapeutic jurisprudence with a pre-charge diversion model. The Houston Jail Diversion program, run through the Judge Emmett Mental Health Diversion Center in Harris County, allows police officers to refer individuals with persistent mental health issues, who have engaged in a lower-level misdemeanour, to a supported residential treatment program before proceeding with charges. This model is designed to assist the individual with their mental, behavioural, and social needs, enabling them to avoid criminal conviction and improving their reintegration into society.[35]

These variations highlight how therapeutic jurisprudence approaches can be adapted to meet the needs, legal frameworks, and societal demands of the communities they represent. Whilst still acknowledging a need for criminal accountability they are undertaken in a more humanistic, supportive approach which often leads to long-term benefits.

Challenges and Criticisms of Application

Whilst present research indicates the benefits of therapeutic courts, particularly for those living with mental health and/or neurodivergent conditions, there still remains some criticism, particularly in terms of inconsistent application.

A 2023 Australian study identified one such barrier was perceived gatekeeping by the judiciary and judicial processes themselves, which found only 57% of those who were eligible for diversion into mental health treatment were actually diverted. For individuals who had a prior offending history the rate dropped to 26%.[36]

This same research identified magistrates' decisions were based on a core set of factors with the most influential being:

- Severity of the mental illness or cognitive impairment,
- Treatment availability,
- Seriousness of offence,
- Level of violence.[37]

Such gatekeeping raises practical and ethical concerns given an independent study identified individuals with primary substance use and/or personality disorders were less likely to be diverted than those with psychotic disorders. Thereby leaving a vulnerable cohort with unmet needs and limited options, despite similar risks of incarceration or recidivism.[38] A point which reflects the consequences of academic and clinical focus on terms such as "Serious Mental Illness" creating a diagnostic divide in real-world crisis systems.

Other common barriers faced by mental health and therapeutic courts include the following[39]:

- Limited resourcing,
- Lack of specialist training,
- Stigma,
- Insufficient community supports.

There is also concern as to whether Mental Health Courts only focus on criminal outcomes. A recent study has explored how Mental Health Courts may be seen by some participants as coercive resulting in impediment towards recovery. Seeing those who saw the process as coercive more likely to recidivate than those who saw the therapeutic model as supporting their autonomy.[40]

Concern is also held on how substantial research focus has examined the benefits of therapeutic court processes for offenders, such as reductions in recidivism and increased engagement with clinical support. Whilst relatively little empirical investigation has been undertaken focusing on the experiences and satisfaction of victims whose cases proceed through these courts.[41]

Future Directions

Some critics attribute the challenges with therapeutic courts stem from the foundational framework of therapeutic jurisprudence itself. Questioning whether it is purely a theoretical concept or merely functions as a set of procedural guidelines lacking traditional legal rigidity.[42] In contrast, supporters hold this flexibility is in fact the cornerstone of its strength, allowing individualised problem-solving approaches to specific needs of the individual.[43]

Current research is increasingly exploring the potential of therapeutic jurisprudence beyond the realm of criminality. In particular, looking at how these principles can enhance civil and family court process by improving accessibility and support for individuals with behavioural health challenges.[44] Such integration into the broader judicial system has potential to improve perceptions of fairness in court processes as a whole rather than being seen as isolated, occasional, and tokenistic gestures.

Supporters' further emphasis the necessity of embedding therapeutic approaches into the education of future practitioners. This is inclusive of not only legal professionals, but also mental health and police practitioners.[45] Integrating principles of trust, self-determination, and procedural fairness into professional education can affect values and bias, in turn affecting both institutional procedures and culture operating within the justice system

Conclusion

Mental Health Courts (and similar models operating under the framework of therapeutic jurisprudence) represent a significant shift in how the justice system approaches offenders with behavioural health needs. These courts offer police and the broader legal system a mechanism to address criminal behaviour through alternative pathways which recognise an individual's behavioural, health, cognitive, or functional conditions which may play a role in their offending.

This distinction is crucial, as while some individuals may be entirely unable to stand trial due to severe impairment, others are simply unfit for or harmed by standard court proceedings.[46] Mental Health Courts aim to meet this complex balance of victims' rights and need for accountability with an approach that is trauma informed, flexible, and humane. In doing so, there is increased likelihood of effective treatments and long-term rehabilitation.

While some concerns remain about the overall effectiveness of therapeutic courts, it is important to recognise that for individuals with diminished cognitive capacity, who may not meet the legal threshold for being unsound of mind, there should still be a pathway within the justice system that supports, rather than solely punishes. This approach further allows police to take on a supportive role, working towards addressing the root cause of criminal behaviour. Ultimately, this enables a justice system that is not just reactively, but proactively addressing the cause of criminal behaviour. After all, the role of policing and the justice system is as much about preventing crime as it is in enforcing the law.

Tactical Resolution (Use-of-Force)

The following section for some readers may contain subject matter which will be confronting or triggering, as it will openly discuss the use of police force and fatal police engagement of individuals in crisis.

In recent years, there has been growing momentum to restructure behavioural health crisis response systems. At its core is the belief that reducing the reliance on police during mental health emergencies will lead to more effective outcomes for individuals experiencing psychological distress. However, much of the broader focus is on eliminating police involvement due to perceptions regarding police use-of-force.

As a result, jurisdictions have increasingly adopted non-police mobile crisis response team (CRT) models, such as clinician-led mobile crisis units, paramedic response teams, and co-responder teams. These non-police response systems and collaborative response models represent a substantive improvement over the previously "police-only" model of crisis response seen three to four decades ago post deinstitutionalisation. However, despite significant investments in systemic reform and frontline officer training, available data has not consistently demonstrated a measurable reduction in police use-of-force incidents.[47]

While there is an expansive emerging shift in reducing police engagement in crisis globally, any examination of crisis response must be prepared to acknowledge the complex reality in which police use-of-force is applied. Although a highly sensitive and confronting aspect of response, there is need for robust discussion on those unavoidable and possibly necessary applications of force for public safety. As Baker and Pillinger (2020) argued, incidents resulting in police use-of-force or death after contact with police cannot be seen as a 'police' only issue, but rather as a symptom of broader healthcare system failures.[48] The following discussion will attempt to hold such a robust examination.

Use-of-Force: A Complex and Incomplete Metric

Whilst police behavioural health calls for service (BHCFS) have risen significantly, the frequency of officer-involved fatalities has not increased at the same pace. This suggests that use-of-force statistics may not accurately reflect the broader progress made through systemic reform.

In the US, it's estimated that 5–20% of all police service calls involve behavioural health concerns.[49] While the volume of total incidents and police-citizen engagements can clearly be shown to have risen, there is still no centralised or definitive count of BHCFS incidents across jurisdictions. Nonetheless, several trends suggest significant shifts:

- In 2015, US police agencies reported 995 fatal shootings, with 261 involving individuals with mental health issues.
- By 2024, total fatal shootings rose to 1,173 (a 16% increase), while those with identified mental health factors declined to 173 (a 40% decrease).[50]

Similar patterns have been observed in Australia:

- Some jurisdictions report up to 30% of all police service calls now involve behavioural health.
- Between 2018 and 2024, total call volume rose by 80%, yet fatal police encounters increased marginally from 17 to 18 annually (a 5% increase), including both mental health and other incidents.[51]

These trends suggests that while overall fatalities have increased, mental health-related deaths in some jurisdictions have decreased proportionally, supporting claims of improved triage processes, collaborative response models, and harm reduction strategies for most jurisdictions.

Selection Bias and Police Involvement in High-Risk Incidents

A critical factor in understanding use-of-force rates, despite systems reforms, is the evolving role police hold in behavioural health crisis response. As systems adapt and new crisis response models emerge, police agencies increasingly serve as responders of last resort, called only to deal with the most severe, volatile, or high-risk situations.[52]

As most non-police crisis teams explicitly exclude situations that involve the following[53]:

- Weapons,
- Active violence,
- Ongoing criminal activity,
- Imminent threats to public safety.

This call risk triaging subsequential generates a structural bias where police are concentrated in the most dangerous encounters. Consequently, police are disproportionately called to the situations most likely to escalate. An operational reality supported by US research showing 87% of non-police crisis teams reported that police were considered a partner agency, especially in cases involving potential violence or firearms.[54]

When Tactical Resolution Is Unavoidable

While tragic, the following examples highlight the realities of triaging bias, due to high-risk events these incidents dictated tactical police intervention:

- **Joel Cauchi – Bondi Junction, Australia (2024)**
  Known to mental health services, Cauchi fatally stabbed six people and injured ten others at a shopping centre. The incident ended only after police applied lethal force.[55]
- **David Dalhover – Covington, USA (2024)**
  Released early from a court-ordered evaluation, Dalhover held a knife to his partner's chest during a police response. Officers fatally engaged him after he threatened to kill her.[56]
- **Odichukwumma Igweani – Milton Keynes England (2021)**
  Following mental health deterioration and lack of service access, Igweani killed a bystander and barricaded himself with a child. Lethal force was used after non-lethal attempts failed.[57]

These cases emphasise certain calls leave police officers with no option than immediate tactical intervention, reaffirming the unique legal authority and operational capacity of police in high-risk situations. Regardless, fatal encounters inevitably draw intense and emotionally charged public attention, often creating a perception of police use-of-force as a primary response. In reality, while these incidents have a significant impact on society, they remain statistically rare.[58]

Supported by US studies which found that deaths caused by police actions occurred in only[59]

- Approximately 3 in 1,000,000 police-citizen contacts,
- Approximately 9 in 100,00 arrests, and
- Approximately 2 in 100 assaults on officers.
- And most US police officers, approximately 95%, never discharge their firearms during their careers.[60]

On an international scale, fatal encounters with police remain similarly uncommon[61]:

- Australia, typically remains under 20 incidents per year,
- United Kingdom, averages fewer than 30 incidents per year.

These statistics demonstrate fatal use-of-force, although requiring absolute oversight and accountability, represent statistical outliers rather than standard operational outcomes.

Possibilities for Improving Police Tactical Resolution

This perspective change on police lethality should not stop calls for improvement of police response in volatile situations however, it highlights a need to reframe only questioning "How to cease police involvement?" to a parallel question "How can police be better equipped and supportive when involvement is unavoidable?"

Discussions will inevitably return to a focus on training. Whilst, continuous improvement in police training is crucial, it can't solve everything. Behavioural health crises are often unpredictable, especially when substance use is involved. In Australia, data shows that 57% of people with a diagnosed mental illness who were fatally shot by police had also used drugs or alcohol. Such unpredictable variables make even the best-trained officers' job harder.[62]

As criminology lecturer Emma Ryan aptly stated[63]:

> Every critical incident carries specific and different dynamics, and officers cannot realistically be trained for every possible scenario.

That's why training alone isn't enough. Officers need an increased array of effective tools at their disposal. When verbal commands don't work, and lethal force feels like the only option, there needs to be something in between. That's where a growing range of innovative less-lethal technologies have emerged to fill this gap such as:

- Conducted Energy Devices (eg. TASER),
- Pepper or Oleoresin Capsicum (OC) spray,
- Impact Munitions (Bean Bag & Rubber rounds),
- Remote Restraint Devices (eg. BolaWrap).

Yet, despite their availability, the implementation and distribution of such tools have been globally inconsistent.

In the United States, a US Government Accountability Office report showed that back in 2005, only about 7,000 of the 18,000 police agencies had begun using conducted energy devices (CED). By 2023, it is still reported not all officers are equipped with the devices as standard issue during patrol.[64]

A similar trend exists in the United Kingdom. In 2019, the National Police Chiefs Council found only 14% of English police officers had received CED training.[65] And despite CED being introduced in the UK in 2003, 2023 Metropolitan Police data showed only 22% of officers had been CED trained.[66]

This lack of access to less-lethal options regularly prompts concern among officers themselves, who argue such failures to provide less-lethal tools compromises their effectiveness in managing high-risk scenarios safely.[67]

Nevertheless, these tools are not without limitations. A recent US study examining 258 police shootings found that in over one-third of cases, CEDs failed. Sometimes, these failed attempts made the situation worse.[68]

These findings point to important ethical, operational, and legal considerations for policymakers and police leadership. Restricting access to less-lethal tools may reduce officers' response options and effectiveness. Affording officers more choices between verbal commands and lethal force could enhance safety, improve outcomes, and save lives during police encounters.

The Overlooked Outcome

While public discourse often centres on victims of police shootings, as we rightly should, we must also acknowledge the toll these events take on police personnel. Even when the use-of-force is deemed justified, officers are often subjected to intense public scrutiny, protracted internal and judicial investigations, and the emotional weight of having taken a life.

Research repeatedly shows officers who are involved in fatal encounters frequently face the following outcomes[69]:

- Elevated risk of post-traumatic stress disorder (PTSD),
- Occupational burnout,
- Premature retirement from service.

These outcomes are rarely acknowledged as consequences during discussions of broader systems failures of crisis response and management. Discussions which may look at a lack of inter-sector collaborations, inadequate community health services, or lack of police training, yet fail to acknowledge limitations in access to less-lethal options or influence of triaging bias.

In this environment, compounded by evocative media coverage, the well-being of officers, whether involved in an incident or not, can be irreversibly compromised, ultimately affecting the performance and resilience of those tasked with responding to society's most complex and high-risk situations.

Conclusion

The evolution of crisis response frameworks toward non-police models marks a positive step in aligning services with community health needs. However, expectations that police can be entirely removed from BHCFS are not yet supported by operational realities.

Non-police response expansion has moved many crises away from police and use-of-force. Yet inadvertently this may be concentrating the most volatile and potentially dangerous crisis to be triaged towards police response. Simply those situations with a higher likelihood of rapid escalation and confrontation. That aside the data shows the normative outcome is a safe and peaceful resolution with fatal encounters being those tragic outliers.

Moving forward, we need to ensure when those volatile incidents do arise, everyone involved is safe, and outcomes are humane as possible. Therefore, meaningful reform discussions might focus on the following:

- Clearer data and evaluation of who responds to what and when,
- Better training in de-escalation and behavioural health,
- Wider access to less-lethal tools,
- Stronger mental health support for officers.

Ultimately, a more open, robust, and balanced conversation is needed, one which acknowledges both the objective to reduce harm and the reality some complex, high-risk incidents will inevitably necessitate a tactical, police-led resolution. The priority should be to ensure those responses are well-informed, properly supported, and equipped with a broad range of resolution options, including access to less-lethal options. We also need to be willing to confront an uncomfortable truth – even in a system built focusing on safety, humane, dignified and accountable frameworks, there will remain rare outlying incidents where some level of force is required to prevent serious harm.

Observational Summary

The reality is not all behavioural health calls can, or should, be resolved in a clinical framework, which will see police remaining first-responders to many behavioural health calls. These situations are often complex, involving individuals with a multitude of competing needs, while at times impacting on families, bystanders, and the wider community.

In these moments, police officers are required to make rapid decisions balancing safety, risk, legal obligations, and potential impact on third parties, often in the absence of, or ability to, engage clinical support. This chapter examined three key aspects of non-clinical police responses: Tactical Disengagement, Judicial Management, and Tactical Resolution.

Tactical Disengagement

Tactical Disengagement refers to a deliberate decision by police officers to withdraw from a BHCFS engagement when continued involvement could escalate the situation or cause harm. It is not abdication of responsibility, rather it is a strategic decision focused on the safety of ***all those involved***. This approach recognises not all situations require forceful interventions and that police presence can sometime exacerbate the situation. Rather, a delayed or alternative approach, particularly with other sectors, may result in safer and just outcomes. Despite its success, ***tactical disengagement*** remains predominately applied in North America and yet to expand globally.

Judicial Management

Often delivered through therapeutic jurisprudence programs such as Mental Health Courts, participants are seen as individuals rather than standard defendants. They provide a specialised judicial setting for defendants whose offending may be affected by mental illness, cognitive, substance use, or general behavioural health challenges. These courts aim to address underlying offending behaviour causation. They also allow for another tier of judicial management between traditional criminal courts and often more restrictive unsoundness-of-mind processes. For police, these courts enable positive action to address accountability for offending, support treatment, enable prison diversion, and foster long-term rehabilitation, rather than retaining a punitive focus.

Tactical Resolution

Tactical Resolution, or using force to resolve incidents, remains the most controversial non-clinical outcome to BHCFS. Force may be applied through the direct physical restraint, deployment of less-lethal weapons, or on rare occasions fatal resolution. These incidents often attract a high level of public scrutiny and can fuel commentary on the criminalisation of behavioural health. It is essential though to pause and acknowledge two key realities. First, there are some situations where force is necessary to prevent imminent harm. Second, research consistently shows tactical resolution is more likely an outcome when officers lack sufficient training or are limited in their access to alternative force options. This highlights the importance of inter-agency collaborations, expanding alternative less-lethal force availability, understanding triaging bias, and enhancing police officer education.

Summary

Police responses to BHCFS are dynamic, complex, and require split second decision-making. While not each decision may be the most appropriate, officers can only operate within the framework of options supplied to them by government, their own policing agency, or the broader crisis system.

Improving training, expanding access to alternative force options, and strengthening cross-sector collaborations will increase a police officers' non-clinical resolution spectrum.

There is also a pressing need to recognise the impact that repeated reliance on non-clinical outcomes to resolve BHCFS, such as courts or use-of-force, has on police officers themselves, with rising rates of PTSD, damage to morale, and loss of policing experience from the frontline having a flow-on impact on the crisis care system.

Ultimately, there is a pressing need for outcomes to reflect fully integrated and collaborative justice and health systems that can deliver informed, compassionate, and flexible policing models.

Notes

1 MacIsaac, A., Baldwin, S., Semple, T., & Bennell, C. (2024). Exploring the relationship between officer safety and de-escalation in a simulated crisis encounter. *Police Quarterly.* https://doi.org/10.1177/10986111241289885; Ellis, A. (2024, December 13). *Matching care to need: 5 Facts on how to improve behavioral health crisis response.* The Council of State Governments (CSG) Justice Center. https://csgjusticecenter.org/2024/12/13/matching-care-to-need-5-facts-on-how-to-improve-behavioral-health-crisis-response/.

2 Davies, G., & Dawson, S. E. (2024). Contextualizing and defining de-escalation in policing. *Police Practice and Research*, *26*(1), 19–38. https://doi.org/10.1080/15614263.2024.2386578.

3 Lamb, H. R., Weinberger, L. E., & DeCuir, W. J. (2002). *The Police and Mental Health. Psychiatric Services* (Washington, D.C.); *Psychiatry Services*, *53*(10), 1266–71. https://10.1176/appi.ps.53.10.1266

4 California Court of Appeal, First District, Division 2. (1988). *ADAMS v. CITY OF FREMONT (1988) Nos. A074965, A075279.* https://caselaw.findlaw.com/court/ca-court-of-appeal/1288866.html.

5 United States Court of Appeals, Ninth Circuit. (2003). *Drummond ex rel. Drummond v. City of Anaheim (2003) No. 02 55320.* https://caselaw.findlaw.com/court/us-9th-circuit/1371011.html

6 United States Court of Appeals, Ninth Circuit. (2024). *Scott v. Smith (2024) Nos. 23-15480.* https://caselaw.findlaw.com/court/us-9th-circuit/116433900.html

7 United States Court of Appeals, Ninth Circuit (2024). *Scott v. Smith (2024) Nos. 23-15480.* https://caselaw.findlaw.com/court/us-9th-circuit/116433900.html.

8 O'Sullivan, Teresa. (2022). *Inquest in the death of Ian Fackender Coroners* (File No. 2017/00264782). Coroners Court of New South Wales. https://coroners.nsw.gov.au/coroners-court/download.html/documents/findings/2022/Ian_Fackender_findings.pdf.

9 State Coroner's Court of New South Wales. (2023). *Inquest into the death of Todd McKenzie* (File No. 2019/00239447). Magistrate Harriet Grahame,

Deputy State Coroner. https://coroners.nsw.gov.au/documents/findings/2024/Inquest_into_the_death_of_Todd_McKenzie.pdf.

10 Weiss, K. (2023). Suicide by cop and civil liability for police. *Journal of the American Academy of Psychiatry and the Law* Online Mar 2023, JAAPL.220062-22; DOI: 10.29158/JAAPL.220062-22.

11 Cannon, A. M. (2021). *North American Company for Life and Health Insurance v. Michelle Caldwell, et al., No. 22-10534 (11th Cir. 2022).* https://fingfx.thomsonreuters.com/gfx/legaldocs/egvbyyoxwpq/NorthAm%20v%20Caldwell_SDFL%20ruling.pdf

12 United States Court of Appeals, Seventh Circuit. (1997). *PALMQUIST v. SELVIK (1997) No. 96-1114.* https://caselaw.findlaw.com/court/us-7th-circuit/1097073.html.

13 Blackwell, G. (2023). *Reducing recidivism in behavioural health crisis cycles.* www.churchilltrust.com.au/project/the-churchill-fellows-association-of-western-australia-churchill-fellowship-to-establish-diversionary-practices-for-mentally-and-intellectually-disabled-persons-engaging-police/; Lopez, R. (2022). *'But we can't just leave!' How LAPD SWAT implemented a strategic disengagement policy.* www.police1.com/swat/articles/but-we-cant-just-leave-how-lapd-swat-implemented-a-strategic-disengagement-policy-lHT6VGQ1dTv9UN4f/.

14 Blackwell, G. (2023). *Reducing recidivism in behavioural health crisis cycles.* www.churchilltrust.com.au/project/the-churchill-fellows-association-of-western-australia-churchill-fellowship-to-establish-diversionary-practices-for-mentally-and-intellectually-disabled-persons-engaging-police/; Lopez, R. (2022). *'But we can't just leave!' How LAPD SWAT implemented a strategic disengagement policy.* www.police1.com/swat/articles/but-we-cant-just-leave-how-lapd-swat-implemented-a-strategic-disengagement-policy-lHT6VGQ1dTv9UN4f/.

15 Lopez, R. (2022). *'But we can't just leave!': How LAPD SWAT implemented a strategic disengagement policy.* www.police1.com/swat/articles/but-we-cant-just-leave-how-lapd-swat-implemented-a-strategic-disengagement-policy-lHT6VGQ1dTv9UN4f/.

16 Alanez, T. (2021, July 20). *Boston police emphasize de-escalation, disengagement in mental health calls.* Boston Globe. www.bostonglobe.com/2021/07/20/metro/boston-police-emphasize-de-escalation-disengagement-mental-health-calls/; Oliveira, P., Mitchell, J., & Sous, A. (n.d.). *New Bedford Police Department, Office of the Chief of Police Research & Development.* www.mass.gov/doc/new-bedford-police-commissioners-new-directive-so-21-30/download#:~:text=Boston%20Police%20Dept%20has%20implemented%20a%20strategic%20disengagement,for%20harm%20against%20officers%20or%20the%20civilian%20himself.

17 San Francisco Police Department. (n.d.). *General order disengagement procedures.* www.sf.gov/sites/default/files/2022-10/PoliceCommission101922-DGO%20Disengagement%20Procedures%20%28Clean%29%2010.13.22%20Police%20Commission.pdf.

18 Gov1. (2019, December 26). *Police in Kansas City learn to 'tactically disengage' to avoid violent confrontations.* www.gov1.com/public-safety/articles/police-in-kansas-city-learn-to-tactically-disengage-to-avoid-violent-confrontations-INkmllwTn4T29OUj/.

19 News South Wales Courts. (2023). *A summary of the New South Wales Police Use of Force Manual.* NSW Police Force Use of Force Manual. https://rlc.org.au/sites/default/files/2023-05/NSW%20Police%20Use%20of%20Force%20Manual.pdf.
20 College of Policing. (2020). *Conflict management using de-escalation, communication and negotiation guidelines.* https://assets.college.police.uk/s3fs-public/2020-09/Conflict-management-guidelines.pdf
21 Portland.Gov. (n.d.). *0850.20 Police response to mental health crisis.* www.portland.gov/policies/police-directives/arrest-detentions-court-0800/085020-police-response-mental-health-crisis; San Francisco Police Department. (n.d.). *General order disengagement procedures.* www.sf.gov/sites/default/files/2022-10/PoliceCommission101922-DGO%20Disengagement%20Procedures%20%28Clean%29%2010.13.22%20Police%20Commission.pdf.
22 Hartvigsson, T. (2023). Between punishment and care: Autonomous offenders who commit crimes under the influence of mental disorder. *Criminal Law, Philosophy, 17*, 111–34. https://doi.org/10.1007/s11572-021-09595-4.
23 Farrugia, L. (2024). Community and police officer attitudes towards offenders with mental health conditions. *Current Issues in Criminal Justice*, 1–16. https://doi.org/10.1080/10345329.2024.2425151.
24 United Nations. (n.d). *Department of Economic and Social Affairs Social Inclusion, Convention on the Rights of Persons with Disabilities (CRPD), Article 12 – Equal recognition before the law.* https://social.desa.un.org/issues/disability/crpd/article-12-equal-recognition-before-the-law.
25 Legislation.gov.uk. (n.d). *Criminal Procedure (Insanity and Unfitness to Plead) Act 1991.* www.legislation.gov.uk/ukpga/1991/25/contents; California Public Law. (n.d). Inquiry into the competence of the defendant before trial or after conviction, Chapter 6. https://california.public.law/codes/penal_code,_part_2,_title_10,_chapter_6; NSW Legislation. (n.d). *Mental Health and Cognitive Impairment Forensic Provisions Act 2020.* https://legislation.nsw.gov.au/view/whole/html/inforce/2021-03-24/act-2020-012
26 International Commission of Jurists. (2022). *Implementing the CRPD in criminal justice systems* (Briefing Paper). www.icj.org/wp-content/uploads/2022/12/Briefing-Paper-Implementing-The-CRPD-In-Criminal-Justice-Systems-Access-to-Justice-Knowledge-Hub.pdf.
27 Simonsson, P., Farwell, M. M., & Solomon, P.L. (2020). Judicial perspectives on mental health courts: The role of psychiatric disorder and violence risk. *International Journal of Law and Psychiatry, 70*, 101562. https://10.1016/j.ijlp.2020.101562
28 Howieson, J.A. (2023). A framework for the evidence-based practice of therapeutic jurisprudence: A legal therapeutic alliance. *International Journal of Law and Psychiatry, 89*, 101906. https://10.1016/j.ijlp.2023.101906.
29 Howieson, J. A. (2023). A framework for the evidence-based practice of therapeutic jurisprudence: A legal therapeutic alliance. *International Journal of Law and Psychiatry, 89*, 101906. https://10.1016/j.ijlp.2023.101906.
30 Jalain, C., Lucas, P., & Higgins, G. (2024). Assessing the effectiveness of mental health courts in reducing recidivism: A systematic review with meta-analysis.

Justice Evaluation Journal, *7*, 1–19. 10.1080/24751979.2024.2373245. www.researchgate.net/publication/382063508_Assessing_the_Effectiveness_of_Mental_Health_Courts_in_Reducing_Recidivism_A_Systematic_Review_with_Meta-analysis.

31 Soon, Y. L., Singh, S., Greenberg, D., Rae, N., Korobanova, D., Dixon, C., & Dean, K. (2024). Impact of mental health court diversion on reoffending: A direct comparison of diverted and undiverted groups. *International Journal of Forensic Mental Health*, *23*(4), 484–98. https://doi.org/10.1080/14999013.2024.2390107.

32 Lordelo, J. P. (2024). Therapeutic justice and problem-solving courts: A critical and comparative analysis. *Beijing Law Review*, *15*, 2253–64. https://doi.org/10.4236/blr.2024.154125.

33 NHS England. (n.d). *Mental health treatment requirements (MHTRs)*. www.england.nhs.uk/commissioning/health-just/mental-health-treatment-requirements/

34 Magistrates Court of Western Australia. (n.d). *Magistrates Court of Western Australia*. www.magistratescourt.wa.gov.au/default.aspx.

35 Blackwell, G. (2023). *Reducing recidivism in behavioural health crisis cycles*. www.churchilltrust.com.au/project/the-churchill-fellows-association-of-western-australia-churchill-fellowship-to-establish-diversionary-practices-for-mentally-and-intellectually-disabled-persons-engaging-police/.

36 Macdonald, C., Weatherburn, D., & Lappin, J. (2024). Diversion into mental health treatment: A survey of magistrates and treatment plans. *Psychiatry, Psychology and Law*, *32*(3), 354–72. https://doi.org/10.1080/13218719.2024.2313985.

37 Macdonald, C., Weatherburn, D., & Lappin, J. (2024). Diversion into mental health treatment: a survey of magistrates and treatment plans. *Psychiatry, Psychology and Law*, *32*(3), 354–72. https://doi.org/10.1080/13218719.2024.2313985.

38 Soon, Y. L., Singh, S., Greenberg, D., Rae, N., Korobanova, D., Dixon, C., & Dean, K. (2024). Impact of mental health court diversion on reoffending: A direct comparison of diverted and undiverted groups. *International Journal of Forensic Mental Health*, *23*(4), 484–98. https://doi.org/10.1080/14999013.2024.2390107.

39 Hailemariam, M., Bustos, T. E., Montgomery, B. W., et al. (2024). Mental health interventions for individuals with serious mental illness in the criminal legal system: A systematic review. *BMC Psychiatry*, *24*, 199. https://doi.org/10.1186/s12888-024-05612-7; Lowder E. M., Rade C. B., & Desmarais, S. L. (2018). Effectiveness of mental health courts in reducing recidivism: A meta-analysis. *Psychiatric Services*, *69*(1), 15–22. doi: 10.1176/appi.ps.201700107. Epub 2017 Aug 15. PMID: 28806894.

40 Pratt, C., Yanos, P. T., Kopelovich, S. L., Koerner, J., & Alexander, M. J. (2013). Predictors of criminal justice outcomes among mental health courts participants: The role of perceived coercion and subjective mental health recovery. *International Journal of Forensic Mental Health*, *12*(2), 116–25. doi: 10.1080/14999013.2013.791351. PMID: 24039547; PMCID: PMC3770483.

41 Otto, H. D. (2020). *A review of literature on mental health court goals, effectiveness, and future implications.* Illinois Criminal Justice Information Authority; Howieson, J. (2023). A framework for the evidence-based practice of therapeutic jurisprudence: A legal therapeutic alliance. *International Journal of Law and Psychiatry, 89,* 101906, ISSN 0160-2527, https://doi.org/10.1016/j.ijlp.2023.101906.
42 Kawałek, A. (2024). Strengthening the theoretical commitments underpinning therapeutic jurisprudence research: Ontology and epistemology. *Liverpool Law Review, 45,* 73–103. https://doi.org/10.1007/s10991-023-09329-7.
43 Howieson, J. A. (2023). A framework for the evidence-based practice of therapeutic jurisprudence: A legal therapeutic alliance. *International Journal of Law and Psychiatry, 89,* 101906. https://10.1016/j.ijlp.2023.101906.
44 Segal, M., & Gur, A. (2025). Using therapeutic jurisprudence principles to enhance access to legal proceedings for persons with disabilities: The ICCAP model. *International Social Work.* https://doi.org/10.1177/00208728251319495.
45 Kawałek, A. (2024). Strengthening the theoretical commitments underpinning therapeutic jurisprudence research: Ontology and epistemology. *Liverpool Law Review, 45,* 73–103. https://doi.org/10.1007/s10991-023-09329-7; Howieson, J. A. (2023). A framework for the evidence-based practice of therapeutic jurisprudence: A legal therapeutic alliance. *International Journal of Law and Psychiatry, 89,* 101906. https://10.1016/j.ijlp.2023.101906.
46 Young, J., Davis, F., Wardale, S., Vassos, M., Van Dooren, K., Nankervis, K., & Lennox, N. (2018). Severity of cognitive disability and mental health court determinations about fitness to stand trial. *Journal of Intellectual Disability Research, 62*(2), 126–39. doi:10.1111/jir.12468.
47 Marcus, N., & Stergiopoulos, V. (2022). Re-examining mental health crisis intervention: A rapid review comparing outcomes across police, co-responder and non-police models. *Health & Social Care in the Community, 30,* 1665–79. https://doi.org/10.1111/hsc.13731; Rogers, M. S., McNiel, D. E., & Binder, R. L. (2019). Effectiveness of police crisis intervention training programs. *Journal of the American Academy of Psychiatry and the Law* Online Sep 2019, JAAPL.003863-19; doi: 10.29158/JAAPL.003863-19
48 McDaniel, J., Moss, K., & Pease, K. (Eds.). (2020). *Policing and mental health: Theory, policy and practice* (1st ed.). Routledge. www.routledge.com/Policing-and-Mental-Health-Theory-Policy-and-Practice/McDaniel-Moss-Pease/p/book/9781032336848.
49 Kyprianides, A., & Bradford, B. (2025). Policing and mental health: A rapid evidence assessment of the patterning of police activity. *The Police Journal.* https://doi.org/10.1177/0032258X251318210; Wood, J. D., Watson, A. C., & Fulambarker, A. J. (2017). The "gray zone" of police work during mental health encounters: Findings from an observational study in Chicago. *Police Quarterly, 20*(1), 81–105. doi: 10.1177/1098611116658875. Epub 2016 Jul 13. PMID: 28286406; PMCID: PMC5342894; Katz, G. (2024). Rethinking law enforcement approaches to mental health crises. *American Police Beat.*

https://apbweb.com/2024/10/rethinking-law-enforcement-approaches-to-mental-health-crises/#:~:text=Some%20research%20studies%20have%20estimated%20that%20at%20least,this%20demand%20has%20been%20increasing%20for%20many%20departments.

50 The Washington Post. (2025). *Fatal force.* www.washingtonpost.com/graphics/investigations/police-shootings-database/.

51 Australian Institute of Criminology. (2024). *Deaths in police custody and custody-related operations.* www.aic.gov.au/publications/sr/sr49

52 Quattlebaum, M., & Tyler, T. (2020). Beyond the law: An agenda for policing reform. *Boston University Law Review, 100*(3), 1017.

53 Eugene. (2025). *CAHOOTS.* www.eugene-or.gov/5129/CAHOOTS; White Bird Clinic. (2025). *CAHOOTS (Crisis Assistance Helping Out on the Streets).* https://whitebirdclinic.org/cahoots/; Pope, L. G., Patel, A., Fu, E., Zingman, M., Warnock, A., Ellis, S., & Compton, M. T. (2023). Crisis response model preferences of mental health care clients with prior misdemeanor arrests and of their family and friends. *Psychiatric Services, 74*(11), 1163–70. https://doi.org/10.1176/appi.ps.20220363.

54 Erickson, B. R., Pope, L. G., Compton, M. T., Dixon, L. B., Odes, R., Looper, P., & Goldman, M. L. (2025). Mobile Crisis Teams' reliance on law enforcement for multiple key functions. *Psychiatric Services, 76*(4), 421–22. https://10.1176/appi.ps.20240346.

55 Coroners Court of New South Wales. (2026, February 5). *Inquest into the deaths at Westfield Bondi Junction: Executive summary.* https://coroners.nsw.gov.au/documents/bondi-junction-inquest/findings/Inquest_into_the_deaths_at_Westfield_Bondi_Junction_Summary.pdf.

56 Lyons, V. (2024, July 13). *NKY police shooting suspect allegedly given early release from psych hospital days before deadly incident, 9 WCPO ABC Cincinnati.* www.wcpo.com/news/local-news/kenton-county/taylor-mill/nky-police-shooting-suspect-allegedly-given-early-release-from-psych-hospital-days-before-deadly-incident; Sanderson, E. (2024, July 12). *Prosecutor clears officer in fatal shooting of suspect during reported hostage situation.* WLWT5. www.wlwt.com/article/hostage-situation-officer-involved-shooting-taylor-mill/61583078.

57 Cummings, S. (2023, August 16). *Odichukwumma Igweani: Prevention of future deaths report [2023-0296].* Courts and Tribunals Judiciary. www.judiciary.uk/prevention-of-future-death-reports/odichukwumma-igweani-prevention-of-future-deaths-report/

58 Rogers, M. S., McNiel, D. E., & Binder, R. L. (2019). Effectiveness of police crisis intervention training programs. *Journal of the American Academy of Psychiatry and Law, 47*(4), 414–21. doi: 10.29158/JAAPL.003863-19. Epub 2019 Sep 24. PMID: 31551327.

59 Johnson, R. (2019). *Dispelling the myths surrounding police use of lethal force.* Dolan Consulting Group, July 2016. dolanconsultinggroup.com/wp-content/uploads/2019/02/Dispelling-the-Myths-Surrounding-Police-Use-of-Lethal-Force.pdf.

60 Katz, G., (2025). *Misconceptions about police violence.* https://apbweb.com/2025/01/misconceptions-about-police-violence/

61 Australian Institute of Criminology. (2024). *Deaths in police custody and custody-related operations.* www.aic.gov.au/publications/sr/sr49; Independent Office for Police Conduct. (2024, October). *Deaths during or following police contact Statistics for England and Wales 2023/24.* file:///C:/Users/dash_/Downloads/Annual-deaths-statistics-report-England-and-Wales-202324.pdf.
62 Australian Institute of Criminology. (2013). *Police shootings of people with a mental illness.* Research in practice no. 34. Canberra: Australian Institute of Criminology. www.aic.gov.au/publications/rip/rip34
63 Ryan, E. (2025, April 3). *How should police officers use force? The Kristian White case is an insight into what the community thinks.* https://policinginsight.com/feature/opinion/how-should-police-officers-use-force-the-kristian-white-case-is-an-insight-into-what-the-community-thinks/
64 United States Government Accountability Office. (2005, May). *Taser weapons: Use of tasers by selected law enforcement agencies*; Report to the Chairman, Subcommittee on National Security, Emerging Threats and International Relations, Committee on Government Reform, House of Representatives, p. 25; Bowling, R. (2023, November 10). *History of the TASER: How it became an essential police tool.* Officer.com. www.officer.com/tactical/less-lethal/article/21251746/history-of-the-taser-how-it-became-an-essential-police-tool; Brean, B. (2022, July 30). In-depth: Why don't all police have Tasers? www.whec.com/archive/in-depth-why-dont-all-police-have-tasers/.
65 National Police Chiefs Council. (March 2019). *Working group on less lethal weapons, TASER® – Fifteen years on, an analysis of TASER® use in British policing.* www.npcc.police.uk/SysSiteAssets/media/downloads/publications/publications-log/2020/an-analysis-of-taser-use-in-british-policing.pdf
66 Metropolitan Police. (2023). *Data on Taser usage from January 2013 to July 2023, Freedom of information request reference no: 01.FOI.23.030484.* www.met.police.uk/foi-ai/metropolitan-police/disclosure-2023/august-2023/data-taser-usage-january2013-july2023/.
67 Walker, N. (2024, May 9). *Equipping UK police: The debate on expanding Taser accessibility.* Peel Solutions. https://peelsolutions.co.uk/equipping-uk-police-the-debate-on-expanding-taser-accessibility/#:~:text=Taser%20availability%20varies%20across%20the,more%20restrictive%20policies%20in%20place.
68 Caputo, A., Gilbert, C., Hing., G., & Pederson, N. (2019). *Tased, then shot – APM reports.* https://features.apmreports.org/taser-shootings/.
69 Papazoglou, K., & Andersen, J. P. (2014). A guide to utilizing police training as a tool to promote resilience and improve health outcomes among police officers. *Traumatology*, *20*(2), 103–11; Komarovskaya, I., Maguen, S., McCaslin, S. E., et al. (2011). The impact of killing and injuring others on mental health symptoms among police officers. *Journal of Psychiatric Research*, *45*(10), 1332–36.

6 The Question of Behavioural Health Training for Police

Introduction

As new programs evolve to reduce policing's role in behavioural health calls for service (BHCFS), one thing remains clear: police won't be stepping away from these situations entirely.[1] There are still many scenarios, especially those involving heightened risk, where officers are the only ones available to respond. That reality drives a fair and growing public demand: if police are going to be involved in these situations, they need the right kind of training.

Many police agencies still provide only cursory crisis training, with United States and Australian policing agencies, typically delivering less than one full day focusing on behavioural health crisis to new recruits.[2] In England, the average officer gets just 90 minutes of e-learning, however, some jurisdictions have started to build more in-depth courses lasting two to five days, but these are the exception, not the rule.[3]

What's more concerning is the near-total absence of mandatory, ongoing training once officers are on the job. Leaving officers with little opportunity to refresh or build contemporary skills, relying on only their academy training. This creates a significant mismatch between public expectations and the actual preparedness of frontline officers.

There's growing scepticism about whether we'll see a global shift towards comprehensive crisis response training for all officers anytime soon. Instead, those departments who do deliver any training tend to focus their efforts on select teams. *Crisis Intervention Teams International* (CITI) is an internationally recognised leader in training programs, yet illustrates this ideology stating "*CIT training is to prepare a select group of patrol officers... with a specialization in assisting people in crisis*" rather than aiming for broad implementation across agencies.[4]

Yet targeted programs raise questions about effectiveness when undertaken in isolation, with a recent study in England finding the impact of a one-day training course showed no noticeable improvement in how officers

DOI: 10.4324/9781003749585-6

handled mental health crises, six months later.[5] The takeaway? Brief and selective training sessions just don't cut it.

Policing leadership need only ask their own officers and many will say they feel ill equipped, with an Australian survey of police recruits revealing they felt unprepared for behavioural health situations, pointing to training that was fragmented, outdated, or too theoretical.[6] Results which reinforce public concern about whether police are adequately prepared for real-world crisis response.

While police training understandably prioritises command and control, tactics, and responding to high-threat situations to ensure officer safety, it is important this narrative doesn't dominate. Especially at the expense of empathy and communication skills, or reinforcing problematic stereotypes, particularly towards danger. This imbalance can increase the risk of escalation and reinforce implicit bias towards people in crisis.[7]

The United Kingdom College of Policing, acknowledged this in their 2020 guidelines on *Conflict Management Using De-escalation, Communication, and Negotiation*, noting personal safety remains a dominant narrative with a focus on physical techniques, with "*generally much less investment in the development of more specialist negotiation skills that are necessary for the safe resolution of these encounters.*"[8]

In the absence of formalised training many officers rely upon trial and error or mentoring from experienced officers to learn on the job. Yet agencies that default to this approach adopt a practice that is risky for everyone involved.[9] Especially as police forces tend to be experiencing a shortage of seasoned officers compared to years past.

As mentioned, some agencies have commenced adopting training for select groups of officers, however, they can't be everywhere and often can't be the first on scene. So, when officers without that training respond to BHCFS, they often fall back on what they know best, tactical control, not crisis communication.[10]

In 2015 the US *President's Task Force on 21st Century Policing* argued at recommendation 5.6 that crisis intervention training should be integrated into both academy and ongoing professional development, given officers felt more confident, better equipped to engage, and delayed rushing to resolution having undertaken behavioural health training.[11] A call supported by a survey of Los Angeles police who completed a 40-hour training program, where participants stated they were less likely to rush into a situation and more willing to slow things down, with a focus on de-escalation.[12]

The question, therefore, isn't whether police should receive behavioural health crisis training, this is an unequivocal necessity. The real task for police leaders is to define what type of training will actually make a difference. The evidence is clear: checklist-style, one-day, one-an-done workshops aren't enough. Improving both outcomes for people in crisis and trust in policing demands investment in training that's evidenced, grounded in real-world practice, and sustainable. This means investing time and resources to develop officers who can respond not just safely, but compassionately and effectively.

The next big questions we need to answer: **What content should an extended behavioural health crisis training program include, which police receive it, and when should training occur?**

Diagnostic Specific Knowledge

When discussions turn to police behavioural health crisis training, the focus regularly shifts to the familiar question: *How well should police understand specific conditions people are experiencing?* Academics, coronial inquests, and advocacy groups regularly call for 2-8 hours of training on individualised neurological conditions, mental health disorders, or substance use problems.[13]

But in reality, this demographic-specific approach runs into serious limitations. The *Diagnostic and Statistical Manual of Mental Disorders*, lists nearly 300 disorders, and adding to this are calls for training on intersectionality with factors such as age, sexuality, cultural background, First Nations identity which only expand the scope of training.[14] Delivering any meaningful insight would demand hundreds of training hours, an unrealistic and unsustainable demand on any policing agency.

Even narrowing the focus to only on the "most common" or "highest-risk" groups raises concerns. Prioritising certain disorders or demographics risks reinforcing harmful stereotypes, especially when data about which conditions are most commonly encountered in crisis is limited or unreliable. Crisis presentations also don't always align clinically with diagnostic or demographic profiles. A person with autism, someone experiencing a psychotic episode, and someone intoxicated might all display similar behaviours like confusion, agitation, or distorted reality. Even within the mental health field, misdiagnosis is a challenge.[15]

Too narrow a focus, or over emphasis of specific groups may be counter-productive and may unintentionally embed organisational and personal bias in how officers perceive and react to crisis.[16] So, let's also be clear: police officers *are not clinicians*. Expecting officers to develop clinical-level recognition of individual conditions is unrealistic, especially when many healthcare professionals spend years specialising in just one.

Training Needs To Be Practical, Not Clinical

This call to step away from overly clinical training for police was highlighted by the U.S. Department of Justice report *Improving Responses to People with*

Mental Illnesses: Strategies for Effective Law Enforcement Training which clearly stated:

> When discussing mental illnesses, coordinators and trainers from medical and mental health professions, as well as people with mental illnesses and their family members, should avoid overusing clinical terminology or diagnoses. Instead, content should be presented in clear terms and focus on behaviours that officers are likely to observe. Similarly, coordinators and trainers should avoid presenting too much information or detail that is not directly relevant to a law enforcement officer. [17]

Simply, prioritising clarity and practicality in police training should guide design. Not overloading technical content with clinical details. The goal isn't to make officers experts on mental illness, but to help them recognise signs, respond safely, and connect people to appropriate help.

Despite these challenges, agencies have continued to respond to external pressure in training development and delivery. The *Crisis Intervention Team* (CIT) model is widely recognised as a gold standard. Its 40-hour training program, which hasn't significantly changed since its 2010 launch, devotes roughly 40% of its curriculum, that's about two full days, to demographic-specific instruction.[18]

More recently, the International Association of Chiefs of Police (IACP) launched a new training called Crisis Response and Intervention Training (CRIT). Developed in 2022, IACP acknowledges that CRIT is based on the CIT training framework. As the IACP states, its goals include[19]:

- *Expanding officers' knowledge of mental health conditions, substance use disorders, and intellectual and developmental disabilities;*
- *Creating connections with people with lived experience;*
- *Enhancing officers' awareness of community services;*
- *Emphasising the de-escalation of crisis situations; and*
- *Supporting officer safety and wellness.*

Yet just like the CIT foundation CRIT retains a heavy demographic-specific structure.[20] But it's worth noting that demographic emphasis varies across other US regional CIT programs as shown on the Bureau of Justice Assistance website[21]:

- **Utah CIT** dedicates 12 hours (30%) to ten demographic-specific sessions
- **Houston CIT** devotes 10 hours (25%) to nine sessions
- **Clermont County CIT** allocates just 5 hours (14%) across four sessions

Reflecting the diverse approaches to incorporating demographic specificity within the broader context of behavioural health training in contemporary, revised programs.[22] Though a constant across many of these programs is a returning focus on a training session labelled "Serious Mental Illness".[23]

At first glance, the discussion may appear to argue against any clinical training for police officers. But that is not the case. The key is to understand police officer's role in crisis response: safety – keeping people safe, not to create first-response clinicians. A point highlighted ironically, in the International Association of Chiefs of Police (2018) report, *Responding to Persons Experiencing a Mental Health Crisis* which made it clear police are not expected to diagnose clinical conditions.[24] Instead, officers need only an ability to recognise behaviours to assist in deciding upon applying behavioural health, first aid or traditional policing tactics to ensure safety.

Accordingly, training should remain broad overviews of mental illness, intellectual and developmental disabilities (IDD), substance use disorders, and comorbidity. Along with an overview of understanding differences between suicidality and non-suicidal self-injury, which can span all behavioural health presentations, to understand when an individual causes harm to themselves it is not always an attempt to die.[25]

Ideally police training would reduce current excessive clinical content into less than a day, leaving time to equip officers to learn more trauma-informed care and de-escalatory approaches.[26] To illustrate this shift the following scenarios as set out in Table 6.1 are based on the author's operational experience and illustrate what crisis actually looks like in practice. It shows how diagnostic specific training would (or would not) affect the engagement and outcome accordingly.

Finally, the risk of overly clinical focus on conditions can be seen in a 2021 study of German police officers.[27] While officers could reliably identify schizophrenia, they struggled to recognise signs of PTSD, mania, personality disorders, or other behavioural health conditions. The researchers attributed this directly to their training, which focused heavily on schizophrenia.[28] It's a clear illustration of how focusing narrowly on certain disorders can result in officers missing other signs that are just as relevant during acute crisis response.

Behavioural Health Training Content

Having explored the limitations of diagnostic and demographic-specific training, we return to the initial questions: **What content should an extended behavioural health crisis training program include, which police receive it and when should training occur?**

The first of these questions: what content actually matters, forms the foundation of the next section of this chapter. Recognising a need to reimagine what genuinely is needed by police as frontline responders, that is less ability to identify specific diagnosis, brings us to realise there

Table 6.1 Behavioural Health Crisis Call for Service Training Scenario

Police attendance required for distressed person on traffic overpass bridge looking as though they may be at risk of self-harm.

Subject One:	Subject Two:	Subject Three:
Schizophrenia Homeless Non-compliant with treatment Co-occurring substance use Acquired Brain Injury	Nil mental illness history Substance Use (methylamphetamine) Past low level criminal offending	Schizophrenia Compliant with treatment Tertiary educated Employed LGBTQI+
Presentation: States they are seeking the golden horn, as directed by God, to bring them prosperity. This has resulted in the subject being in the unsafe location. Happy to engage with police. Proceeds to explain how with police present it is clear this is not the location of the horn, as it will only be revealed to those who are chosen. They are happy to move to another location with police, and recommence the search another time.	Presentation: Is unable to remain still, responding to people who are not present, and appears extremely concerned for their own welfare. Telling unseen persons to back away. Highly agitated and continues to tell those unseen people to take care as they are a well-known underworld figure with powerful friends. They are unwilling to engage with police, stating police are working with those wishing to harm them. Police are aware they have no significant criminal history or involved in organised crime.	Presentation: They appear slightly agitated, standing still, and leaning over the railing looking towards the passing traffic. They tell police calmly they have come to this location intending to end their life. They explain they have reached this point given the sudden and unexpected death of their long-term partner of more than 20yrs in a workplace accident. They are reluctantly engaging with police, due to a sense of hopelessness, emotional distress, and loss of future focus.

Summary:

These real-world examples show the limits of detailed diagnostic specific training in resolving acute crisis effectively.

Subject One is clearly experiencing delusional thinking but is cooperative, easily guided away from harm and may need to be assessed by clinical professionals.

However, Subject Two has no mental illness history and their behaviour is far less cooperative, almost combative, requiring a different approach to ensure safety. Similarly Subject Three is less combative but still reluctant to engage with police, although they have a mental illness, it is the situational crisis police will have to navigate to ensure safety.

It is the presenting behaviours, risk, and threat – not diagnostic profile – that drives police and first-responders' decision-making in times of imminent crisis.

are more universal principles that support safer, dignified, and decisive outcomes.

These foundational principles are:

- **Procedural Knowledge:**
  Helping police know their powers ensures a *procedurally just* approach
- **Relational Approaches:**
  Helping officers slow down, see the person not the problem and build trust
- **Trauma-Informed Care:**
  Understand how past trauma shapes current behaviours, fosters empathy, and reduces re-traumatisation
- **De-escalation Training:**
  Helping offices to focus on communication, not just control, to reduce harm

As seen in the earlier bridge scenario, these skills are applicable across most crisis presentations. When responders must react immediately to ensure safety, these principles provide the tools to engage respectfully, effectively and justly, regardless of a person's social circumstances, identity or diagnostic profile.

Each of these principles will be explored in detail in the sections that follow.

Procedural Knowledge

When we think about police training for behavioural health crisis situations, the focus is on empathy, communication, and de-escalation and rightly so. So why start the discussion on police behavioural health training here on legislation, procedures and procedural justice? Because discussions too often commence in the "how" of crisis response, *how* to talk someone down, *how* to calm a tense situation. But before officers can confidently apply de-escalation or behavioural health knowledge, they need to understand the legal context they're operating in.

That is where the key piece of the training debate regularly overlooks: *procedural knowledge*. Without a solid understanding of the laws, protocols, and judicial principles that underpin crisis response, even the best intentions can lead to poor outcomes.

So, what exactly does this procedural foundation look like? Officers must be grounded in:

- **Local Legislation and Case Law**:
  Officers must be conversant in local mental health legislation and aware of powers available to them, and just as importantly, when they are not

available. Case law adds nuance, showing how courts have interpreted these powers in real-life scenarios.

- **Behavioural Health-Specific Judicial Systems**:
  In many jurisdictions specialist courts or diversion programs exist. Officers need to know how these systems work so that the judicial system can also be supportive and not solely punitive in action.
- **Departmental Protocols**:
  Every agency has its own internal policies that guide officer behaviour in crisis situations. Understanding these ensures consistency, accountability, and alignment with broader agency goals
- **Inter-Agency Guidelines**:
  Police rarely work alone in these situations. Crisis responses often involve mental health professionals, social workers, or paramedics. Officers need to be familiar with memorandums of understanding, referral protocols, and collaborative guidelines that make these partnerships work.

Basic procedural and legislative knowledge extends beyond crisis roles for police. But in terms of crisis response work, knowing the rules isn't enough. Officers need to understand how to apply these rules fairly, especially in high-pressure moments, to retain community trust. That's where the concept of *procedural justice* comes in.

Central to a *procedurally just* approach is understanding how legislated authority is applied. For police attending a behavioural health crisis call for service, this means acting in ways that are[29]:

- **Dignified and Respectful**: Treating individuals with humanity, even in challenging circumstances.
- **Principled and Neutral**: Making decisions free from personal bias—based on facts and observed behaviour, not assumptions.
- **Trustworthy**: Upholding integrity and transparency in all actions. Building credibility through consistency and accountability.
- **Inclusive of Individual Voices**: Allowing individuals (and carers) to express their perspectives during interactions

Procedural justice becomes especially important in situations like involuntary apprehension, incarceration, or court referral, where the stakes are high and individuals may already feel powerless.[30] Research has shown procedurally just interactions improve public perceptions of police legitimacy. Conversely, the misuse or misinterpretation of legislated powers can severely undermine public trust and the efficacy of mental health legislation.[31]

The Australian case *State of New South Wales v Talovic [2014]* helps illustrate why this matters. Police officers detained Mr. Talovic based solely on advice from a third-party claiming he had made suicidal statements. The court found officers never independently assessed his condition. Instead, they acted—likely out of concern for liability—without verifying if the criteria for lawful apprehension under mental health legislation were actually met.

The court ruled that the officers had not acted on reasonable grounds and awarded damages to Mr. Talovic. The case sent a clear message: procedural shortcuts, even with good intentions, can cause harm and erode public trust.[32]

In real-world policing, especially when lives or safety are at stake, officers often default to what they know best—traditional police responses. That's why it's so important to start training with a strong procedural foundation, grounded in legislation, agency protocol, and a clear understanding of procedural justice approaches. Only then can we layer on behavioural health insights in a way that's meaningful and effective.

The Relational Approach: Slowing Down to See the Person

At its heart, a relational approach is about treating people in crisis as people first, not threats to neutralise, problems to be solved, or another incident report to complete. This approach asks Police officers to slow down, actively listen, and develop trust to better understand the needs of the person in crisis.[33] A relational approach encourages officers to reflect on implicit biases or cultural norms within policing which might influence their assumptions or reactions to individuals in crisis.[34]

This approach isn't just about making compassionate officers. It closely aligns with *procedural justice* principles, which are based on fairness, dignity, respect and importantly lawfulness.[35] It's also safer. A 2024 Canadian study on officer safety during de-escalation found:

> Relational de-escalation strategies appeared to be particularly important and were associated with higher levels of officer safety.[36]

This dual benefit, enhancing both public and officer safety during crisis interventions, makes a relational approach critical in modern policing which is becoming seen as more and more institutional.

Trauma-Informed Care: Understanding the "Why" Behind the Behaviour

A high proportion of individuals who experience behavioural health crisis have a history of trauma, which if ignored or mishandled, can either escalate the present incident or worse compound the individual's trauma history.[37]

A Trauma-Informed Care approach is a framework for understanding how past trauma shapes present behaviour. It shifts the focus from "what's wrong with this person?" to "what has this person experienced?" This shift helps officers reframe presenting behaviours which appear threatening or defiant as survival strategies.[38]

Statistics support how prevalent trauma is in crisis. A study of high-secure forensic hospitals in England found that over 95% of patients had experienced significant trauma or abuse, often stemming from Adverse Childhood Experiences (ACEs).[39] While conducted in a healthcare setting the same statistics can be seen in the justice system.

A 2023 U.S. study of individuals with mental illness found that ACEs scores were a clear predictor of arrest rates.[40] With a 2024 global review of nearly 30,000 participants finding individuals who had committed crimes exhibited higher ACEs scores compared to the general population.[41]

Incorporating trauma-informed practices into crisis response gives officers a way to recognise these patterns and enhance de-escalation effectiveness during crises by reframing a subject's combative or resistant behaviours as adaptive survival responses.[42]

Additionally, implementing trauma-informed strategies works. With studies identifying that trauma-informed interventions can ease crisis symptoms for up to three months afterward.[43] Resulting in fewer repeat calls, less demand on services, and improved outcomes for the person in crisis and the community at large.

Enhanced Communication and De-Escalation Training

Around the world, police agencies are being urged to improve communication and de-escalation training. Skills essential in crisis situations with a view to enhancing opportunities for safe, peaceful resolution of behavioural health incidents.[44]

However, there's no universal definition, and as a result, success is often measured by whether officers used force or not. While that's a helpful metric, it doesn't capture the full picture.[45]

Policing discourse must acknowledge that predominately de-escalation training is designed for incidents of suicidality, non-suicidal self-injury, or erratic behaviour. During a crisis, normal thinking and communication often breaks down. And the primary aim of de-escalation interventions is to help individuals re-establish their baseline, so they can engage with services or make safe decisions.[46]

But it's important during post incidents analysis to truly understand where de-escalation fits and where it doesn't. This type of training isn't intended for every high-risk scenario. If someone is armed and actively threatening others, or if police are executing a warrant or intervening in ongoing violence, the focus will inevitably shift back to safety and tactical response.[47]

Rather, de-escalation training aims to:

- Fostering cultural change within police agencies,
- Reducing reliance on restrictive practices or unwarranted involuntary apprehension,
- Enhancing understanding what is driving behaviour, and
- Ensuring that restrictive interventions, when necessary, are conducted in the safest and most dignified manner.[48]

One model that's commonly referenced by agencies in de-escalation training development is the Behavioural Change Stairway Model (BCSM), originally developed by the FBI, often called the *FBI Stairway Model.* It's since been updated and renamed the Behavioural Influence Stairway Model (BISM) though both versions are actively being used in training.[49] A global survey of nearly 200 hostage negotiators found about half regularly used BCSM or BISM in real-world situations.[50]

These models are based on the following frameworks[51]:

- **BCSM** uses five steps: Active Listening → Empathy → Rapport → Influence → Behavioural Change
- **BISM** refines this to four stages: Empathy → Rapport → Trust → Influence

Both models emphasise the principle of *time* as a crucial advantage in negotiation, advocating for police officers to adopt a measured pace aligned with the subject's state, while maintaining focus on the negotiation agenda.[52]

At their core, these models reinforce what we've already explored, effective crisis response depends on relational approaches. Trust, empathy, clear communication, and an ability to acknowledge an individual's traumatic history.[53] When those elements are in place, even the most volatile situations have a greater chance of being resolved peacefully.

A Police Behavioural Health Training Framework

At this point it's fair for readers to expect a training framework, something tangible, to summarise the ideas explored so far. And while a course outline will be presented shortly, it's important to be clear: this isn't being proposed as the *ideal*, or *definitive* model.

Instead, what follows should be seen as a practical starting point. A framework to prompt further discussion, guide local course development, and encourage training teams to tailor their own programs. Every jurisdiction faces unique demands, with its own mix of resources, political pressures, agency priorities, and research evidence. That's why flexibility and local adaptability are key.

This program is built around the principles examined so far. These aren't just abstract ideas; they directly reflect commonalities within the majority of behavioural health-related calls experienced on the frontline. Supporting the officer's role as a layperson whose primary duty in is to ensure safety. Those principles again are the following:

- Procedural Knowledge
- Trauma-Informed Care
- Relational Approaches
- Communication and De-escalation

Two further considerations affect how training will be effective and credible. First, without a serious investment in scenario-based learning, officers won't be able to meaningfully transfer classroom knowledge into the high-pressure reality of behavioural health crisis situations. Theory alone is never enough.

Second, any program shorter than 40 hours risks falling short of its purpose. While agencies face real limitations around funding, time, and staffing, cursory training fails to prepare officers for real-world crisis response. Further, courts, media, and the wider public are becoming more aware of what agencies are, or are not, training their staff in. Superficial training practices places agencies in undefendable positions, diminishes agency credibility and affects wider community trust. Communities increasingly expect policing to invest in credible, evidence-informed, and contemporary programs.

Table 6.2 outlines a proposed framework that re-centres the purpose of police training and offers a practical foundation for agencies to build upon. This training schedule is developed with the following broad considerations:

- The session titles indicate recommended training sessions – the dot points are only entered to assist in discussion of the session's objective
- Day One – Sessions should be delivered by sworn police officers, preferably from the agency's mental health team (i.e., co-responders) who have both theoretical and practical knowledge
- Day Two – Sessions titled 'Behavioural Health Clinical Overview' and 'Suicidality versus Non-Suicidal Self-Harm' should be delivered by delivered by Co-Responder clinicians (where available) as they already have insight to both police and health culture and operational reality
- Day Three – Session delivered by appropriate professional, preferrable with training experience in police and judicial settings
- Days Four and Five – Sessions managed by police trainers with assistance from co-responder personnel to assess and feedback to participants

Table 6.2 Training Framework

Day One – Procedural Justice	*Day Two – Relational Approaches*	*Day Three – Trauma Informed*	*Day Four – De-Escalation*	*Day Five – Scenario-Based Training*
Course Introduction **Legislation and Policy** Mental Health Acts Powers Apprehension Powers Search Powers Force Powers of Entry Associated Legislation Criminal Codes Firearms Codes	**Behavioural Health Clinical Overview** Explain differences between: • Mental Illness • Intellectual Disability • Neurodiversity • Substance Use Explain differences and commonalities: • Presentation / Symptoms • Risks Explain differences between therapies: • Psychopharmaceutical • Talk therapies • Behaviour Therapies • Other treatments	**Trauma-Informed Care and Practice** Types of trauma: Direct Intergenerational Vicarious Explain Adverse Childhood Experiences (ACEs) Impact of ACEs on-Substance Use Self-harm Incarceration Unemployment	**Communication and De-escalation** Building rapport, empathetic listening Utilisation of FBI Behavioural Influence Stairway Model Reinforcement of relational approaches and need to utilise time	**Scenario-Based Training** This second session should be increased in difficulty. More non-compliant subjects, or interfering bystanders etc. Still no involvement of weapons or direct threats to students.

Meal Break	**Meal Break**	**Meal Break**	**Meal Break**	**Meal Break**
Mental Health Courts Understanding judicial processes for persons with Mental Illness and/or IDD **Coronial and Judicial Reviews** A Procedural Justice look at judicial directions like: Stuart V Kirkland-Veenstra [2009] State of New South Wales v Talovic	**Suicidality v. Non-Suicidal Self-harm** Raise awareness as to the difference these presentations have for individuals and for response **Emotional Break**	**Trauma-Informed Care and Practice** Impact of trauma on victims of crime or serious incidents – memory recall–statementtaking Understanding some combative presentations are auto-response for self-protection – Fight Flight Freeze Fawn Flail How to manage presentation in informed approach – empoweringautonomy	**Scenario-Based Training** First scenario-based training session is to focus on the previous de- escalation training. In simple non-confrontational incidents	**Scenario-Based Training** These scenarios can incorporate more challenging scenes and at discretion of training staff inclusion of weapons, without subjects forcing incident to a use-of-force ending though. Recommend having Co-Responder staff on site to assist in feedback and again build trust in capacity by students **Graduation and Certification**
Co-Responders Intro and Info Session from co-responder team. With advice on local key stakeholders and resources	**Officer Wellness** Session from HR Support, vicarious trauma, agency resources, i.e., EAP, etc			

Importance of Scenario-Based Training

A 2022 survey of Australian police recruits recorded they believed there was a real need for Scenario-Based Training (SBT), specific for behavioural health crisis.[54]

Well-designed scenarios are intentionally built to include intellectual, technical, and ethical challenges.[55] They are realistic, dynamic, unique, and unpredictable.[56] It's not about memorising responses, it's about learning how to respond flexibly and professionally particularly in dynamic high-stakes situations.[57] Helping recruits move beyond theory and embedding practical skills like critical thinking, teamwork, and effective communication.

Research from Norway, although use-of-force training focused, offers insights regarding SBT:

> For simulated training to be efficient, students must be exposed to both low-threat and high-threat scenarios, to learn how to vary their means of force in accordance with an ever-changing situation. [58]

For scenario training to be effective, it needs adequate time in training schedules. International models, such as Crisis Intervention Team International and the IACP's CRIT framework, dedicate roughly a quarter of training time to scenarios.[59] Future training programs should follow this lead, allocating at least a full day, or ideally more to scenario-based learning. This gives participants the ability to consolidate their knowledge and skills, across multiple crisis scenarios with increasing levels of complexity.

Emphasis on scenario training also aligns with the US Bureau of Justice Assistance guide, *Improving Responses to People with Mental Illnesses: Strategies for Effective Law Enforcement Training* which stresses the importance of observable behaviours and actionable strategies in training.[60] Likewise, the U.K. College of Policing highlighted the need for greater de-escalation, negotiation and communication skills, acknowledging current training isn't practical enough.[61] Clearly both these directions to improve officer skills can only be achieved through scenario-based learning.

Skills like de-escalation can't be mastered by participants in a lecture or online course. Skills need to be practiced, tested, and refined through experience. Scenario-based training gives officers the opportunity to do exactly that.

When Scenarios Miss the Point: Rethinking the "Hearing Voices" Exercise

The "Hearing Voices" exercise, where officers role play experiencing auditory hallucination by other trainees whispering behind participants, appears in many training programs.[62] The idea is to build empathy for people who hear voices. But there's a risk here.

Its brief and simplistic nature risks reinforcing stereotypes, especially as trainers often unwittingly emphasise themes of "command and control". Unintentionally reinforcing the idea that people experiencing psychosis are dangerous. In reality, that's not what the majority crisis calls look like.

Data from the *Adult Psychiatric Morbidity Survey* of over 33,000 people, published in the *British Journal of Psychiatry* (2015) found only 4% of individuals reported hallucinations in the past year. With a similar Norwegian survey finding just 0.88% of people experienced daily hallucinations.[63] Interestingly, olfactory hallucinations occur at a similar rate of 4%, yet there is no comparable push to expose trainees to noxious odours.[64] These statistics challenge the prevailing narratives around 'Serious Mental Illness' and highlights how some training scenarios might be more about drama than accuracy.[65]

A more constructive use of this exercise for crisis training is to shift away from the diagnostic, hallucination narrative to a more trauma-informed approach, which highlights how sensory overload, like ambient noise, radio chatter, or even disengaged peripheral first-responders can increase stress for everyone involved. Reframing this exercise through the trauma lens helps officers recognise how environmental and past experience factors, not just symptomology, can affect outcomes.

Who Should Learn and When?

I'm always willing to learn, although, I do not always like being taught
Sir Winston Churchill

Having now explored the limitations of diagnostic and demographic-specific training, and what content more appropriately will assist officers to address acute crisis we return to the final aspects of the training question. Which police should receive training and when should training occur?

First, let's begin with the question of *Who?*

Research consistently shows when behavioural health training is cursory and selective it can lead to inconsistent response practices and the overuse of coercive measures.[66] Alternatively, officers with comprehensive training are less likely to involuntary apprehend individuals in crisis. They demonstrate improved de-escalation skills, and more likely to support voluntary care before resorting to the criminal justice system.[67] Further, officers report a greater sense of confidence in responding to crisis calls and more likely to view individuals experiencing crisis as less threatening, leading to safer outcomes.[68]

Ironically, the benefits of behavioural health training extend beyond public perception, but has significantly beneficial results for their agencies. Effective training is linked with decreases in uses of force, fewer trips to emergency departments, reduced downtime, improved working relations with external stakeholders, and importantly, improved public trust in police.

The answer here may be brief but the takeaway is simple: behavioural health training shouldn't be restricted to select units or officers as a voluntary course; it should be universal. All officers, including those in leadership roles, should complete comprehensive behavioural health training. Ultimately, behavioural health understanding and skills should become embedded in the culture of policing to the extent use-of-force training has evolved.

This leads us to a more contemporary and complex question: *When should training be delivered?* We will examine this question in two parts:

- Academy Training
- In-Service Training

Academy Training

The police academy serves as the foundation where recruits gain essential knowledge and are introduced to agency culture before encountering the realities of frontline policing. Consequently, many advocates argue behavioural health training should be integrated into academy curricula. Believing this early training can set the tone of a career.[69]

Researchers suggest the quality and depth of training provided in academy programs significantly influences an officer's ability to support individuals experiencing crisis in the community from day one. Some argue that without robust training in this area, newly graduated officers will struggle to fulfil their mandate to protect the public effectively.[70]

However, it is important to consider the significant challenges faced by individual police academy students. Recruits are under intense pressure, attempting to absorb a huge amount of information, in high-pressure environments. Training covers legislation, tactics, policies, procedures, driver training, first aid and more, condensed in just a few months. By graduation they are expected to master everything from firearms handling and traffic law to family violence policy, courtroom documentation, and, of course endless streams of paperwork.

All without the context of real-world policing experiences. As a result, some recruits may struggle to fully grasp and reflect on the relevance of many of these concepts, yet alone crisis response. Crisis Intervention Teams International highlights this challenge, stating: "training officers before they have experience in the field makes it challenging for officers to integrate their skills."[71]

The U.S. Department of Justice echoed this concern in a 2012 review of the Portland Police Bureau's training, stating:

> New recruits in a basic police academy are not generally ready to receive, absorb and implement critical information about how mental illness calls need a different response than the more common police calls. Trainees at that level are overwhelmed with information and generally lack the maturity that experience brings them on the street.[72]

This raises an important question: what is a more effective alternative to delivering this training to academy recruits?

The Los Angeles Police Department (LAPD) delivers a progressive approach, placing a 40-hour, face-to-face *Mental Health Intervention Training* (MHIT) course at the later stages of probation instead.[73] At this point in their career, probationary officers have completed the academy but are still undergoing structured learning. This model gives officers time to develop context, reflect on personal real-world experiences, and better understand the importance of the training, while allowing the department a chance to address early career biases and attitudes.

As CITI puts it, this kind of training outside of the academy "rejuvenates officers and reminds them that they can make a difference."[74]

In-Service Training

However, recruit or probationary training alone is not enough to automatically improve police officer decision-making at crisis calls for an officer's career.[75] For real change to occur, police leadership must treat crisis response as a core policing skill, one supported by policies, cross sector collaboration, and continuous improvement in practice.[76]

As Bittner argued back in 1970, policing has long relied on paramilitary, crime-focused training models, based on principles from two centuries past.[77] Today's challenges call for something different: officers not just tactically skilled, but able to also combine empathy, problem-solving, and an ability to work across sectors. Changing culture within policing requires leadership-driven messaging and reform that embeds 21st-century community values expected of modern policing practice.

This cultural shift aligns with CITI's idea of *rejuvenating* officers and reminding them they can make a difference flows into the concept of ongoing in-service training, delivered to seasoned officers. Policing is a long career, and like any skill set, behavioural health competencies need to be refreshed and updated. Most agencies already acknowledged this principle, requiring officers to regularly requalify in firearms and defensive tactics. So why not apply the same standard to crisis response training?

Research supports the value of ongoing, structured refresher courses, ideally delivered annually, just like firearms and tactic refreshers.[78] With evaluation of in-service training in New Mexico finding officers who received continuous, updated behavioural health training acknowledged an increase in confidence and better outcomes in real-world situations.[79]

These courses do not need to be as extensive as initial training but can consist of one- or two-day sessions. Some jurisdictions are already leading the way here. For example, California's POST and Texas's TCOLE both mandate regular initial and ongoing behavioural health training be delivered to all police officers, setting a strong precedent for continuous professional development in policing ideology.[80]

To emphasis the point CITI stress refresher training "*reminds them they can make a difference*."[81] Something especially important for officers who've been on the job a long time and may feel disconnected from the original values that drew them into the profession.

Observational Summary

The question of whether police require training is past the point of debate. Across the globe communities are demanding all officers undergo comprehensive behavioural health training. Training that commences in the formative stages of an officer's career, ideally during their probationary period rather than academy, but this is only the beginning. Cultural shifts can only occur when behavioural health training becomes a critical skill embedded in ongoing training programs, mirroring the use-of-force refresher training ethos that has become routine within modern police agencies.

The real debate now should focus on not if police should train, but rather what they should be trained in?

Most discussions focus on expanding diagnostic knowledge in a raft of conditions, overlayed with the intersectionality of factors such as sexual identity, cultural diversity, first nations experiences, veteran status and so many more. Calls often driven by academics, advocacy, political agendas, and even police recruits are on the surface well intentioned. But these calls overlook a fundamental reality, the volume and complexity of such content make it impractical for police agencies to dedicate sufficient time or resources to teach to any appropriate standard.

Further, such calls are frequently coming from a distant reality to how frontline crisis work presents. Real-world crisis response for policing occurs when situations are imminent, high-risk, dynamic, and definitely in a non-clinical environment. Assuming more clinical detail will result in better frontline decision-making is either optimistic, or at worst perpetuating biases and stigma during time of elevated crisis.

A more effective approach is building strong foundational skills, as called for by Bittner as far back as the 1970's focusing on empathy, problem-solving, and collaboration.[82] These skills are far more transferable across diagnostic or social factors during crisis, providing officers dynamic tools to apply during real-world crisis calls. Those skills are based in the following principles:

- Procedural Knowledge
- Relational Approaches
- Trauma-Informed Care
- Communication and De-escalation Skills

Developing these foundational skills enables officers to be more dynamic and responsive to those individuals before them, rather than becoming bogged down in trying to recall overly complex clinical assumptions about what they think they are seeing before them. Without these skills, officers are likely to revert to more embedded practices, often those coercive tactics from a different era. With these skills, however, officers are more likely to make ethical, informed, person-centred decisions, that enhance safety, reduce use-of-force, and reflect the 21st century culture communities expect of modern policing. These principles form the cornerstone of training development and reflect the professional approach to crisis explored here in this chapter.

Training Footnote

And one final thought to leave with you.

Substantial attention in crisis debate, and even judicial directions, focus on development and expansion of police training for behavioural health crisis. This has seen the rapid roll-out of specialist training delivered by practitioners, service providers, and peer trainers to be a part of programs such as the International Association of Chiefs of Police's new 40-hour *Crisis Response and Intervention Training*.[83] What receives less attention in these debates is the other side of the system: preparing health professionals to work effectively with police and emergency responders.[84]

Health professionals and clinical providers rarely receive any training that addresses the realities of policing, such as police powers, operational constraints, use-of-force capacity, or the lack of clinical understanding frontline officers have.[85] This imbalance has real consequences. Operational experience highlights families are often advised by health practitioners to call police requesting actions beyond authority or capacity, such as enforcing medication compliance, compelling appointment attendance, or returning voluntary patients to health facilities. When police decline to respond or action these requests that are beyond their capacity, families understandably become frustrated or confused, advising they were told "this is what police will (or must) do" by a practitioner.

If we want a truly integrated and effective crisis response system, training parity between the health and police sectors is essential. Without it we risk building a one-sided model requiring police to continually adjust their practices, while health professionals remain unchallenged, or just unaware of the realities of policing's role in crisis response. Addressing this imbalance will be another step towards a fully functioning systems-based response, based on genuine understanding and collaboration between sectors to meet the needs of people in crisis.

Notes

1 Koziarski, J., Ferguson, L., & Huey, L. (2021). Shedding light on the dark figure of police mental health calls for service. *Policing: A Journal of Policy and Practice*. https://doi.org/10.1093/police/paac006.

2 Cohen, G., & Bagwell, M. (2023). The state of mental health training in basic police curricula: A national level examination. *Journal of Public Affairs Education*, *29*(3), 327–49. https://doi.org/10.1080/15236803.2023.2179235; Judiciary UK. (2024). *Response from Sussex Police, Inquest Ryan Ouslem*. www.judiciary.uk/wp-content/uploads/2024/09/2024-0511-Response-from-Sussex-Police-1.pdf; Bratina, M. P., Carrero, K. M., Kim, B., & Merlo, A. V. (2018). Crisis intervention team training: When police encounter persons with mental illness. *Police Practice and Research*, *21*(3), 279–96. https://doi.org/10.1080/15614263.2018.1484290; Blackwell, G (2023). *Reducing recidivism in behavioural health crisis cycles*. www.churchilltrust.com.au/project/the-churchill-fellows-association-of-western-australia-churchill-fellowship-to-establish-diversionary-practices-for-mentally-and-intellectually-disabled-persons-engaging-police/.

3 Cohen, G., & Bagwell, M. (2023). The state of mental health training in basic police curricula: A national level examination. *Journal of Public Affairs Education*, *29*(3), 327–49. https://doi.org/10.1080/15236803.2023.2179235.

4 Usher, L., Watson, A., Bruno, R., Andriukaitis, S., Kamin, D., Speed, C., & Taylor, S. (2019). *Crisis Intervention Team (CIT) programs: A best practice guide for transforming community responses to mental health crises* (p. 122). Memphis: CIT International. www.cit.memphis.edu/resources/best-practices-guide.pdf.

5 Scantlebury, A., Fairhurst, C., Booth, A., McDaid, C., Moran, N., Parker, A., Payne, R., Scott, W., Torgerson, D., Webber, M., & Hewitt, C. (2017). *Effectiveness of a training program for police officers who come into contact with people with mental health problems: A pragmatic randomised controlled trial*. https://doi.org/10.1371/journal.pone.0184377.

6 Morgan, M., & Miles-Johnson, T. (2022). Responding to persons with mental illness (PWMI): Police recruit perceptions of mental health response training and engagement. *Cogent Social Sciences*, *8*(1). https://doi.org/10.1080/23311886.2021.2020469.

7 Morgan, M., & Miles-Johnson, T. (2022). Responding to persons with mental illness (PWMI): Police recruit perceptions of mental health response training and engagement. *Cogent Social Sciences*, *8*(1). https://doi.org/10.1080/23311886.2021.2020469; Glaser, J. (2024). Disrupting the effects of implicit bias: The case of discretion & policing. *Daedalus*, *153*(1), 151–73. https://doi.org/10.1162/daed_a_02053.

8 United Kingdom College of Policing. (2020). *Conflict management using de-escalation, communication and negotiation: Guidelines.* https://assets.college.police.uk/s3fs-public/2020-09/Conflict-management-guidelines.pdf.

9 Wilson, J. M., & Miles-Johnson, T. (2024). The police staffing crisis: Evidence-based approaches for building, balancing, and optimizing effective workforces. *Policing: A Journal of Policy and Practice*, *18*, paae044. https://doi.org/10.1093/police/paae044; Police Federation England & Wales. (2024). *Why police officers are leaving and why retention is crucial.* www.polfed.org/news/latest-news/2024/why-police-officers-are-leaving-and-why-retention-is-crucial/; Miles-Johnson, T., & Morgan, M. (2022). Operational response: Policing persons with mental illness in Australia. *Journal of Criminology*, *55*(2), 260–81. https://doi.org/10.1177/26338076221094385.

10 Reuland, M. & Schwarzfeld, M. (2008). *Improving responses to people with mental illnesses: Strategies for effective law enforcement training.* www.govinfo.gov/content/pkg/GOVPUB-J26-PURL-LPS116900/pdf/GOVPUB-J26-PURL-LPS116900.pdf.

11 President's Task Force on 21st Century Policing. (2015). *Final report of the President's Task Force on 21st Century Policing.* Office of Community Oriented Policing Services. https://cops.usdoj.gov/pdf/taskforce/taskforce_finalreport.pdf.

12 Martinez, C. (2021). *Los Angeles Police Department's mental health intervention training: A quantitative study* (Publication No. 29261604) [Doctoral dissertation, Touro University Worldwide]. ProQuest Dissertations & Theses Global. www.proquest.com/openview/0ffd9ca53e0d81c1d51f4b7d1cdfd751/1?pq-origsite=gscholar&cbl=18750&diss=y.

13 Morgan, M., & Miles-Johnson, T. (2022). Responding to persons with mental illness (PWMI): Police recruit perceptions of mental health response training and engagement. *Cogent Social Sciences*, *8*(1). https://doi.org/10.1080/23311886.2021.2020469; Lavoie, J., Alvarez, N., & Kandil, Y. (2022). Developing community co-designed scenario-based training for police mental health crisis response: A relational policing approach to de-escalation. *Journal of Police and Criminal Psychology*, *37*, 587–601. https://doi.org/10.1007/s11896-022-09500-2; Gardner, S. (2022, December 3). *College of policing – Neurodiversity training to better support the public.* www.college.police.uk/article/neurodiversity-training-better-support-public; Kenney, C. K., Sreckovic, M. A., Wallace, M., et al. (2024). Autism training for law enforcement officers: Perceptions

from the field. *Journal of Autism and Developmental Disorders.* https://doi.org/10.1007/s10803-024-06587-w.

14 American Psychiatric Association. (2022). *Listing of DSM-5-TR diagnoses and new ICD-10-CM codes.* www.psychiatry.org/getmedia/de1bf4c9-c75e-4e89-add8-3dd6e9c29de9/APA-DSM5TR-ICD10CM-Code-Updates-092022.pdf; Morgan, M., & Miles-Johnson, T. (2022). Responding to persons with mental illness (PWMI): Police recruit perceptions of mental health response training and engagement. *Cogent Social Sciences, 8*(1). https://doi.org/10.1080/23311886.2021.2020469; Lavoie, J., Alvarez, N., & Kandil, Y. (2022). Developing community co-designed scenario-based training for police mental health crisis response: A relational policing approach to de-escalation. *Journal of Police and Criminal Psychology, 37,* 587–601. https://doi.org/10.1007/s11896-022-09500-2; Gardner, S. (2022, December 3). *College of policing – Neurodiversity training to better support the public.* www.college.police.uk/article/neurodiversity-training-better-support-public; Kenney, C. K., Sreckovic, M. A., Wallace, M., et al. (2024). Autism training for law enforcement officers: Perceptions from the field. *Journal of Autism and Developmental Disorders.* https://doi.org/10.1007/s10803-024-06587-w.

15 Bradford, A., Meyer, A. N. D., Khan, S., et al. (2024). Diagnostic error in mental health: A review. *BMJ Quality & Safety, 33*(9), 663–72. https://doi.org/10.1136/bmjqs-2023-016879.

16 Glaser, J. (2024). Disrupting the effects of implicit bias: The case of discretion & policing. *Daedalus, 153*(1), 151–73. https://doi.org/10.1162/daed_a_02053.

17 Reuland, M., & Schwarzfeld, M. (2008). *Improving responses to people with mental illnesses: Strategies for effective law enforcement training.* www.govinfo.gov/content/pkg/GOVPUB-J26-PURL-LPS116900/pdf/GOVPUB-J26-PURL-LPS116900.pdf.

18 Usher, L., Watson, A., Bruno, R., Andriukaitis, S., Kamin, D., Speed, C., & Taylor, S. (2019). *Crisis Intervention Team (CIT) programs: A best practice guide for transforming community responses to mental health crises* (p. 128). Memphis: CIT International. www.cit.memphis.edu/resources/best-practices-guide.pdf

19 Bureau of Justice Assistance. (2022). *Crisis response and intervention training (CRIT).* https://bja.ojp.gov/events/crisis-response-and-intervention-training-crit; International Association of Chiefs of Police. (2022). *Crisis response and intervention training (CRIT) toolkit.* www.informedpoliceresponses.com/crit-toolkit.

20 International Association of Chiefs of Police. (2022). *Crisis response and intervention training (CRIT) toolkit.* www.informedpoliceresponses.com/crit-toolkit.

21 Bureau of Justice Assistance. (n.d.). *Office of Justice Programs Training, Police-Mental Health Collaboration (PMHC) Toolkit.* https://bja.ojp.gov/program/pmhc/training.

22 Bureau of Justice Assistance (n.d.). *Office of Justice Programs Training, Police-Mental Health Collaboration (PMHC) Toolkit.* https://bja.ojp.gov/program/pmhc/training.

23 Usher, L., Watson, A., Bruno, R., Andriukaitis, S., Kamin, D., Speed, C., & Taylor, S. (2019). *Crisis Intervention Team (CIT) programs: A best practice guide for transforming community responses to mental health crises* (p. 128). Memphis: CIT International. www.cit.memphis.edu/resources/best-practices-guide.pdf; Bureau of Justice Assistance. (n.d.). *Bureau of Justice Assistance – Police-Mental Health Collaboration (PMHC) Toolkit – CIT UTAH Academy PDF.* https://bja.ojp.gov/sites/g/files/xyckuh186/files/media/document/CIT%20Utah%20Training%20Curriculum.pdf.

24 International Association of Chiefs of Police. (2018). *Responding to persons experiencing a mental health crisis (August 2018).* IACP Law Enforcement Policy Center. www.theiacp.org/sites/default/files/2021-07/Mental%20Health%20Crisis%20Response.

25 World Health Organization. (2016). *Practice manual for establishing and maintaining surveillance systems for suicide attempts and self-harm.* World Health Organization. https://iris.who.int/handle/10665/208895; Hamza, C. A., Stewart, S. L., & Willoughby, T. (2012). Examining the link between nonsuicidal self-injury and suicidal behavior: A review of the literature and an integrated model. *Clinical Psychology Review, 32*(6), 482–95. https://doi.org/10.1016/j.cpr.2012.05.003.

26 Lavoie, J., Alvarez, N., & Kandil, Y. (2022). Developing community co-designed scenario-based training for police mental health crisis response: A relational policing approach to de-escalation. *Journal of Police and Criminal Psychology, 37*, 587–601. https://doi.org/10.1007/s11896-022-09500-2.

27 Wittmann, L., Groen, G., Hampel, P., Petersen, R., & Jörns-Presentati, A. (2021). Police officers' ability in recognizing relevant mental health conditions. *Frontiers in Psychology, 12.* https://doi.org/10.3389/FPSYG.2021.727341.

28 Wittmann, L., Groen, G., Hampel, P., Petersen, R., & Jörns-Presentati, A. (2021). Police officers' ability in recognizing relevant mental health conditions. *Frontiers in Psychology, 12.* https://doi.org/10.3389/FPSYG.2021.727341.

29 Morgan, M. M. (2022). Contradictions between community-oriented police training and paramilitary police training: Implications for police recruit mental health response training. *Journal of Police and Criminal Psychology, 37*, 876–91. https://doi.org/10.1007/s11896-022-09537-3.

30 Morgan, M. M. (2022). Contradictions between community-oriented police training and paramilitary police training: Implications for police recruit mental health response training. *Journal of Police and Criminal Psychology, 37*, 876–91. https://doi.org/10.1007/s11896-022-09537-3.

31 Morgan, M. M. (2022). Contradictions between community-oriented police training and paramilitary police training: Implications for police recruit mental health response training. *Journal of Police and Criminal Psychology, 37*, 876–91. https://doi.org/10.1007/s11896-022-09537-3.

32 State of New South Wales v Talovic [2014] NSWCA 333. www.caselaw.nsw.gov.au/decision/54a63edf3004de94513dc542.

33 Lavoie, J., Alvarez, N., & Kandil, Y. (2022). Developing community co-designed scenario-based training for police mental health crisis response: A relational policing approach to de-escalation. *Journal of Police and Criminal Psychology*, *37*, 587–601. https://doi.org/10.1007/s11896-022-09500-2.

34 Garcia, V. (2005). Constructing the 'other' within police culture: An analysis of a deviant unit within the police organization. *Police Practice and Research*, *6*(1), 65–80. https://doi.org/10.1080/15614260500047283.

35 Lavoie, J., Alvarez, N., & Kandil, Y. (2022). Developing community co-designed scenario-based training for police mental health crisis response: A relational policing approach to de-escalation. *Journal of Police and Criminal Psychology*, *37*, 587–601. https://doi.org/10.1007/s11896-022-09500-2.

36 MacIsaac, A., Baldwin, S., Semple, T., & Bennell, C. (2024). Exploring the relationship between officer safety and de-escalation in a simulated crisis encounter. *Police Quarterly*. https://doi.org/10.1177/10986111241289885.

37 Nizum, N., Yoon, R., Ferreira-Legere, L., Poole, N., & Lulat, Z. (2020). Nursing interventions for adults following a mental health crisis: A systematic review guided by trauma-informed principles. *International Journal of Mental Health Nursing*, *29*, 348–363. https://doi.org/10.1111/inm.12691.

38 Nizum, N., Yoon, R., Ferreira-Legere, L., Poole, N., & Lulat, Z. (2020). Nursing interventions for adults following a mental health crisis: A systematic review guided by trauma-informed principles. *International Journal of Mental Health Nursing*, *29*, 348–363. https://doi.org/10.1111/inm.12691

39 Goodman, H., Papastavrou Brooks, C., Price, O., & Barley, E. A. (2020). Barriers and facilitators to the effective de-escalation of conflict behaviours in forensic high-secure settings: A qualitative study. *International Journal of Mental Health Systems, 14,* 59. https://doi.org/10.1186/s13033-020-00392-5.

40 Ashekun, O., Zern, A., Langlois, S., & Compton, M. (2023). Adverse childhood experiences and arrest rates among individuals with serious mental illnesses. *Journal of the American Academy of Psychiatry and the Law, 51*(3), 325–34. https://doi.org/10.29158/JAAPL.220096-22.

41 Pessoa, T. M. G., & Almeida, T. C. (2024). The link between adverse childhood experiences and mental health in offenders: A systematic review. *Crime & Delinquency*. https://doi.org/10.1177/00111287241242478.

42 Goodman, H., Papastavrou Brooks, C., Price, O., & Barley, E. A. (2020). Barriers and facilitators to the effective de-escalation of conflict behaviours in forensic high-secure settings: A qualitative study. *International Journal of Mental Health Systems, 14,* 59. https://doi.org/10.1186/s13033-020-00392-5.

43 Sweeney, A., Clement, S., Filson, B., & Kennedy, A. (2016). Trauma-informed mental healthcare in the UK: What is it and how can we further its development? *Mental Health Review Journal*, *21*(3), 174–92, https://doi.org/10.1108/MHRJ-01-2015-0006; Registered Nurses' Association of Ontario. (2017). *Crisis intervention for adults using a trauma-informed approach: Initial four weeks of management* (3rd ed.). Retrieved February 5, 2026, from https://rnao.ca/bpg/guidelines/crisis-intervention.

44 Krameddine, Y. I., & Silverstone, P. H. (2015). How to improve interactions between police and the mentally ill. *Frontiers in Psychiatry, 5,* 186. https://doi.org/10.3389/fpsyt.2014.00186.
45 MacIsaac, A., Baldwin, S., Semple, T., & Bennell, C. (2024). Exploring the relationship between officer safety and de-escalation in a simulated crisis encounter. *Police Quarterly.* https://doi.org/10.1177/10986111241289885.
46 Vecchi, G., Van Hasselt, V., & Romano, S. (2004). Crisis (hostage) negotiation: Current strategies and issues in high-risk conflict resolution. www.gocit.org/uploads/3/0/5/5/30557023/crisis__hostage__negotiations.pdf.
47 Engel, R. S., Corsaro, N., Isaza, G. T., & McManus, H. D. (2022). Assessing the impact of de-escalation training on police behavior: Reducing police use of force in the Louisville, KY metro police department. *Criminology & Public Policy, 21,* 199–233. https://doi.org/10.1111/1745-9133.12574.
48 Lavelle, M., Ferreira, A. L., Dixen, S., & Berring, L. L. (2024). De-escalation in mental health care settings. In N. Hallett, R. Whittington, D. Richter, & E. Eneje (Eds.), *Coercion and violence in mental health settings.* Cham: Springer. https://doi.org/10.1007/978-3-031-61224-4_15.
49 Vecchi, G. M., Wong, G. K., Wong, P. W., & Markey, M. A. (2019). Negotiating in the skies of Hong Kong: The efficacy of the Behavioral Influence Stairway Model (BISM) in suicidal crisis situations. *Aggression and Violent Behavior, 48,* 230–39. https://doi.org/10.1016/j.avb.2019.08.002.
50 Johnson, K. E., Thompson, J., Hall, J. A., & Meyer, C. (2017). Crisis (hostage) negotiators weigh in: The skills, behaviors, and qualities that characterize an expert crisis negotiator. *Police Practice and Research, 19*(5), 472–89. https://doi.org/10.1080/15614263.2017.1419131; Vecchi, G. M., Wong, G. K., Wong, P. W., & Markey, M. A. (2019). Negotiating in the skies of Hong Kong: The efficacy of the Behavioral Influence Stairway Model (BISM) in suicidal crisis situations. *Aggression and Violent Behavior, 48,* 230–239. https://doi.org/10.1016/j.avb.2019.08.002.
51 Johnson, K. E., Thompson, J., Hall, J. A., & Meyer, C. (2017). Crisis (hostage) negotiators weigh in: the skills, behaviors, and qualities that characterize an expert crisis negotiator. *Police Practice and Research, 19*(5), 472–489. https://doi.org/10.1080/15614263.2017.1419131; Lavoie, J., Alvarez, N., & Kandil, Y. (2022). Developing community co-designed scenario-based training for police mental health crisis response: A relational policing approach to de-escalation. *Journal of Police and Criminal Psychology, 37,* 587–601. https://doi.org/10.1007/s11896-022-09500-2.
52 Johnson, K. E., Thompson, J., Hall, J. A., & Meyer, C. (2017). Crisis (hostage) negotiators weigh in: the skills, behaviors, and qualities that characterize an expert crisis negotiator. *Police Practice and Research, 19*(5), 472–489. https://doi.org/10.1080/15614263.2017.1419131; Lavoie, J., Alvarez, N., & Kandil, Y. (2022). Developing community co-designed scenario-based training for police mental health crisis response: A relational policing approach to de-escalation. *Journal of Police and Criminal Psychology, 37,* 587–601. https://doi.org/10.1007/s11896-022-09500-2.

53 Johnson, K. E., Thompson, J., Hall, J. A., & Meyer, C. (2017). Crisis (hostage) negotiators weigh in: the skills, behaviors, and qualities that characterize an expert crisis negotiator. *Police Practice and Research*, *19*(5), 472–489. https://doi.org/10.1080/15614263.2017.1419131; Lavoie, J., Alvarez, N., & Kandil, Y. (2022). Developing community co-designed scenario-based training for police mental health crisis response: A relational policing approach to de-escalation. *Journal of Police and Criminal Psychology*, *37*, 587–601. https://doi.org/10.1007/s11896-022-09500-2.

54 Morgan, M., & Miles-Johnson, T. (2022). Responding to persons with mental illness (PWMI): Police recruit perceptions of mental health response training and engagement. *Cogent Social Sciences*, *8*(1). https://doi.org/10.1080/23311886.2021.2020469.

55 Shipton, B. (2023). Scenario-based learning. In: *Signature pedagogies in police education*. Springer Briefs in Criminology. Cham: Springer. https://doi.org/10.1007/978-3-031-42387-1_4; Stenshol, K., Risan, P., Knudsen, S., & Sætrevik, B. (2023). An explorative study of police student's decision-making in a critical incident scenario simulation. *Police Practice and Research*, *25*(4), 401–18. https://doi.org/10.1080/15614263.2023.2268789.

56 O'Neill, J., O'Neill, D. A., Weed, K., Hartman, M. E., Spence, W., & Lewinski, W. J. (2018). Police academy training, performance, and learning. *Behaviour Analysis in Practice*. 2018 Dec 18; *12*(2), 353–72. doi: 10.1007/s40617-018-00317-2. Erratum in: *Behaviour Analysis in Practice*. 2019 Jan 24; *12*(2), 373–4. https://doi.org/10.1007/s40617-019-00332-x.

57 O'Neill, J., O'Neill, D. A., Weed, K., Hartman, M. E., Spence, W., & Lewinski, W. J. (2018). Police academy training, performance, and learning. *Behaviour Analysis in Practice*. 2018 Dec 18; *12*(2), 353–72. doi: 10.1007/s40617-018-00317-2. Erratum in: *Behaviour Analysis in Practice*. 2019 Jan 24; *12*(2), 373–4. https://doi.org/10.1007/s40617-019-00332-x.

58 Stenshol, K., Risan, P., Knudsen, S., & Sætrevik, B. (2023). An explorative study of Police student's decision-making in a critical incident scenario simulation. *Police Practice and Research*, *25*(4), 401–18. https://doi.org/10.1080/15614263.2023.2268789.

59 Usher, L., Watson, A., Bruno, R., Andriukaitis, S., Kamin, D., Speed, C., & Taylor, S. (2019). *Crisis Intervention Team (CIT) programs: A best practice guide for transforming community responses to mental health crises* (p. 128). Memphis: CIT International. https://citinternational.org/bestpracticeguide; Bureau of Justice Assistance. (2022). *Crisis response and intervention training (CRIT)*. https://bja.ojp.gov/events/crisis-response-and-intervention-training-crit; International Association of Chiefs of Police. (2022). *Crisis response and intervention training (CRIT) toolkit*. www.informedpoliceresponses.com/crit-toolkit

60 Reuland, M., & Schwarzfeld, M. (2008). *Improving responses to people with mental illnesses: Strategies for effective law enforcement training*. www.govinfo.gov/content/pkg/GOVPUB-J26-PURL-LPS116900/pdf/GOVPUB-J26-PURL-LPS116900.pdf; United Kingdom College of Policing. (2020). *Conflict management using de-escalation, communication and negotiation: Guidelines*.

College of Policing Limited. https://assets.college.police.uk/s3fs-public/2020-09/Conflict-management-guidelines.pdf.

61 Reuland, M., & Schwarzfeld, M. (2008). *Improving responses to people with mental illnesses: Strategies for effective law enforcement training*. www.govinfo.gov/content/pkg/GOVPUB-J26-PURL-LPS116900/pdf/GOVPUB-J26-PURL-LPS116900.pdf; United Kingdom College of Policing. (2020). *Conflict management using de-escalation, communication and negotiation: Guidelines*. College of Policing Limited. https://assets.college.police.uk/s3fs-public/2020-09/Conflict-management-guidelines.pdf

62 Bureau of Justice Assistance. (n.d.). *Bureau of Justice Assistance Police-Mental Health Collaboration (PMHC) Toolkit*. https://bja.ojp.gov/program/pmhc/training.

63 Kråkvik, B. (2015). Prevalence of auditory verbal hallucinations in a general population: A group comparison study. *Scandinavian Journal of Psychology*, *56*(5), 508–15. https://doi.org/10.1111/sjop.12226.

64 Vedul-Kjelsås, E. (2021). Olfactory hallucinations in a population-based sample. *Psychiatry Research*, *299*, 113853. https://doi.org/10.1016/j.psychres.2021.113853.

65 Yates, K., Lång, U., Peters, E. M., et al. (2021). Hallucinations in the general population across the adult lifespan: Prevalence and psychopathologic significance. *The British Journal of Psychiatry*, *219*(6), 652–58. https://doi.org/10.1192/bjp.2021.100.

66 Morgan, M., & Miles-Johnson, T. (2022). Responding to persons with mental illness (PWMI): Police recruit perceptions of mental health response training and engagement. *Cogent Social Sciences*, *8*(1). https://doi.org/10.1080/23311886.2021.2020469.

67 Hassell, K. D. (2020). The impact of Crisis Intervention Team Training for police. *International Journal of Police Science & Management*, *22*(2), 159–70. https://doi.org/10.1177/1461355720909404.

68 Hassell, K. D. (2020). The impact of Crisis Intervention Team Training for police. *International Journal of Police Science & Management*, *22*(2), 159–70. https://doi.org/10.1177/1461355720909404; Crisanti, A. S., Fairfax-Columbo, J., Duran, D., et al. (2022). Evaluation of Ongoing Crisis Intervention Team (CIT) training for law enforcement using the ECHO Model. *Journal of Police and Criminal Psychology*, *37*, 863–75. https://doi.org/10.1007/s11896-022-09529-3.

69 Morgan, M. M. (2022). Contradictions between community-oriented police training and paramilitary police training: Implications for police recruit mental health response training. *Journal of Police and Criminal Psychology*, *37*(4), 876–91. https://doi.org/10.1007/s11896-022-09537-3.

70 Cohen, G., & Bagwell, M. (2023). The state of mental health training in basic police curricula: A national level examination. *Journal of Public Affairs Education*, *29*(3), 327–49. https://doi.org/10.1080/15236803.2023.2179235.

71 Usher, L., Watson, A., Bruno, R., Andriukaitis, S., Kamin, D., Speed, C., & Taylor, S. (2019). *Crisis Intervention Team (CIT) Programs: A best practice*

guide for transforming community responses to mental health crises (p. 128). Memphis: CIT International. https://citinternational.org/bestpracticeguide.

72 U.S. Department of Justice. (2012). *Investigation of the Portland police bureau.* U.S. Department of Justice Civil Rights Division and U.S. Attorney's Office for the District of Oregon. http://media.oregonlive.com/portland_impact/other/PPB%20Letter%20of%20Findings.pdf

73 Blackwell, G. (2023). *Reducing recidivism in behavioural health crisis cycles.* www.churchilltrust.com.au/project/the-churchill-fellows-association-of-western-australia-churchill-fellowship-to-establish-diversionary-practices-for-mentally-and-intellectually-disabled-persons-engaging-police/.

74 Usher, L., Watson, A., Bruno, R., Andriukaitis, S., Kamin, D., Speed, C., & Taylor, S. (2019). *Crisis Intervention Team (CIT) Programs: A best practice guide for transforming community responses to mental health crises* (p. 128). Memphis: CIT International. https://citinternational.org/bestpracticeguide.

75 Freeze, S. M., & Campbell, M. A. (2024). Police officer decision-making during mental health calls: A qualitative study. *Journal of Police Criminology and Psychology*, *39*, 358–69. https://doi.org/10.1007/s11896-024-09656-z.

76 Adebowale, L. (2013). *Independent commission on mental health and policing report.* https://amhp.org.uk/wp-content/uploads/2017/08/independent_commission_on_mental_health_and_policing_main_report.pdf.

77 Cohen, G., & Bagwell, M. (2023). The state of mental health training in basic police curricula: A national level examination. *Journal of Public Affairs Education*, *29*(3), 327–49. https://doi.org/10.1080/15236803.2023.2179235.

78 Krameddine, Y. I., & Silverstone, P. H. (2015). How to improve interactions between police and the mentally ill. *Frontiers in Psychiatry*, *5*, 186. https://doi.org/10.3389/fpsyt.2014.00186.

79 Crisanti, A. S., Fairfax-Columbo, J., Duran, D., et al. (2022). Evaluation of Ongoing Crisis Intervention Team (CIT) training for law enforcement using the ECHO Model. *Journal of Police Criminology and Psychology*, *37*, 863–75. https://doi.org/10.1007/s11896-022-09529-3.

80 Texas Commission on Law Enforcement. (2024, December). *Training requirements.* Texas Commission on Law Enforcement. www.tcole.texas.gov/content/training-requirements; State of California Commission on Peace Officer Standards and Training. (2024, December). *Crisis intervention behavioural health training.* State of California Commission on Peace Officer Standards and Training. https://post.ca.gov/crisis-intervention-behavioral-health-training.

81 Usher, L., Watson, A., Bruno, R., Andriukaitis, S., Kamin, D., Speed, C., & Taylor, S. (2019). *Crisis Intervention Team (CIT) Programs: A best practice guide for transforming community responses to mental health crises* (p. 128). Memphis: CIT International. https://citinternational.org/bestpracticeguide.

82 Cohen, G., & Bagwell, M. (2023). The state of mental health training in basic police curricula: A national level examination. *Journal of Public Affairs Education*, *29*(3), 327–49. https://doi.org/10.1080/15236803.2023.2179235.

83 Bureau of Justice Assistance (2022). *Crisis Response and Intervention Training (CRIT).* https://bja.ojp.gov/events/crisis-response-and-intervention-training-crit; International Association of Chiefs of Police. (2022). *Crisis Response and Intervention Training (CRIT) Toolkit.* www.informedpoliceresponses.com/crit-toolkit.

84 Steadman, H., & Morrissette, D. (2016). Police responses to persons with mental illness: Going beyond CIT training. *Journal of Psychiatric Services.* https://doi.org/10.1176/appi.ps.201600348.

85 Lopez Wright, F., & Kessler, J. (2024, February). *Preparing law enforcement agencies for embedded clinicians (The Council of State Governments Justice Center).* The Council of State Governments Justice Center. https://csgjusticecenter.org/publications/preparing-law-enforcement-agencies-for-embedded-clinicians.

7 Systemic Barriers to Crisis Management

Introduction

This section will look at the key barriers that, in the author's experience, regularly undermine long-term success in crisis response and management, particularly for individuals who find themselves locked in patterns of chronic crisis cycling.

Each factor is examined in terms of its individual impact upon systems, yet it is essential to recognise that these factors will rarely occur in isolation. Most factors will arise at sometime during the development or operational life of crisis response systems. The real challenge is whether communities and sectors can adopt a broader systems-thinking perspective to anticipate, adapt, and overcome such factors. For a single barrier may reduce the effectiveness of a program, but on its own, it is seldom terminal.

However, when several factors are allowed to emerge unchecked simultaneously, programs can become overwhelmed and vulnerable, often at the very moment when a programs potential for innovative and transformative support in the community is most desperately needed.

Operational Barriers to Crisis Response

This section introduces several key barriers which restrict the progression of interventionist programs to fully develop crisis management systems. The barriers discussed here reflect those the author has observed through operational experience; however, they are not an exhaustive record of challenges faced in crisis system reform. Each barrier is discussed as a brief overview, acknowledging that these issues are complex in their own right, warranting greater research, debate, and policy reform to bring effective change.

The Wrong Pockets Problem

Despite attention from community and advocacy groups, funding has remained a persistent barrier to implementing effective crisis management

DOI: 10.4324/9781003749585-7

systems. The *World Health Organisation Mental Health Atlas 2024* indicates on average countries allocate only around 2% of national health expenditure on mental health, a figure that often results in understandable criticism.[1] However, as with most behavioural health issues funding, challenges are not just about ***how much*** is spent but increasingly ***how it is distributed*** across programs targeting crisis response and management.[2]

The Australian Productivity Commission highlighted this point, indicating funding distribution has created a competitive market in the crisis sector.[3] McGorry and colleagues (2025) argue that such competitive funding decisions are reinforced by outdated and commercialised frameworks embedded in government policies.[4] Short-term grants, unclear oversight, and fragmented service providers greatly impact how funding allocations are utilised effectively in a broader system. This competitive funding environment is a classic example of the "*wrong pockets*" problem.

Simply, the *wrong pockets* analogy represents a failure in systems-thinking. When one part of the system believes they carry the cost of an intervention, when the financial benefit is realised elsewhere.[5] In behavioural health, the co-responder model clearly illustrates this problem. Police and community mental health invest in crisis teams, yet the measurable savings are realised in emergency departments, reduced ambulance call-outs, lower incarceration rates, and reduced demand on crisis stabilisation centres. This can lead to siloed thinking where agencies paying the bills feel the spending is irrational, eventually leading to withdrawal of services.[6]

Yet, from a systems perspective, the spend is rational and long-term benefits may be realised in broader systems improvements. McGorry and colleagues (2025) suggest there is a need for mandatory impact analyses of mental health funding spends, similar to environmental impact statements, to evaluate the risks and rewards of policies before funding allocation.[7]

In the *Mental Health Workforce* report (2020) the Australian Productivity Commission addressed this, recommending funds from Commonwealth, State and Territory governments be pooled under Regional Commissioning Authorities (RCA).[8] RCAs would centrally manage funding and cost across mental health, alcohol and other drugs, neurodiversity, and psychosocial support streams, reducing the siloed and competitive landscape – instead developing a systems-based approach of shared accountability and shared benefits for sustainable crisis management systems.[9]

Ultimately, no matter how much governments invest in crisis management, systems will continue to fail unless sectors work together. Not just to share data or reducing demand, but to recognise funding is a shared social investment rather than a competitive marketplace. A process which can only improve if governments reduce current competitive financial frameworks which produce siloed and narrow focused programs. Adopting a systems-thinking approach encourages sectors to view resources, inclusive of funding, to be seen as investment in aligned priorities, ensuring funding goes into the *right pockets,* at the right pressure points, for the benefit of the system as a whole.

Risk Shifting

Inter-sector crisis response is often weakened by the less spoken of, but highly significant practice of professional *risk shifting*, also described as *defensive practice* or *liability avoidance*.[10] This practice deserves far more attention in current debates about reducing police involvement, given to date there is limited acknowledgement of how frequently clinicians themselves initiate police attendance, often as a strategy to reduce personal or organisational liability.

The UK government commissioned report *Picking Up the Pieces* (2018), called out this pattern directly, finding roughly 10% of behavioural health calls to police appeared to reflect organisational risk being shifted from other service providers, particularly at the end of the day when services were closing.[11] Similar habits were identified in the United States, where surveys of 911 call takers show they often dispatch police rather than non-police responders whenever there are indicators of harm present, mainly due to concerns of liability.[12]

Risk shifting, however, is not a one-way problem. Police also engage in risk shifting, especially at incidents involving suicidality. Officers may default to involuntary apprehension even when their initial assessment suggests limited imminent risk. The Australian case of *Talovic v NSW* (2014) illustrates this, where police officers apprehended a man despite limited evidence of acute danger, primarily to avoid potential liability.[13]

Recent international changes to police procedures, such as Right Care, Right Person and, to some extent, Disengagement policies, can also be understood as institutional risk shifting. While reducing police presence at crisis incidents is beneficial, a driver of such changes is clearly the blame-shifting pressures – particularly with court rulings directly holding police responsible for negative outcomes.[14]

Importantly though, risk shifting cannot be solely attributed to decisions from individuals or within singular organisations. Risk shifting practices are often influenced by broader blame-allocation pressures: coronial inquests, litigation, media commentary, and politicised agendas which often seek to individualise accountability for negative outcomes. When fatalities or adverse incidents are framed as isolated professional failings rather than symptoms of systemic failure, sectors and individual actors are more inclined to shift risks elsewhere.

A systems-based perspective emphasises that risk shifting does not resolve underlying problems.[15] It merely transfers responsibility and strain onto other areas of an already dysfunctional system and further erodes trust, collaboration, and impedes viable crisis systems.[16] Recognising and reducing the culture of risk shifting, or defensive practice, is essential for building sustainable cohesive, accountable, and truly person-centric crisis systems.

Media

Media has an enormous impact on shaping public opinion and influencing policy reform. As media consumption becomes faster, more fragmented, and increasingly global – often with fewer layers of accountability or editorial oversight – its capacity to harm or support social issues grows. Within this landscape, Clifford's (2021) study of police and behavioural health crisis reporting shows how coverage frequently reinforces a simplistic dualistic narrative.[17] Fatal encounters, in particular, are often framed through 'vulnerable versus responsible' or 'victim versus villain' storylines. Clifford argues that these "abstract, over-simplified and archetypal" narratives obscure the complexity of events and hinder preventative efforts.[18] Such emotionally charged coverage only serves to reinforce simplistic public perceptions of what police and first responders do at crisis incidents.

This pattern is not a new phenomenon. A 2012 Australian review of mental illness and the media found news coverage often increased public beliefs that individuals experiencing behavioural health challenges are violent and encouraged greater social distancing.[19] United States researchers likewise found more than half of behavioural health stories focused on violence, with interpersonal violence receiving more reporting than suicide, despite suicide being more common.[20] Such reporting has real-world consequences. When crisis is viewed through a stigmatised lens, incidents can be reported as more dangerous than they are, increasing the likelihood they default to police rather than other services, and raise the prospect of coercive outcomes.

The complexity of media influence doesn't just shape how public call for help, it also influences how people in crisis engage with police. Succar and colleagues (2024) found media coverage of routine policing had little effect on public perception, while national level reporting of police misconduct or abuse, particularly towards vulnerable groups, significantly impacted public perception.[21] This framing can influence how those experiencing a crisis perceive police. With accounts of Australians who had been subject to a police behavioural health crisis response in 2025 reporting feeling fearful, anticipated harmful or coercive outcomes and considered themselves as 'lucky' when no brutality occurred.[22]

These findings show how media narratives, whether from established outlets or freelance sources, act as a systems-level barrier. By shaping public expectations, influencing political agendas, and affecting inter-sector relationships, media coverage can significantly impact the direction of system reform. Too often, reporting focuses on coercive control or violence, and presents these events as typical rather than the outliers, ultimately reinforcing stigma and undermining efforts to build broader systems-based, continuous-care models of crisis management.

Legislation and Policies

The World Health Organisation has identified that many countries are still relying upon outdated legal and policy frameworks to manage crisis response.[23] One of the most common legislative issues is how police are often structured as the only sector with capacity to intervene in situations of acute crisis.

The United Kingdom's Mental Health Act 1983, particularly Section 135 & 136, illustrates this with police set as the only sector empowered to take a person into immediate care or control without a warrant, and empowered to enter a private property to enforce involuntary apprehension.[24] Although Australian states each have their own mental health legislation, in practice they are the same: with police being the only ones empowered to determine the need for emergency involuntary apprehension (aside from authorised mental health professionals), and the only ones legally permitted to use force to enter buildings to enact these powers.[25]

UK legislation creates another unusual barrier: police can't actually use Section 136 powers in anyone's home, even if they have lawfully entered and are physically present with someone actively indicating an intention to self-harm.[26]

These legal boundaries clearly misalign to current community expectations. Expectations that police involvement in crisis is reduced, yet those who would fill this gap – such as peer-teams, ambulance personnel, or community responders – do not have legal authority to act or physically apprehend a person in acute crisis when at risk. Simply, legislation sets the framework where police are the only agents who can act decisively, even when society is asking for change.

The challenge becomes even more complex when we look at how legislation defines mental illness. Most mental health acts use broad clinical sounding language – for example, a person who is affected by a serious impairment of thought, mood, volition, perception, or cognition.[27] This assumes responders, particularly police, can interpret and apply these definitions during dynamic, and at times high-risk, moments of acute crisis, even though they are not clinically trained. At the same time, legislation expects they are able to diagnose the persons behaviour is not due to conditions such as intoxication, dementia, autism, or other conditions often *excluded* from the legal definition of mental illness[28].

Western Australia's *Mental Health Act 2014* creates this exact dilemma for police, where Section 156 allows them to apprehend a person they reasonably suspect has a mental illness and to be taken into care to for safety.[29] However, Section 6(2) lists several conditions which *are not* considered mental illness under the Act, including intellectual disability, substance use, and others. This creates an operational paradox: police must act within the law, yet many of those who experience behavioural health crisis fall outside the legal definitions of mental illness, even when they need urgent support.

These legal boundaries, an inability to act in a person's home and narrow legislated definitions of mental illness, place police in impossible positions. The law sets strict rules to their power, yet officers often feel morally compelled to intervene and prevent a perceived risk. This sets police on a path which may appear procedurally unjust, a concern raised by Asquith and Bartkowiak-Théron (2017) who found such interventions, even when well intentioned, can leave long-lasting psychological scars for those in crisis.[30]

Legislation also reinforces a reactive model of crisis response through strict rules regarding data and information-sharing. Many laws prevent proactive information-sharing, even when to do so may help identify individuals at risk. Instead, information can usually only be shared once a person has reached an acute crisis point.

For example, Western Australia's *Mental Health Regulations* permits disclosure to prevent imminent serious risk, and US *Health Insurance Portability and Accountability Act* rules grant disclosure to police only in situations of acute imminent risk.[31] These examples acknowledge information-sharing can assist in crisis, but limits such collaboration to the moment of crisis itself.

Together these examples illustrate how legislation shapes, and often restricts, how crisis systems can operate. When laws position police as primary responders, narrowly define behavioural health, and limit proactive collaborations, it becomes increasingly difficult to progress crisis systems to more health-based or community led models, regardless of how much society or police call for change.

Meaningful reform requires legislators to realign laws to support how behavioural health is understood in terms of crisis presentation, capacity for collaboration of sectors, and empowering non-police responders. Until then, police will remain locked in by law to a larger role in crisis that either they or communities expect.

Terminology

In de-escalation training, participants are continuously reminded 'what you say matters'. Language can prevent conflict, reduce confusion, and affect outcomes during crisis negotiations. It seems ironic that researchers, policy makers, industry professionals and even advocates will fall victim to those very traps they caution frontline responders to avoid when debating crisis systems and reform.

How frontline crisis response is delivered is influenced by how those in perceived positions of authority describe principles, problems, and proposed reform. Many of these terms have been addressed, but when discussing barriers to crisis system reform it is useful to bring them together. The following examples represent a small collection of frequently used terms the author considers particularly harmful. They are not an exhaustive, nor examined in depth here, but they highlight themes worth recognising.

- **Persons with Serious Mental Illness** – As discussed in Chapter 1, crisis is rarely clinical, or presents in isolation from co-occurring factors. Narrowing research, policy, or operational capacity to a select diagnostic profile category limits the ability to build inclusive and effective response systems.
  The author suggests the terms *Behavioural Health* and *Persons with Behavioural Health* as more inclusive and accurate terms for crisis management systems.
- **Frequent Flyers** – Although there is no adopted definition for individuals experiencing repeated patterns of crisis, terms such as *frequent flyers, high demand, or repeat consumers* have stigmatising undertones. They imply individuals have a willingness or choice in acute crisis episodes, when in reality many people become trapped in these cycles due to systems failures rather than their own personal agendas.
  The author suggests the term *Chronic Crisis Cycling*, which describes the pattern rather than labelling the person. While acknowledging that individuals may become locked in crisis cycles through their own actions, there is a need to look at broader systemic gaps in service.
- **Law Enforcement** – This term will be examined further later in this chapter, but it inadequately reflects the extent of duties society expects of police. Framing police officers as only enforcers of law, narrows and overly simplifies their broad role in maintaining community safety, emergency coordination, and facilitating social cohesion.
  The author suggests returning to the terms *Police* and *Policing* to more accurately describe police officers and their functions.
- **Mental Health Call for Service** – As outlined in Chapter 1, this term is often wrongly applied by frontline responders, particularly police. It narrows a range of behavioural health-related incidents in one diagnostic cluster, unintentionally establishing implicit bias before they attend the scene. This can clearly affect outcomes.
  The author suggests adopting *Behavioural Health Calls for Service* to align with a more inclusive behavioural health framework.

- **Gatekeepers** – Police have routinely been described as gatekeepers to mental health services, a term that implies some clinical authority to determine who receives appropriate healthcare. Originally used by scholars to highlight gaps in community mental health delivery, it has become a somewhat redundant way of framing police involvement in behavioural health crisis.
  The author suggests that in a fully functioning systems-based crisis management model, police would become *Activators,* initiating service providers to deliver the requisite care to manage the crisis.

Recognising how language affects progress is part of the process to developing an inclusive systems-based approach, which shifts from crisis response to crisis management.

"Defund the Police" and Crisis Response

Public outrage in the United States after a series of fatal police encounters, with the notable prominent deaths of Breonna Taylor and George Floyd, came to ahead in 2020, sparking widespread protests and political debate under the banner "Defund the Police".[32] The movement gained global support, with demonstrations and calls for police defunding also occurring in the United Kingdom and Australia.[33] The core message was to raise concerns about police excessive use of force, particularly against marginalised groups, while highlighting deeper problems in crisis response and social services. Many organisers argued for removing police from crisis response and reinvesting their budgets into community-based teams and social services.

This section examines how framing reform in strongly oppositional terms, even when grounded in genuine concern, may in itself become a barrier to system reform. Narratives that delegitimise policing risk polarising sectors, unsettling collaborations, and obscures the complexity and at times acute risks that crisis presents, along with the benefits of multi-sector approaches.

What Does "Defund the Police" Actually Mean?

Calls to reduce policing's role in behavioural health crisis is not new. Lamb and Weinberger argued in 2005, that shifting police funding to social services could reduce the criminalisation of individuals with behavioural health issues.[34] However, the current debate tends to focus more on police use of force.

A major challenge facing the movement is its own lack of clarity. Proponents span a wide spectrum: from total abolition to simply divesting portions of budgets to social services.[35] Smith and colleagues (2024) suggest this division, along with an absence of any clear framework, resulted in broader public opinion opposing the movement.[36]

Despite such divisions, there is wide support for greater investment in health care, housing, education, and other social services which can prevent individuals escalating to a crisis point that requires police intervention. Quattlebaum and Tyler (2020) stress though that removing police without genuine alternatives may increase risks to both individual and public safety.[37] Fleetwood & Lea (2022) similarly argue that defunding is not about punishing police, but should be about redirecting resources to community safety and security.[38]

Has Funding Been Reinvested?

Following the 2020 protests, US jurisdictions implemented reductions in police expenditure, typically from 1% to 10%.[39] However, changes were often seen as cosmetic through budget shifts such as postponing recruitment, limiting overtime, or eliminating specialist units, rather than substantial financial reforms.

Regardless, the movement did revitalise broader conversations on changing health and social service capacity. Notably, several jurisdictions established non-police crisis response programs, including Minneapolis' Behavioural Crisis Response, Durham's Community Safety Department, New York's B-HEARD, and Dayton's Mediation Response Unit.[40] These programs marked a progressive shift in public policy.

Meanwhile, the United Kingdom provides a working example of what defunding outcomes can look like. Since 2009, due to austerity measures, policing numbers have reduced by more than 19,000 officers, creating significant frontline pressures.[41] In response, UK policing adopted the Right Care, Right Person (RCRP) model to reduce police involvement in behavioural health calls and redirect these incidents to other health and social services.[42] However, reinvestment into those sectors did not match the reduction of police resources or their withdrawal from crisis response. As a result, those sectors similarly became overstretched seeing gaps in service delivery to crisis.

However, Hoang and Benjamin (2023) found, that although initial budget cuts after the 2020 protests were modest- and unlikely to satisfy those calling for reform- most police budgets have since returned to pre-defund levels or increased.[43] A point attributed in part to the fact that many of the changes introduced in the midst of politicised defund policy reform, were not embedded in long-term policy frameworks and simply short-term agendas.

Unintended Consequences

Research suggests several unintended outcomes emerged from the defund movement. Ebbinghaus and colleagues (2025) found there was "policy backlash," where some cities actually increased police budgets in response to public safety concerns during the protests.[44] With other studies finding political officials, who openly supported defunding often failed to secure re-election, raising questions about the long-term sustainability of reforms introduced.[45]

Lum and colleagues (2021) argued some policy changes moved faster than the available evidence, resulting in significant gaps in understanding the scale and nature of police calls, or why some individuals choose to call police rather than social services.[46] This latter point, that some individuals refuse clinical support preferring a police response, has been evidence by several studies and illustrates an additional complication in assuming services can simple be substituted.[47]

Increased anti-police sentiment in itself also carries risks at the individual level. Media and social media narratives – which focus on police misconduct or divisive narratives – have been linked to increasing fear in vulnerable groups, leading some individuals to delay or avoid seeking help, or to display increased fight, flight, freeze behaviours when police arrive.[48] At the same time, police officers report reduced morale, reduced feelings of community support and increased concerns for their own safety.[49] This dynamic, often described as "The Ferguson Effect," can reduce an officers' willingness to engage in proactive policing, creating further tensions when required to engage in social welfare roles.[50]

Koziarski and Huey (2021) caution against removing police from all non-criminal welfare roles arguing to do so can reduce trust, ability to identify emerging community issues and reduces proactive crime prevention.[51] Reducing police budgets also raises questions on how it affects police capacity to respond to crime. With the London's Metropolitan Police highlighting how officers freed from behavioural health calls, after the implementation of Right Care, Right Person were able to respond to an estimated 500 additional robberies per month.[52] Had these officer hours been removed in line with strict defunding principles, such gains would not have been possible. These points suggest a more considered approach is needed when debating how funding and resourcing is allocated across sectors.

Conclusion

A broader question is whether the appeal of the "defund the police" movement and messaging reflects more than concerns about policing, but also deeper systemic and social failings? Decades of underinvestment in social services have created systemic gaps resulting in policing increasingly been called upon to fill the void. In this context, police may have unwittingly become the public face of broader institutional breakdowns.

Framing police as the sole problem risks oversimplifying a complex issue. The movement itself is divided, from total abolition to simple divestment, illustrating the danger of narrowly focusing on a punitive discourse. Such an approach further overlooks how reducing police resources can impact their capacity to respond to crime.

Ultimately, defund the police movement highlights the need for social services, policing, and governments to move beyond politicised slogans and work collaboratively towards evidence-lead, systems-based approaches to behavioural health crisis.

Policing as Law Enforcement

Policing is routinely referenced as "Law Enforcement", yet this term is historically inaccurate in what police work entails. It also sets a possibly harmful and oversimplified understanding of a police officer's role in society. "Law Enforcement" clearly fails to encapsulate the broad expectations society has of police, for policing has always been so much more than just enforcing legislation.

Although the term is predominately used in North American contexts, the United Kingdom, Australia, and New Zealand are not immune to this institutionalised framing of their role in society. These commonwealth jurisdictions often invoke the "Peelian Principles" as the doctrine of identity, using these principles to situate their core function as crime fighting.

As the reader will now appreciate, a barrier to successful crisis response management is terminology. Labels such as "law enforcement" and deference to the Peelian Principles shape organisational identities, frame culture, and can inhibit contemporary procedurally just practices. This section will examine how these terms, and in some respect even mythology, affect progressive communities from tackling many complex social issues with support of the unique capacity police can bring to management systems.

Policing or Law Enforcement

The term 'law enforcement' is widely used to reference police agencies, particularly in North America. Its rise can be traced back to 1960s, when the Law Enforcement Assistance Administration (LEAA) was established to manage federal funding to address surging crime rates across the nation.[53] This program likely embedded the language *law enforcement* into institutional frameworks and professional identity.

Over time, the term has become entrenched in North American academic, policy, industry, and cultural discussions. When institutionalised, this framing can set a tone with real-world consequences. For example, some police leaders publicly reinforce the notion that police functions are solely to enforce the law. Sacramento County Sheriff Jim Cooper used his podcast to reinforce this narrative, to justify his agencies withdrawal from mental health incidents after the Ninth Circuit Court of Appeals ruled police may lose qualified immunity when dealing with non-criminal matters.[54] While his response to the ruling is understandable, such statements can produce a false narrative of what society expects of police, particularly in terms of non-criminal matters.

Professor of Criminology Michael Rowe argues that policing has always been more than 'law enforcement'.[55] Police discretion gives individual officers and policing command collectively the capacity to enforce certain laws and not others. This flexibility goes against the concept of law enforcers. Even in the 1970s Bittner (1970, p. 42) was challenging police as 'law enforcers', emphasising communities regularly call on police to assist in non-criminal matters.[56] He cautioned by suggesting crime control is the only serious work of police it can be detrimental to the morale of officers, particularly when their non-criminal work is degraded by their colleagues and command.

Use of Peelian Principles to Narrow Functionality

United Kingdom and commonwealth police agencies mirror their North American counterparts with a law enforcement-centric narrative, deferring to the "Peelian Principles". These principles hark back to a newly formed Metropolitan Police of the 1820s and Sir Robert Peel's nine principles he issued to new constables to guide their conduct.[57] Built around the primary doctrine of policing by consent, contemporary policing leadership holds that these principles also guide that the core function of policing is the maintenance of law and order.

Evidence of this law enforcement focus came from then Chief Inspector of Constabulary Andy Cooke's 2021 opening statement at the *State of Policing: Annual Assessment* by asserting "The Peelian Principles remind us that the police are the public and the public are the police. But they also remind us that the basic mission for which the police exist is to prevent crime and disorder."[58] A similar point was made by Chief Constable Anderson during the 2023 Health and Social Care Committee review of Right Care, Right Person. When asked whether the Peelian Principles extend to protecting individuals in crisis, he rejected this broader interpretation, rather telling the Committee – "*the point I am making is that a police officer is trained as a cop. They are there to deter and detect crime.*"[59]

However, just as Rowe and Bittner argue that the term 'Law Enforcement" fails to capture what society expects of police, contemporary scholars voice similar concerns about policing leaderships reliance upon the Peelian Principles, to narrow policing's function. Just as use of 'law enforcement' narrows focus, this present practice also ignores the reality of what is expected of policing in modern society.

This comes from two key issues. First is the question of relevance: whether to rely on principles that were developed two centuries ago in Georgian England retain any meaningful capacity to guide policing in today's twenty-first-century society.[60] Today's policing operates within vastly different societal norms, trans-national crime, technological advancements in offending and crime fighting, population expansion and understanding of psycho-social factors make continued observance of nineteenth-century doctrines appear increasingly nostalgic rather than practical.

Second there is the actual validity of the Peelian Principle mythology itself. Most scholars now recognise that the familiar 'nine principles' were not authored by Sir Robert Peel, but a creation of academic Charles Reith in 1948, over a hundred years after Peel's time as commissioner.[61] Even on this account it still makes these principles the better part of a hundred years out of date. More importantly scholars argue that when the nine principles are read fully, they are at most vague in their direction and certainly do not hold that policing's role is purely to maintain law and order.

A clear example is looking collectively at principles 7 and 9[62]:

#7 – To maintain at all times a relationship with the public that gives reality to the historic tradition that *the police are the public and that the public are the police*, the police being only members of the public who are paid to give full time attention to duties which are incumbent on every citizen *in the interests of community welfare and existence.*

#9 – To recognise always that the test of police efficiency is the absence of crime and disorder, and *not the visible evidence of police action in dealing with them.*

These two principles indicate even within the mythology of the Peelian Principles there is recognition that policing is not only about law enforcement. The concluding principle makes this explicit, highlighting policing success is not measured by the enforcement of laws but in the ability of police to prevent crime; a standard calling for proactive, preventative, and socially engaged police. This clearly aligns closely with principle 7, which emphasises police are part of the wider community ("the police are the public") supporting "community welfare". Together, these principles suggest policing has a responsibility to engage in broader social welfare and crime prevention strategies, rather than reactive law enforcement roles.

These conflicting interpretations are echoed in academic debates, leading some to ask, if academics cannot agree on the foundations and specifics of the Peelian Principles how can policing leadership who attempt to invoke them not experience similar confusion or disagreement.[63]

Policing beyond Crime

A clear aside in the behavioural health debate to illustrate the limits of a 'law enforcement' narrative can be seen in the many roles police and society are willing to accept beyond crime. As Andrews (2025) notes, the Peelian Principles, just like the term law enforcement, are routinely invoked to reinforce a narrow criminogenic mission. Yet, frontline officers spend much of their time on welfare-based crises: that is, behavioural health, family violence, and missing persons.[64]

A simple example is missing persons. Australian data shows that of approximately 38,000 missing persons reported to police annually, 99.5% are resolved with the majority not resulting in a criminal outcome.[65] The United Kingdom and United States are impacted more so with each having hundreds of thousands of missing persons reports managed by police annually, mostly also resolved without a criminal outcome.[66] Yet each jurisdiction willingly establishes dedicated missing persons units.

Similarly, police globally are often called upon to assume the role of incident command during disasters and unusual hazards, such as Western Australia Police being responsible for 'falling space debris', under local emergency management legislation.[67] Accordingly despite policing insisting their core function is crime, both police and society expect more. Police willingly establish themselves as indispensable social responders in areas such as missing persons, family violence, and emergency coordination, even as they seek to distance themselves from behavioural health work – a contradiction that exposes the rift between organisational identity messaging and operational realities.

Why the "Law Enforcement" Narrative Harms Crisis Management

There is no doubt that police are far from ideal as default behavioural health crisis responders. However, there is a proportion of calls where police are the most suitable, and sometimes only, sector able to respond. When these moments arise, the problem is not the presence of police, but the environment that has been cast around policing. When academic, social, and institutional narratives repeatedly reinforce an ideology that police only respond through an enforcement lens, it can only heighten the sense of distrust and agitation felt by those in crisis and those responding.

A narrative focused on enforcement can build a culture of warrior style policing.[68] Where police are trained and called upon with an expectation to utilise coercive measures, including a reliance on using force. Whilst ignoring the reality, police are also expected and do perform social work duties effectively.[69] This enforcement and warrior mentality can inadvertently increase the use of force as a default response even in non-criminal settings.[70]

When considering procedurally just interventions this enforcement lens creates concern. Police framed as enforcers called to act upon transgressions, rather than problem solves working within communities, can affect how officers perceive the public and reduce procedurally just outcomes.[71] Further this framing is counter-intuitive to the Peelian Principles policing leaders lean upon in terms of policing by consent or that the police are themselves the public.[72]

Crisis response requires empathy, a de-escalatory mindset, and problem-solving focused on non-punitive outcomes. Skills and thought processes which may feel threatening to an officer's identity when operating in an enforcement and warrior dominated narrative.[73] A challenge to identity which can be compounded by an officers own organisational messaging when leaders describe social welfare issues as distractions to the 'real police work' of crime fighting.[74]

Summary

The idea that police exist in communities to only fight crime and enforce laws clearly misrepresents what communities expect, and those broader social roles policing leadership routinely embrace. Whilst not every crisis requires a police response, when police *are* required, both policing leadership and elements of society have hamstrung effective crisis capacity by narrowing policing focus, and reducing procedurally just practices by using terms such as 'law enforcement' or reliance on mythologised principles from centuries past.

Such a narrow ideology regarding policing's 'core functions' is incongruent with policing's own willingness to accept a wide array of non-criminal responsibilities. Police attend overwhelming numbers of missing persons reports, act as incident commanders during disaster and unusual hazards, and respond to non-violent family disputes – none of which seem to provoke the concern behavioural health crisis work generates. The question becomes, not whether society and police leadership accept social welfare incidents are a core function of police work, this is already evident in practice. The real question is why behavioural health has become so divisive and emotive within policing, to a point organisational culture is distorting the realities of what police actually do.

To address this policing and society must reimage the position police hold within their community (police are the public). Police will always be there to investigate crime and ensure procedurally just outcomes for transgression; but they are also mobile social problem solvers relied upon every day in communities across the globe. Although this reimagining process must be undertaken with a degree of caution. Agencies better placed to solve such social welfare problems cannot continue to absolve themselves of their 24/7 responsibilities simply because police have historically filled their gaps.

Observational Commentary

This chapter has brought together several persistent barriers that undermine the creation of effective, collaborative, systems-based crisis management systems. Illustrating also how these barriers tend to reinforce a divisive public narrative about policing's role in crisis, a division that regularly distracts from meaningful systems reform.

Public debates such as "defund the police" and emphasis on a "law enforcement" culture appear to come from opposite sides of the police-community divide, yet both ultimately call for a change in crisis management. The defund movement often frames police involvement as only negative, focusing on physical harm. Policing's emphasis of on law enforcement, appears focused on resourcing pressures, organisational culture, and liability concerns. Despite their differences, both perspectives overlook one reality: communities expect a broader social role of police, one where police go beyond the simple enforcement of criminal laws.

Language also shapes how sectors, advocates, and communities understand crisis. Terms such as "serious mental illness", "frequent flyers", and "law enforcement" subtly reinforce fragmented, reactive, crisis response models. Combining such stigmatising language with the defund and law enforcement narratives narrows concepts of crisis, ultimately impacting on the ability to enable broader systems-based perspectives which crisis presently needs. Such language and narratives can only contribute to siloed sectors falling prey to: the *wrong pockets problem.*

A pattern many crisis systems and those within them know too well. One sector invests in effective programs; however, the benefit is realised downstream by other sectors and soon organisational leadership begin to question the expense. Even when those on the frontline or evidence is indicating wider gains across systems. This problem creates the following predictable barrier patterns:

- Resourcing withdrawal to return benefits to their own sector
- Risk shifting to other sectors, often coupled with blame-shifting for systems failures
- Widening gaps in inter-sector collaboration

- Police returning to the role of 24/7 default responders in the absence of system-wide reform

Importantly, these barriers rarely arise in isolation. Evolving rather as interconnected symptoms of communities failing to address behavioural health crisis through a systems-based lens.

Understanding these barriers, even though the list presented here is not exhaustive, is essential for developing and maintaining crisis management systems that are safe, effective, and dynamic. A systems-based approach requires acknowledging how these barriers affect reform, recognising the roles each sector plays, and avoid the trap of divisive, isolated, sector-versus-sector thinking which has dominated debate.

The following chapter examines systems-based thinking in more detail, looking at how leaders who adopt this way of thinking support progressive, collaborative, whole of community models that communities are increasingly demanding.

Notes

1 World Health Organization. (2025). *Mental health atlas 2024.* World Health Organization. https://iris.who.int/server/api/core/bitstreams/5897b3c7-2848-47a7-ba22-0a7902342a81/content; Crime and Justice Institute. (2024). *Behavioral health crisis response landscape analysis.* www.cjinstitute.org/assets/sites/2/2024/05/AV-Crisis-Response-Report.pdf

2 Crime and Justice Institute. (2024). *Behavioral health crisis response landscape analysis.* www.cjinstitute.org/assets/sites/2/2024/05/AV-Crisis-Response-Report.pdf; Mental Health Association. (2021). *Submission to Productivity Commission into Mental Health* www.pc.gov.au/__data/assets/pdf_file/0012/243111/sub538-mental-health.pdf.

3 Mental Health Association. (2021). *Submission to Productivity Commission into Mental Health.* www.pc.gov.au/__data/assets/pdf_file/0012/243111/sub538-mental-health.pdf.

4 McGorry, P., Gunasiri, H., Mei, C., Rice, S., & Gao, C. X. (2025). *The youth mental health crisis: Analysis and solutions. Frontiers in Psychiatry, 15,* Article 1517533. https://doi.org/10.3389/fpsyt.2024.1517533.

5 Kleinman, R., & Patel, V. (2024). *4 targets of opportunity for addressing the behavioral health crisis.* Brookings Institution. www.brookings.edu; Roman, J. K. (2015). *Solving the wrong pockets problem: How pay for success promotes investment in evidence-based best practices.* Urban Institute. www.urban.org/sites/default/files/alfresco/publication-pdfs/2000427-Solving-the-Wrong-Pockets-Problem.pdf.

6 College of Policing. (2023, October). *Right Care Right Person – Humberside Police.* www.college.police.uk/support-forces/practices/smarter-practice/right-care-right-person.

7 McGorry, P., Gunasiri, H., Mei, C., Rice, S., & Gao, C. X. (2025). *The youth mental health crisis: Analysis and solutions. Frontiers in Psychiatry, 15*, Article 1517533. https://doi.org/10.3389/fpsyt.2024.1517533.

8 Australian Government Department of Health. (2023). *Mental health workforce: Labour market analysis (Final report).* www.health.gov.au/sites/default/files/2023-01/mental-health-workforce-labour-market-analysis-final-report.pdf

9 Australian Government Department of Health. (2023). *Mental health workforce: Labour market analysis (Final report).* www.health.gov.au/sites/default/files/2023-01/mental-health-workforce-labour-market-analysis-final-report.pdf

10 Lorenc, T., Khouja, C., Harden, M., et al. (2024). Defensive healthcare practice: Systematic review of qualitative evidence. *BMJ Open, 14*, e085673. https://doi.org/10.1136/bmjopen-2024-085673; Ahmed, N., Barlow, S., Reynolds, L., Drey, N., Begum, F., Tuudah, E., & Simpson, A. (2021). Mental health professionals' perceived barriers and enablers to shared decision-making in risk assessment and risk management: A qualitative systematic review. *BMC Psychiatry, 21*(1), 594. https://doi.org/10.1186/s12888-021-03304-0; Mullen, R., Admiraal, A., & Trevena, J. (2008). Defensive practice in mental health. *The New Zealand Medical Journal, 121*(1286). https://pubmed.ncbi.nlm.nih.gov/19098951/.

11 Her Majesty's Inspectorate of Constabulary and Fire & Rescue Services. (2018). *Policing and mental health: Picking up the pieces* (Report). https://assets-hmicfrs.justiceinspectorates.gov.uk/uploads/policing-and-mental-health-picking-up-the-pieces.pdf.

12 Hedden-Clayton, B., Carl, A., Swanson, L., Comartin, E., & Kubiak, S. (2025). Deflecting people experiencing a mental health crisis from the criminal-legal system at dispatch: Findings from calls-for-service reports and statewide survey data. *Evaluation and Program Planning, 114*, 102727. https://doi.org/10.1016/j.evalprogplan.2025.102727.

13 State of New South Wales v. Talovic. (2014). *87 NSWLR 512.* www.caselaw.nsw.gov.au/decision/54a639bfe4b0b4e1d63f8a4c.

14 United States Court of Appeals, Ninth Circuit (2024) Scott v. Smith (2024). *Nos. 23-15480.* https://caselaw.findlaw.com/court/us-9th-circuit/116433900.html; United States Court of Appeals, Ninth Circuit (2003). *Drummond ex rel. Drummond v. City of Anaheim (2003) No. 02-55320.* https://caselaw.findlaw.com/court/us-9th-circuit/1371011.html; O'Sullivan, T. (2022). *Inquest in the Death of Ian Fackender* Coroners (File No. 2017/00264782). Coroners Court of New South Wales. https://coroners.nsw.gov.au/coroners-court/download.html/documents/findings/2022/Ian_Fackender_findings.pdf.

15 McNab, D., McKay, J., Shorrock, S., Luty, S., & Bowie, P. (2020). Development and application of 'systems thinking' principles for quality improvement. *BMJ Open Quality, 9*(1), e000714. https://doi.org/10.1136/bmjoq-2019-000714; Jordans, M. J. D. (2024). Applying systems theory to global mental health. *Cambridge Prisms: Global Mental Health, 12*, e2. https://doi.org/10.1017/gmh.2024.147.

16 McNab, D., McKay, J., Shorrock, S., Luty, S., & Bowie, P. (2020). Development and application of 'systems thinking' principles for quality improvement. *BMJ Open Quality, 9*(1), e000714. https://doi.org/10.1136/bmjoq-2019-000714; Jordans, M. J. D. (2024). Applying systems theory to global mental health. *Cambridge Prisms: Global Mental Health, 12*, e2. https://doi.org/10.1017/gmh.2024.147.
17 Clifford, K. (2021). *Policing, mental illness and media: The framing of mental health crisis encounters and police use of force.* Palgrave Macmillan.
18 Clifford, K. (2021). *Policing, mental illness and media: The framing of mental health crisis encounters and police use of force.* Palgrave Macmillan.
19 Pirkis, J., & Francis, C. (2012). *Mental illness in the news and information media: A critical review.* Everymind. https://s3-ap-southeast-2.amazonaws.com/everymind/assets/Uploads/Mental-illness-in-the-news-and-information-media-A-critical-review.pdf.
20 McGinty, E. E., Kennedy-Hendricks, A., Choksy, S., & Barry, C. L. (2016). Trends in news media coverage of mental illness in the United States: 1995–2014. *Health Affairs, 35*(6), 1121–29. https://doi.org/10.1377/hlthaff.2016.0011.
21 Succar, R., Ramallo, S., Das, R., Barak Ventura, R., & Porfiri, M. (2024). Understanding the role of media in the formation of public sentiment towards the police. *Communications Psychology, 2*, Article 11. https://doi.org/10.1038/s44271-024-00059-8.
22 Randall, R., Kennedy, H., Karanikolas, P., Bashfield, L., Rayner, A., … Nguyen, F. (2025). '*I was having an anxiety attack and they pepper sprayed me*': police apprehension in mental health contexts in Australia. *Policing and Society, 35*(1), 85–100. https://doi.org/10.1080/10439463.2024.2372354.
23 World Health Organization. (2021). *Mental health crisis services: Promoting person-centred and rights-based approaches.* World Health Organization. https://apps.who.int/iris/handle/10665/341637.
24 Mental Health Act. (1983). *c. 20, ss. 135–36 (U.K.).* legislation.gov.uk. www.legislation.gov.uk/ukpga/1983/20/contents.
25 Mental Health Act 2014 (WA). www.legislation.wa.gov.au; Mental Health Act 2007 (NSW). www.legislation.nsw.gov.au; Mental Health Act 2016 (Qld). www.legislation.qld.gov.au.
26 Mental Health Act 1983, c. 20 (UK). www.legislation.gov.uk/ukpga/1983/20.
27 Mental Health Act 2009 (SA) (Australia). Mental Health Act 2013 (Tas) (Australia). Mental Health Act 2014 (WA) (Australia). Mental Health and Wellbeing Act 2022 (Vic) (Australia).
28 Mental Health Act 2009 (SA) (Australia). Mental Health Act 2013 (Tas) (Australia). Mental Health Act 2014 (WA) (Australia). Mental Health and Wellbeing Act 2022 (Vic) (Australia).
29 Mental Health Act 2014 (WA). www.legislation.wa.gov.au *Mental Health Act* 2007 (NSW); www.legislation.nsw.gov.au; Mental Health Act 2016 (Qld). www.legislation.qld.gov.au.
30 Asquith, N. L., & Bartkowiak-Théron, I. (2017). Police as public health interventionists. In N. Asquith, I. Bartkowiak-Théron, & K. Roberts. (Eds.),

Policing encounters with vulnerability. Cham: Palgrave Macmillan. https://doi.org/10.1007/978-3-319-51228-0_7.
31 Western Australia. (2015). *Mental Health Regulations 2015: Regulation 20 – Prescribed authorised recording, disclosure or use of information*. State Law Publisher. Retrieved November 11, 2025, from https://classic.austlii.edu.au/au/legis/wa/consol_reg/mhr2015237/s20.html; U.S. Department of Health and Human Services. (2003). *Standards for privacy of individually identifiable health information, 45 C.F.R. § 164.512 (Uses and disclosures for which consent, authorization, or opportunity to agree or object is not required)*. Federal Register. Retrieved November 11, 2025, from www.ecfr.gov/current/title-45/subtitle-A/subchapter-C/part-164/subpart-E/section-164.512.
32 Jackson, J., Fine, A. D., Bradford, B., & Trinkner, R. (2023). Social identity and support for defunding the police in the aftermath of George Floyd's murder. *Group Processes & Intergroup Relations*, *26*(4), 833–58. https://doi.org/10.1177/13684302221128230.
33 BBC News. (2020, June 3). *George Floyd death: Thousands join London protest*. BBC News. www.bbc.com/news/uk-52907101; Mitchell, J., & Fisher, J. (2020, June 6). *Black Lives Matter rallies held across Australia to protest against mistreatment and deaths of Indigenous people*. ABC News. www.abc.net.au/news/2020-06-06/black-lives-matter-rallies-held-across-australia/12325442.
34 Quattlebaum, M., & Tyler, T. (2020). Beyond the law: An agenda for policing reform. *Boston University Law Review*, *100*(3), 1017–45; Lamb, H. R., & Weinberger, L. E. (2005). The shift of psychiatric inpatient care from hospitals to jails and prisons. *Journal of the American Academy of Psychiatry and the Law*, *33*(4), 529–34. https://jaapl.org/content/33/4/529.
35 Fegley, T., & Murtazashvili, I. (2023). From defunding to refunding police: Institutions and the persistence of policing budgets. *Public Choice*. Advance online publication. https://doi.org/10.1007/s11127-023-01063-y; Smith, O. K. H., Flick, C., & Michalski, N. D. (2024). To eliminate police or redirect police funds? The impact of framing on public support for defunding the police. *Frontiers in Psychology*, *15*, Article 1439463. https://doi.org/10.3389/fpsyg.2024.1439463; Jackson, J., Fine, A., Bradford, B., & Trinkner, R. (2023). Social identity and support for defunding the police in the aftermath of George Floyd's murder. *Group Processes & Intergroup Relations*, *26*(4), 833–58. https://doi.org/10.1177/13684302221128230; Corley, C., & Reber, M. (2023). Defunding the police: Reflecting on the US experience and lessons learned for Canada. *Journal of Community Safety and Well-Being*, *8*(1), 41–47. https://doi.org/10.35502/jcswb.315.
36 Smith, O. K. H., Flick, C., & Michalski, N. D. (2024). To eliminate police or redirect police funds? The impact of framing on public support for defunding the police. *Frontiers in Psychology*, *15*, Article 1439463. https://doi.org/10.3389/fpsyg.2024.1439463.
37 Quattlebaum, M., & Tyler, T. (2020). Beyond the law: An agenda for policing reform. *Boston University Law Review*, *100*(3), 1017; Fleetwood, J., & Lea, J. (2022). Defunding the police in the UK: Critical questions and practical

suggestions. *The Howard Journal of Crime and Justice, 61*(2), 167–84. https://doi.org/10.1111/hojo.12468.

38 Quattlebaum, M., & Tyler, T. (2020). Beyond the law: An agenda for policing reform. *Boston University Law Review, 100*(3), 1017; Fleetwood, J., & Lea, J. (2022). Defunding the police in the UK: Critical questions and practical suggestions. *The Howard Journal of Crime and Justice, 61*(2), 167–84. https://doi.org/10.1111/hojo.12468.

39 Fegley, T., & Murtazashvili, I. (2023). From defunding to refunding police: Institutions and the persistence of policing budgets. *Public Choice.* Advance online publication. https://doi.org/10.1007/s11127-023-01063-y; DeShazo, J. (2024). Policy windows and protests: Black lives matter protests and calls to defund the police in the United States. *Journal of Public Policy and Administration, 8*(3), 92–101. https://doi.org/10.11648/j.jppa.20240803.15.

40 Gaherty, K. (2023, May 22). *Behavioral crisis response in Minneapolis: Embracing inclusive design in community safety.* National League of Cities. www.nlc.org/article/2023/05/22/behavioral-crisis-response-in-minneapolis-embracing-inclusive-design-in-community-safety/; City of Durham. (n.d.). *Community safety.* Durham, NC: gov. www.durhamnc.gov/4576/Community-Safety; City & State NY. (2022, April). *What to know about NYC's B-HEARD mental health crisis response teams.* www.cityandstateny.com/policy/2022/04/what-know-about-nycs-b-heard-mental-health-crisis-response-teams/366286/; City of Dayton. (n.d.). *Dayton Mediation Response Unit.* https://dayton-mediation-response-unit-daytonohio.hub.arcgis.com/.

41 Fleetwood, J., & Lea, J. (2022). Defunding the police in the UK: Critical questions and practical suggestions. *The Howard Journal of Crime and Justice, 61*(2), 167–84. https://doi.org/10.1111/hojo.12468.

42 Warren, S. (2022, November 1). *Austerity 2.0: Why it's critical for our health that the government learns the lessons of Austerity 1.0.* The King's Fund. www.kingsfund.org.uk/insight-and-analysis/blogs/why-critical-for-health-government-learns-lessons-austerity.

43 Fegley, T., & Murtazashvili, I. (2023). From defunding to refunding police: Institutions and the persistence of policing budgets. *Public Choice.* Advance online publication. https://doi.org/10.1007/s11127-023-01063-y. Corley, C., & Reber, M. (2023). Defunding the police: Reflecting on the US experience and lessons learned for Canada. *Journal of Community Safety and Well-Being, 8*(1), 41–7. https://doi.org/10.35502/jcswb.315; Ebbinghaus, M., Bailey, N., & Rubel, J. (2025, August). The effect of the 2020 Black Lives Matter protests on police budgets: How "Defund the Police" sparked political backlash, *Social Problems, 72*(3), 1198–1215, https://doi.org/10.1093/socpro/spae004.

44 Ebbinghaus, M., Bailey, N., & Rubel, J. (2025, August). The effect of the 2020 Black Lives Matter protests on police budgets: How "Defund the Police" sparked political backlash, *Social Problems, 72*(3), 1198–1215, https://doi.org/10.1093/socpro/spae004.

45 Fegley, T., & Murtazashvili, I. (2023). From defunding to refunding police: Institutions and the persistence of policing budgets. *Public Choice*. Advance online publication. https://doi.org/10.1007/s11127-023-01063-y.
46 Lum, C., Koper, C. S., & Wu, X. (2021). Can we really defund the police? A nine-agency study of police response to calls for service. *Police Quarterly*, *25*(3), 255–80. https://doi.org/10.1177/10986111211035002 (Original work published 2022).
47 Every-Palmer, S., Dunn, A., Langridge, R., & McKenna, B. (2023). Police, ambulance and psychiatric co-response versus usual care for mental health and suicide emergency callouts: A quasi-experimental study. *Australian & New Zealand Journal of Psychiatry*. https://doi.org/10.1177/00048674231177491; Yang, S. M., Gill, C., Kanewske, L. C., & Thompson, P. S. (2018). Exploring police response to mental health calls in a nonurban area: A case study of Roanoke County, Virginia. *Victims & Offenders*, *13*(8), 1132–52. https://doi.org/10.1080/15564886.2018.1512020.
48 Davenport-Klunder, K., Hine, K., & McKillop, N. (2024). Anger, fear, and frozenness: Exploring the emotive aspect of anti-police sentiment. *Journal of Criminal Justice*, *94*, 102269, ISSN 0047-2352, https://doi.org/10.1016/j.jcrimjus.2024.102269.
49 Gau, J. M., Paoline, E. A., & Paul, N. D. (2022). De-policing as a result of public scrutiny: examining officers' perceptions of negative media attention and willingness to engage in self-initiated activity. *Journal of Crime and Justice*, *45*(5), 539–51. https://doi.org/10.1080/0735648X.2021.2024082.
50 Gau, J. M., Paoline, E. A., & Paul, N. D. (2022). De-policing as a result of public scrutiny: examining officers' perceptions of negative media attention and willingness to engage in self-initiated activity. *Journal of Crime and Justice*, *45*(5), 539–51. https://doi.org/10.1080/0735648X.2021.2024082.
51 Koziarski, J., & Huey, L. (2021). #Defund or #Re-Fund? Re-examining Bayley's blueprint for police reform. *International Journal of Comparative and Applied Criminal Justice*, *45*(3), 269–84. https://doi.org/10.1080/01924036.2021.1907604.
52 Police Professional. (2024, May 9). *MPS responding to 500 more robberies every month since launch of Right Care, Right Person*. https://policeprofessional.com/news/mps-responding-to-500-more-robberies-every-month-since-launch-of-right-care-right-person/.
53 Office of Justice Programs. (1996). *LEAA/OJP retrospective: 30 years of federal support to state and local criminal justice* (NCJ 164509). U.S. Department of Justice. www.ncjrs.gov/pdffiles1/nij/164509.pdf.
54 Cooper, J. (2023). *The hard truth on mental health with Sheriff Cooper* [Video]. YouTube. www.youtube.com/watch?v=YpXY6eJOVr4.
55 Rowe, M. (2007). What is policing? In *Introduction to policing* (Chapter 1). SAGE Publications. https://us.sagepub.com/sites/default/files/upm-binaries/19049_01_Rowe_Ch_01.pdf.
56 Bittner, E. (1970). *The functions of the police in modern society: A review of background factors, current practices, and possible role models*. U.S. Government

Printing Office. https://archive.org/details/functionsofpolic0000bitt/page/42/mode/1up.

57 Andrews, T. (2025). The 'Peelian Principles': Their historical and contemporary veracity. *Policing and Society*, *35*(5), 584–602. https://doi.org/10.1080/10439463.2024.2436078.

58 Cooke, A. (2022). Foreword. In *State of policing: The annual assessment of policing in England and Wales 2021* (p. 5). Her Majesty's Inspectorate of Constabulary and Fire & Rescue Services. www.justiceinspectorates.gov.uk/hmicfrs/publication/state-of-policing-the-annual-assessment-2021/.

59 Health and Social Care Committee. (2023). *Oral evidence: Mental Health – Right Care, Right Person (HC1836).* UK Parliament. https://committees.parliament.uk/oralevidence/13663/html.

60 Andrews, T. (2025). The 'Peelian Principles': Their historical and contemporary veracity. *Policing and Society*, *35*(5), 584–602. https://doi.org/10.1080/10439463.2024.2436078.

61 Home Office. (2012). *Definition of policing by consent.* UK Government. www.gov.uk/government/publications/policing-by-consent/definition-of-policing-by-consent; Andrews, T. (2025). The 'Peelian Principles': Their historical and contemporary veracity. *Policing and Society*, *35*(5), 584–602. https://doi.org/10.1080/10439463.2024.2436078.

62 Andrews, T. (2025). The 'Peelian Principles': Their historical and contemporary veracity. *Policing and Society*, *35*(5), 584–602. https://doi.org/10.1080/10439463.2024.2436078.

63 Scott, J. (2010). Evolving strategies: A historical examination of changes in principle, authority and function to inform policing in the twenty-first century. *The Police Journal*, *83*(2), 126–63. https://doi.org/10.1350/POJO.2010.83.2.490.

64 Andrews, T. (2025). The 'Peelian Principles': Their historical and contemporary veracity. *Policing and Society*, *35*(5), 584–602. https://doi.org/10.1080/10439463.2024.2436078.

65 Bricknell, S., & Renshaw, L. (2016). *Missing persons in Australia, 2008–2015* (Statistical Bulletin No. 1). Australian Institute of Criminology. www.aic.gov.au/sites/default/files/2020-05/sb001.pdf; Australian Federal Police. (n.d.). *Missing person investigations in Australia and overseas.* National Missing Persons Coordination Centre. www.afp.gov.au/our-services/national-policing-services/missing-persons

66 National Crime Agency. (2024). *UK Missing Persons Unit statistical report 2023–24.* www.nationalcrimeagency.gov.uk/images/mpu/downloads/UKMPU%20Statistical%20Report%202023-24.pdf; Federal Bureau of Investigation. (2024). *NCIC missing and unidentified person statistics: 2024.* U.S. Department of Justice. www.fbi.gov/file-repository/cjis/2024-ncic-missing-and-unidentified-person-statistics.pdf/view.

67 Western Australia Police Force. (2023). *State Hazard Plan – HAZMAT Annex B: Space Re-entry Debris (SPRED)* (Version 3.03). State Emergency Management Committee. www.wa.gov.au/government/publications/state-hazard-plan-hazmat-annex-b-space-re-entry-debris-spred.

68 Tyler, T. R., & Nobo, C. (2022). Legitimacy-based policing and the promotion of community vitality. In *Elements in criminology*. Cambridge University Press. https://doi.org/10.1017/9781009308014.
69 Andrews, T. (2025). The 'Peelian Principles': Their historical and contemporary veracity. *Policing and Society*, *35*(5), 584–602. https://doi.org/10.1080/10439463.2024.2436078.
70 Tyler, T. R., & Nobo, C. (2022). Legitimacy-based policing and the promotion of community vitality. In *Elements in criminology*. Cambridge University Press. https://doi.org/10.1017/9781009308014.
71 Schaap, D., & Saarikkomäki, E. (2022). Rethinking police procedural justice. *Theoretical Criminology*, *26*(3), 416–33. https://doi.org/10.1177/13624806211056680.
72 Andrews, T. (2025). The 'Peelian Principles': Their historical and contemporary veracity. *Policing and Society*, *35*(5), 584–602. https://doi.org/10.1080/10439463.2024.2436078.
73 Schaap, D., & Saarikkomäki, E. (2022). Rethinking police procedural justice. *Theoretical Criminology*, *26*(3), 416–33. https://doi.org/10.1177/13624806211056680.
74 Papazoglou, K., & Tuttle, B.M. (2018). Fighting police trauma: Practical approaches to addressing psychological needs of officers. *SAGE Open*, *8*(3), 1–12. https://doi.org/10.1177/2158244018794794.

8 Evolving from Crisis Response to Crisis Management

Introduction

Internationally, crisis reform has predominately focused on introducing both police and non-police led co-responder programs and enhancing police training. While these approaches can improve immediate outcomes, their effect is often short lived and based in interventionist frameworks failing to address broader issues to curb the crisis cycle.[1]

Over time, both individuals and systems can become fatigued by the repeated, unresolved pattern of crisis. United Kingdom research illustrates this fatigue risk: with suicide rates remaining constant or even increasing when crisis response teams were introduced without broader systems support.[2] Raising a critical question: are response-only models inadvertently increasing the vulnerability of people, given individuals who crisis cycle through emergency departments face a higher risk of mortality than those with occasional contacts?[3] Yet, these individuals often receive no more intensive follow-up than infrequent presenters, revealing a critical limitation: without long-term coordinated care, chronic crisis cycling will continue.[4]

In contrast, emerging systems-based approaches move beyond reactive interventions. They aim on building stability and wellbeing through proactive, multi-sector collaborations. These models acknowledge chronic crisis cycling creates shared demand and shared risks, making it a shared community responsibility.

There have been recent calls for such reform internationally. The U.S. Crime and Justice Institute's *Behavioral Health Crisis Response Landscape Analysis* (2024) identified proactive "case management is a highly sought after element of the crisis care-continuum".[5] Similarly, the Australian Queensland Governments *Better Crisis Care* (2025) stresses that every individual presenting in crisis should be provided ongoing post crisis support.[6] This includes establishing cross-sector networks, to address underlying drivers of crisis.

DOI: 10.4324/9781003749585-8

Brief interventions will always be affective for some. Yet, every community has a group of individuals whose needs are more complex and persistent, seeing them cycle through crisis. They need support from an integrated, collaborative support system, rather than fragmented sectors. Despite emerging evidence, proactive approaches are still underutilised in behavioural health crisis systems, often as a result of factors such as siloed funding, legal limitations, and competing priorities across sectors.[7] The result is a gap within the continuum of care for those who desperately need it and often impact services the most. An impact that illustrates the limitations of a response-only focused framework.

Moving beyond Crisis Response

> **There comes a time where we need to stop just pulling people out of the river.**
> **We need to go upstream and find out why they're falling in.**

This widely published quote, often attributed to Desmond Tutu without verification, offers a useful metaphor for today's behavioural health crisis systems. It demonstrates the *crisis-crossroads* reached in present debate, policy, and practice. Traditional models focus heavily on the reactive response, only intervening when a person is in acute distress. While essential for emergencies, this approach does little for individuals in patterns of chronic crisis cycling and increases strain on already overburden systems. The metaphor illustrates the need to shift focus upstream, looking towards proactive strategies addressing systemic and structural factors driving patterns of crisis cycling.

Improving crisis response systems, requires looking beyond those rare but high-profile failures dominating public debate. These incidents, while serious, often become over politicised and distort public understanding and narrow the focus. In contrast, effective crisis response succeeds routinely with little public attention.[8] An imbalance that contributes to a divisive landscape which foster blame-shifting between sectors or adoption of rapid, highly visible reform that does little to address causation.

Co-Responder models, whether police or non-police based, are the most prominent forms of rapid reform. These programs are progressive in their own right and promote a collaborative approach to crisis and I remain a strong advocate to their development and expansion. However, co-responder programs typically remain focused on immediate crisis intervention and usually bring together only two sectors. They simply create a band-aid for broader social welfare, health, and service sector gaps, rather than becoming part of a more coordinated whole-of-system approach.

Complex Needs and Chronic Crisis Cycling

Two-sector collaborations remain effective for rapid response to crisis, but they rarely address long-term needs of those locked in patterns of chronic crisis cycling. As the reader by now should realise, chronic crisis cycling is almost never the result of a singular diagnosis or social issue. Rather, repeated cycling reflects a complex mix of needs often remaining unmet in continuous care.

This is where two-sector collaborations lack capacity to address broader social, institutional, judicial, and individual factors which perpetuates crisis cycling. Without broad multi-sector approaches, these collaborations risk keeping vulnerable individuals balancing on the precipice and in a constant state of risk.

We in turn cycle back to Chapter 1, Baldry and Dowse (2019) and their powerful way to illustrate this complexity with their "Complex Needs Web".[9] This web presents a tangible visualisation of the interconnectedness of multiple factors, from health and trauma to social and judicial challenges, which impact on a person's pattern of crisis. Critically, it reimagines past practices of blaming individuals to instead assess how systems themselves affect ongoing crisis cycling.

Such reframing challenges the idea the individual chooses or fails when locked in patterns of crisis and illustrates the complexity of social needs and service delivery gaps which enable ongoing vulnerability. It also prompts a question: are we building systems to respond to the symptoms or are we failing to build the systems required to support a pathway to wellbeing?

Returning to the Complex Needs Web (Figure 8.1) helps to remind us how those 'disadvantageous factors' can contribute to an individual's chronic crisis cycling (Baldry & Dowse, 2013, p.224).[10]. When these factors are visibly identified it becomes clear that reducing chronic crisis cycling requires more than reactive interventions. It calls for a coordinated multi-sectoral approach which addresses the complex and co-occurring needs many vulnerable individuals face.

Moving Forward, Two Critical Changes Are Needed:

1 A spectrum-of-care approach – Crisis care must expand beyond reactive crisis response to include intensive follow-up services, multi-sector collaborations, shared data, and policy reforms. This enables individuals to receive support throughout the entire crisis cycle, not just in acute crisis.
2 A systems-thinking perspective – Crisis must be viewed as a complex web of needs and interactions across housing, social services, disability services, carers, police, justice and hospitals. Chronic crisis cycling is not a linear event but dynamic and unpredictable dependant on service user needs.

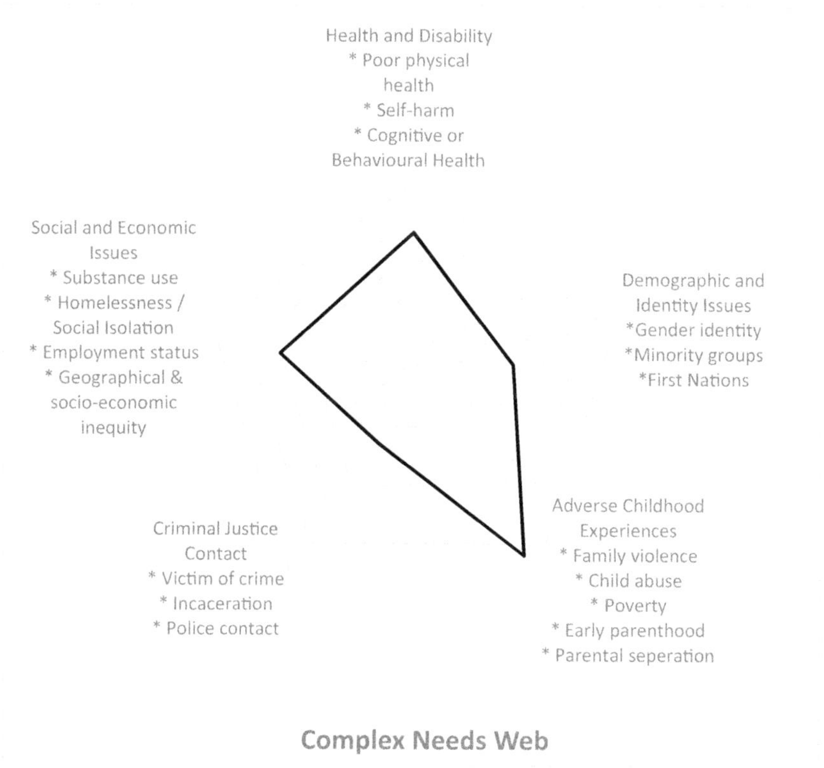

Figure 8.1 Complex Needs Web.

Applying a Systems-Thinking Approach to Crisis

Systems-thinking requires us to look at the bigger picture of crisis, not just acute crisis response. As Jordans (2024) cautioned, "*Single interventions increase the risks for condition-specific approaches and risk forcing policymakers to make choices between mental health promotion, prevention or treatment intervention, rather than adopting a spectrum-of-care approach*".[11]

The Substance Abuse and Mental Health Services Administration in the United States, already addresses this broader view. Their three-stage crisis framework outlines a more expansive response system, outlined as (1) Someone to Contact, (2) Someone to Respond, and (3) A Safe Place for Help.[12] This is an important step towards systems-thinking, but it retains an acute crisis response focus. What is lacking is direction on longitudinal care and recovery.

Emergency Department evidence supports the limits of a reactive-only focus. With approximately 10% of patients returning within 30–60 days, and 70% of those caught in chronic crisis cycling patterns re-presenting within 28days, accounting for nearly 30% of crisis care resources.[13] Such repeat admissions highlight the limitations of reactive-only models. A more effective approach is to actively identify individuals locked in chronic crisis cycling and provide intensive follow-up after an acute crisis incident, otherwise the cycle simply repeats.[14]

One example of proactive follow-up care is the Assertive Community Treatment (ACT) Team in Vancouver, Canada. A partnership between Vancouver Coastal Health and Vancouver Police Department, which reaches out intensively to individuals with complex needs and often treatment resistant.[15] While ACT goes beyond basic crisis response, it remains a two-sector collaboration with a short-term objective, operating inside a larger linear framework.

In contrast, emerging crisis management models advocate for more dynamic approaches, with multi-sector systems-thinking. Such initiatives bring together a broader range of stakeholders such as housing, healthcare, substance abuse treatment, and other social services, to address underlying drivers of crisis cycling. Two successful models are:

- Merseyside High Demand Action Plan, Liverpool, UK.
- Chronic Consumer Stabilization Initiative, Houston, USA.[16]

Both emphasise holistic, wraparound care which supports individuals long after the immediate crisis call for service. They build a "web-of-support" rather than releasing individuals back into the chronic crisis cycle.

Expanding further on this ideology is the *Sequential Intercept Model.* Widely used in North America, it has even been modelled as far as Northern Ireland.[17] It maps a lineal pathway for how individuals move through the justice system from community to arrest, courts, custodial settings, and reintegration. The sequential intercept model has been valuable in promoting diversion points away from the justice system.

But, one critical factor remains: Sequential Intercept Modelling is heavily focused towards individuals already in the justice system. It fails to address broader needs of those in chronic crisis cycling outside of these settings, and fails to return ownership of the crisis care-continuum to health systems.[18]

Systems-Thinking: Moving from Justice to Health

The COVID-19 pandemic highlighted the importance of inter-sector collaboration on health issues which heavily impact communities. Subsequently, both academic and industry leaders acknowledge how health-based challenges can be addressed more dynamically and holistically when multiple sectors collaborate.[19]

Applying these lessons to crisis care, systems-thinking enables a deeper understanding of the complexities of behavioural health problems. This approach helps to uncover the underlying factors which trigger an individual's crisis or reasons behind their chronic crisis cycling.[20] These problems are rarely isolated, often influenced by a range of real-world factors like housing, employment, medical access, and social supports, each creating their own pressures.[21] As Baldry and Andrews (2013) observed, individuals who crisis cycle have complex health *and* social-welfare needs, requiring structural changes to an individual's overall care management.[22]

Social prescribing, examples how systems-thinking is supporting individuals with complex behavioural health challenges. Social prescribing aims to integrate non-clinical care into broader health care plans, recognising how psychosocial factors such as loneliness, low self-esteem, and a lack of autonomy can influence overall wellbeing and vulnerability to acute crisis.[23]

Social prescribing connects individuals into various non-clinical supports such as peer groups, social groups, and local services. Supports often better resourced to address such needs. In doing so, social prescribing demonstrates how systems-thinking can coordinate cross-sectoral support to improve holistic wellbeing and reduce risk.[24] One which optimises not only health and policing services, but also broader multi-sector collaborations, required for the scaling of service delivery in both response and care.[25]

Importantly, such models of care can provide pathways to shift current justice led approaches, such as *sequential intercept model*, back into a health-driven framework. In doing so, systems-thinking repositions crisis care as a health responsibility, being supported by police, justice, and other sectors.

Maintaining Systems and Collaborations

A critical challenge in current debates on crisis care is the dualistic narrative. That is, discussions become locked in setting policing and justice against health and advocacy, as if there must be a black or white answer to who is in or out of the care-continuum. This narrative is divisive, with reliance upon rare but tragic failures to politicise discourse. As Pulido-Gomez et al., (2025) point out, when setbacks occur unsuccessful collaborations respond in a process of "*mutual blaming*", with policymakers and leaders unintentionally compounding divisions and making it hard to evolve.[26]

Rather, successful collaborations focus on "*mutual learning*". Thereby understanding the shared pressures across sectors, which can often improve leadership buy-in.[27] Yet, research indicates such inter-sector collaborations, particularly between frontline workers, health professionals, police, justice, and non-health agents, are not fully embraced by all stakeholders.[28] More crucially policymakers themselves remain hesitant, affecting long-term stable reform.

This resistance could be attributed to perceived unpredictability in policy restructuring, focusing on short-term solutions over long-term strategies.[29] Perspectives that can leave frontline workers believing programs are often narrowly aimed at resourcing and demand reduction over strategies to address the root cause of system-wide pressures. Cox (2024) highlighted this point noting: systems-level changes such as shifting resources, funding or demand pressures, without applying a broader systems perspective can unintentionally harm patient care.[30] A warning particularly relevant given politicised reforms such as *Defund the Police* or *Right Care, Right Person.* Which in some cases, produced the very unintended consequences, Cox warns about.

A systems-thinking lens encourages every sector affected to recognise the complexity that is behavioural health crisis. This complexity makes it easier to understand the need to move beyond two-sector collaborations. True systems-thinking creates space to identify common patterns and pressures across multiple sectors. Yet, this broader integrated, multi-sector approach, appears to be a largely missed opportunity in most jurisdictions.[31]

The Web-of-Support: A Systems-Thinking Approach

One way to capitalise on those missed opportunities is to use systems-thinking to build a broader spectrum-of-care. This approach shifts away from siloed, disconnected sectors, and rigid lineal programs. Rather systems-thinking acknowledges crisis is dynamic, can impact sectors in unpredictable patterns and encourages systems to be viewed in the terms of Capra (1990), who argued that all life is interconnected.[32] A simple way to do this is reimage crisis systems as a "Web-of-Support".

In this reimagining, any disruption at any point on the web creates a ripple effect that to some degree impacts all points on the web. It also acknowledges that different sectors will engage with individuals in crisis at various times, responding to often unpredictable patterns of need rather than through a steady progressive flow of care.

In a Web-of-Support model:

- Crisis can impact the web at anytime, anywhere, with varying degrees of force, sending ripples across the entire system. Yet, the entire structure of the web needs to be ready to respond.
- Each sector is an anchor point of the web, such as emergency responders, police, community mental health, hospitals, in-patient care, carers, advocates, and peer support networks.
- Each strand of the web represents feedback loops and data sharing to the anchor points. Providing constant two-way feedback evenly around the

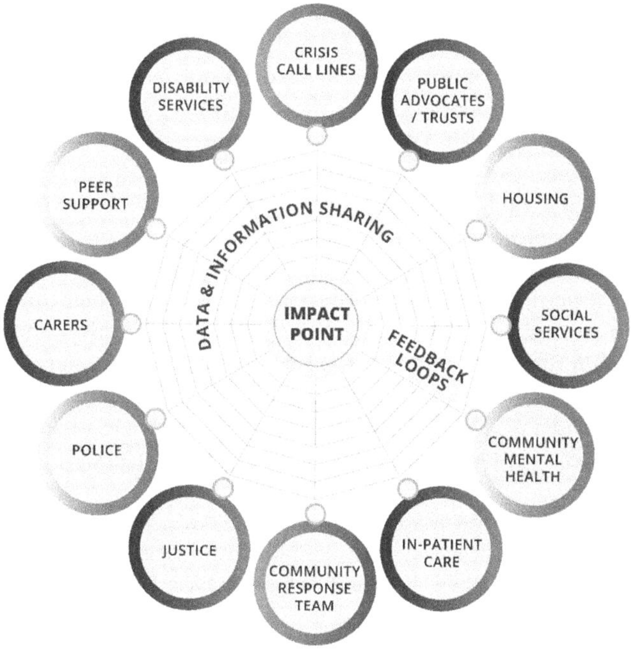

Figure 8.2 Web-of-Support.

web, ensuring all sectors are informed in real time to support the stability and integrity of the web.

- The strength of the web relies upon its integrity. If one strand breaks, the entire system weakens. Therefore, it is essential for each sector to avoid strengthening their own position to the detriment of the web.
- Maintenance is essential. Just as a spider regularly maintains its web, stakeholders must participate in regular collaborative meetings to ensure all sectors are securely integrated and supported, just as much as the individuals the web-of-support is designed for.
- The Web-of-Support model, shown in Figure 8.2, illustrates sectors interconnections through information and feedback, how sectors can be added as needs evolve, and how individuals may impact the web at any point yet still be met with system-wide support.

Need for Longitudinal Approach

Globally, many crisis management systems are emerging to become multi-sector (health, police, service providers, disability service, etc) webs-of-support. Yet, many still remain fragile. Programs commence under well-intentioned leaders, but frequently struggle to embed into the social fabric of communities. Without sustained investment, particularly the critical investment in time to strengthen the web, the strands risk breaking under the shifting winds of political agendas, preventing these networks becoming integral in health and emergency infrastructure.

This challenge is highlighted by Gadsby and Wilding's (2024) research on how systems-thinking can improve public health outcomes in the United Kingdom.[33] Their findings emphasis the complexities of attaining agreement among multiple stakeholders, who each face unique short-term pressures. Pressures which pull at the integrity of the web. In contrast, successful collaborations co-evolve over an extended period of time, building strength in connections.[34] Creating a web-of-support focusing not on short-term fixes, but the anchoring of longitudinal partnerships to create sustained benefits for all sectors.

Case Study: Real-World Benefits of Systems-Thinking beyond Response

The following case study has been adapted from several real-world scenarios and anonymised to illustrative how a systems-thinking approach can disrupt chronic crisis cycling. Highlighting the need to look beyond reactive-only approaches which often fail to achieve long-term gains for both the individual and service providers.

This case study focuses on a service user in their late 40s, with Acquired Brain Injury (ABI), sustained in a horse-riding accident. While they have no other psychiatric diagnosis, their cognitive capacity was assessed as equivalent to 12-14-year-old. Over time, they became fixated on emergency services, leading to frequent high-risk behaviours, impacting on multiple sectors.

They averaged over 15 police behavioural health crisis calls for service a month. Ranging from threats of self-harm, public disturbances to false reports of mass casualty events. Actions designed to elicit urgent police and emergency services responses, creating significant demand and risk.

Their condition did not fit community mental health services charter. Rather, receiving disability services payments and support, however, funding was underutilised, and support service delivery was inconsistent, being limited to basic housing and meal planning.

They were also in the judicial system for criminal matters relating to creating false reports to emergency services.

Initial System Failures

This case highlights how agencies focus on their own strand of a web, often unaware how their response creates a ripple affect across the broader system.

- Police were repeatedly called to respond to public safety threats
- Frontline police, lacking training and understanding, responded with a criminal justice lens rather than therapeutic support
- Emergency response lines were overwhelmed with false alarms, diverting resources from genuine calls for service
- Hospital emergency departments became resistant to frequent police attendance with the individual
- Disability service providers operated with limited insight into the wider impact of the individual's behaviour
- Guardianship effectiveness was compromised due to limited feedback loops from affected frontline services, service providers, and oversight bodies

This fragmentation highlights a weakened support network and classic inter-agency demand shifting. Each sector redirecting responsibility elsewhere, and breaking any strands of collaboration, further entangling the individual in a cycle of crisis.

Applying a Systems-Thinking Approach

Recognising the limitations of reactive responses, police worked to build a collaborative intervention strategy prior to upcoming court processes. A multi-sectoral "web-of-support" was constructed including:

- Public advocate and trustees
- Disability service provider
- Police and emergency services
- Hospital emergency departments

Bringing these stakeholders together, allowed information to be shared and reviewed collectively, which increased understanding of the individual's needs, patterns of behaviours, and gaps in care.

Insights and Interventions

Several key early findings emerged:

- Each agency held partial strands of data which, when combined, revealed the full impact on the web.
- Hospital Emergency Departments reported excessive self-presentations with phantom illnesses or injury, which police and service providers were unaware of.

- Police clarified their limited capacity to intervene in many calls or ED presentations due to legislative constraints.
- Disability funding was underutilised, resulting in a lack of structured care.
- Poor inter-agency communication had enabled maladaptive behaviours to persist.
- The service provider had limited interaction with the individual, resulting in a lack awareness how crisis cycling behaviour impacted the wider web.
- The Public Advocate likewise had limited insight due to fragmented feedback loops from the service provider.
- They had not received a comprehensive cognitive assessment in several years, leaving critical gaps in understanding the individual's needs.
- They lived alone without 24/7 care, family, or social networks. Factors which likely contributed to isolation and observed behavioural patterns.

As part of the systems response, the following actions were taken:

- A broader web-of-support was established, including clinical specialists, disability employment services, and specialist therapeutic court supports.
- A new cognitive assessment revealed a decline of cognitive health resulting in an increase in disability funding.
- Increased funding allowed for a higher-quality service provision to be established with structured daily support.
- The individual was engaged in supported employment providing routine and social engagement.
- Improved housing arrangements were upgraded to shared accommodation, reducing isolation.
- Therapeutic courts addressed outstanding legal matters with a rehabilitative lens.

Outcomes

Within months, coordination of care within the "web-of-support" shifted organically from police to the disability service provider. As responsibility's, feedback, and support across the web improved crisis incidents sharply declined. The individual became more stable and begun to actively participate in their own care planning, demonstrating increased wellbeing.

This intervention required approximately 8–10 months to fully take hold. Though once established it proved to be sustainable, with coordination meetings occurring on an as-needs basis, reflecting stronger intersectoral buy-in, shared accountability, and a resilient web-of-support. This longitudinal stability reinforces how systems-thinking perspectives fosters collaborations which improve not only the individual's situation but also multiple sector's needs.

Key Takeaways

This case illustrates several critical lessons:

- Crisis cycles often persist when sectors on a web remained siloed and communication is fragmented.
- Not all Behavioural Health Crises are rooted in psychiatric conditions
- Systems-thinking enables a shift from reactive crisis management to pro-active, coordinated long-term care across a supportive web.
- Longitudinal investment in inter-agency collaboration strengthens the web, and reduces demand and resourcing pressures evenly across the web.
- Sustainable acute crisis responses systems are improved when complimentary sustainable long-term support management is established.
- *Time*, the need to invest in time to build strong webs, but the results are transformative both financially and socially.

Conclusion

There have been consistent calls for systems-thinking to be adopted to improve the wider health system. It stands to reason, these same systems-thinking approaches should be applied to improving crisis care. Marcus and Stergiopoulos (2022) call for a shift from 'crisis-services' to 'crisis-systems', yet in the real world, crisis systems-thinking often remains limited in practice.[35]

As discussed, many programs labelled as systems-based retain narrow two-sector, reactive interventions. Failing to address long-term challenges for both the individual or broader multi-sectoral demands. Genuine systems-thinking requires consideration of the entire behavioural health crisis cycle, looking at proactive prevention, response, crisis care and long-term wellbeing.

The web-of-support allows sectors to recognise how their actions, or inaction, sends ripples across the broader system. Communities who build a web-of-support develop safety nets for individuals who crisis cycle, regardless of diagnostic profiles, criminogenic risk, or social demographic. Importantly, there is no exhaustive list as to who may act as anchors on the web-of-support. The strength comes from a systems-thinking approach which is adaptable. Enabling the web to evolve and grow as challenges arise and needs change.

Effective crisis management therefore needs communities to move beyond the "police versus health" narrative, realising 'blame-shifting' hinders progress. Whilst recognising multiple anchor points with expanded strands of information and feedback are essential, to effectively support both individuals and communities in need.

The case study demonstrated how a more inclusive, integrated "web-of-support" can foster change and stability for those experiencing chronic crisis cycling, while producing sustainable outcomes. Fortunately, some jurisdictions have already begun to move beyond the reactive response approach towards addressing crisis cycling within a greater continuum of care. The following section will explore these programs, offering valuable insight into how systems-thinking approaches are applied in real-world contexts.

Reviewing Current Management Programs

It is apparent that systems-thinking needs to be applied to crisis systems. To illustrate that this is not purely theoretical ideology, this section will examine real-world examples from across the globe. Initiatives such as Merseyside's High Demand Action Plan (HDAP), Houston's Chronic Consumer Stabilization Initiative (CCSI), to Vancouver's Assertive Outreach Team (AOT), which exemplify proactive, multi-sector approaches to chronic crisis cycling.

Although each program operates within different structures, there are six commonalities that underpin their success. They can be categorised as

- Inclusivity in Chronic Crisis Care
- Integrated Referral Pathways
- Intensive Case Management
- Dedicated Staffing Models
- Police Activated but not Owned
- Data and Information Sharing

Together these principles enable collaborative, cross-sectoral approaches to assist individuals break the crisis cycling pattern, and move towards long-term wellbeing.

Inclusivity in Chronic Crisis Care

Effective behavioural health care programs focus on individuals locked in patterns of chronic crisis cycling. Individuals whose complex cognitive or emotional challenges often fall outside of traditional care frameworks, yet their behaviours create broad community risk. Critically, inclusion is based upon how behaviours impact on broader systems in terms of demand and risk, not by demographic or diagnostic profile criterium.

Mersey Care's Personality Disorder Hub – United Kingdom[36]

Collaborating with emergency services and Merseyside Police, the Personality Disorder Hub supports individuals diagnosed with personality disorders. Despite these individuals often posing a serious risk and service demand, they are frequently excluded from systems designed for 'serious mental illness.' Through tailored intensive and longitudinal care planning, the Personality Disorder Hub works to identify, and address the needs of individuals traditionally marginalised in crisis systems.[37]

Houston's Chronic Consumer Stabilization Initiative – United States[38]

Operated by the Harris Center for Mental Health and Intellectual Developmental Disability, CCSI broadens eligibility to include individuals with neurocognitive disorders alongside mental illnesses. An approach which ensures inclusivity for broader behavioural health crisis care in a singular program.[39]

Police-Assisted Addiction and Recovery Initiative – United States[40]

Developed as a collaboration between police and communities to create non-arrest diversion pathways for individuals who are affected by substance use disorders. Inclusion of individuals with substance use challenges exemplifies inclusivity in behavioural health focused treatment, over traditional judicial outcomes.[41]

Across these programs, the common theme is to shift away from exclusionary diagnostic profiles towards risk-based inclusion. Rather than labelling individuals, the focus is the severity of harm individuals may pose to themselves, others, or service systems. This reframing creates a more inclusive, responsive, and equitable web-of-support for those with the most complex of needs in crisis systems.

Integrated Referral Pathways

As chronic crisis cycling affects all sectors on a web-of-support, successful systems foster equity in referral. Research from the United Kingdom emphasises the importance of integrated care pathways, especially for those with complex needs, to promote open communication and inclusivity.[42] Embedded structured referral networks are also flexible allowing referral from initial engagement to crisis treatment.

Merseyside's High-Demand Action Plan – United Kingdom

Each month, cross-sectoral stakeholders, health, police, ambulance, personality disorder hub, nominate their prospective program participants.[43] After a structured discussion assessing shared demand, risk, and capacity for cross-sector support, all stakeholders equally decide to accept or decline a referral. This collective decision-making exemplifies a systems-thinking approach and improves buy-in.[44]

Los Angeles' Case Assessment and Management Program – United States

Although CAMP is a two-sector program between police and health, it adopts the same equity in referral as Merseyside's HDAP. Through shared case assessment of an individual's risk, CAMP coordinates linkages into appropriate health and social services to promote recovery.[45]

Integrated referral pathways, such as Merseyside's HDAP, encourages cross-sectoral buy-in and coordination of resources. It simplifies access to the collective strength a web-of-support provides, promoting recovery for a broader range of vulnerable people.

Intensive Case Management

The aim of proactive intervention with chronic crisis cycling, is not to "cure" underlying health conditions.[46] Rather the objective is to interrupt the pattern of cycling, stabilise individuals, improve engagement with services and reduce reliance on emergency interventions like police and emergency departments.

Baldery and Andrews (2013) identified that mixed medical and psychosocial models, like Assertive Community Treatment (ACT) and Intensive Case Management (ICM), are effective in delivering coordinated, cross-sectoral support.[47] With research finding collaborative assertive approaches reduce hospitalisation and criminalisation over the medium to long term.[48] In this section, the term *Intensive Case Management* (ICM) is used broadly to cover both ACT & ICM, as they operate within a web-of-support.

Drawing from the author's experience across jurisdictions, three similarities stood out with successful ICM teams:

Low staff-to-client ratios:

The first and critical principle of ICM was personalised service. Evidence shows when low staff-client ratios, such as one case manager for every five to fifteen clients, greater outcomes are achieved with complex clients.[49] For example Liverpool's, *Personality Disorder Hub*, operates at 1:10, with weekly contact aiming to connect individuals into community supports.[50] Houston's Chronic Consumer Stabilisation Initiative, began with 30 clients and two case managers, and retains that 1:15 ratio.[51]

Vancouver's *Assertive Outreach Team (AOT)*, a collaboration between Vancouver Coastal Health and Vancouver Police Department, takes this idea a step further, managing just 25-30 clients as a whole team, with near daily contact focusing on crisis interruption.[52]

Time-limited engagement:

The second element is ICM programs operate within fixed timeframes. They act as bridging programs, not long-term care. Liverpool's P.D Hub operates a 100-week program before referring clients onto other supports. Vancouver's AOT engages intensively for 28 days before transitioning clients to longer-term Assertive Community Treatment Teams.[53] The United Kingdom and Australia, both operate Reconnect programs, to transition individuals with behavioural health challenges back into the community within 12-months of release from prison.[54] These timeframes illustrate ICM is about stabilisation and bridging periods, not to cure.

Crisis cycling interruption:

Post-incarceration ICM models have expanded globally. Slate et al., (2021) reports the U.S. Forensic Assertive Community Treatment (FACT) framework reduces re-arrest, re-hospitalisation, and re-incarceration, while improving program retention and financial outcomes.[55] Similarly, the United Kingdom's *Enhanced Reconnect* and Australia's juvenile *ReConnect* programs, are psychology-led and trauma-informed, supports for individuals with complex behavioural health needs. These programs go beyond treating clinical conditions. They address broader needs such as housing, independent living skills, and connectedness.[56] These programs exemplify the operationalisation of *Social Prescribing* as discussed earlier.

Yet, there is clearly a need to apply these same ICM ideologies earlier in the crisis cycling pattern to avoid incarceration. Programs such as Merseyside's High Demand Action Plan, Los Angele's CAMP, Houston's CCSI, and Vancouvers' AOT exemplify this upstream shift. Their strength lies in collaboration with primary first responders, including police, to reduce reliance on emergency services, acute crisis response, and judicial systems.[57] Houston's CCSI brochure captures this philosophy stating: the objective is "*interrupting the cycle of repeated encounters with law enforcement and repeated psychiatric hospitalizations*".[58] This highlights ICM's broader role is not just for post-incarceration but also preventative.

Intensive Case Management shows how law staffing ratios, time-limited contact, a focus on crisis interruption over cure, and cross-sectoral resources within a web-of-support can achieve rapid results in assisting individuals reduce their reliance on acute crisis systems.

Dedicated Staffing Models

As discussed in the section Intensive Case Management proactive web-of-supports are not built to cure individuals but act as a bridge between crisis and long-term recovery. Yet as Ruud and Friis (2022) note, crisis care remains focused on response, with less attention on continuity or development of therapeutic relationships during the transition from acute to long-term care.[59]

A web-of-support can be that bridge. Its strength however relies upon dedicated staff who can build trust and work confidently across sectors. Merseyside's HDAP, Houston's CCSI and Vancouver's AOT demonstrate this, with each having permanent staffing which provides legitimacy and stability for both service users and inter-sector alike.

Scandinavian research highlights how critical this stability is for individuals with complex mental health needs, using the term "*relational continuity*".[60] Put simply, relational continuity means stability, and knowing who will support you. Studies show that relational continuity can improve quality of life, reduced emergency department presentations and lower rates of suicidality and mortality.[61]

Ruud and Friis also highlight how individuals with complex psychiatric disorders often experience division due to over-specialisation across multiple sectors.[62] They call for more integrated, multi-sector teams that can provide stable support through different phases of illness.[63] Continuity of care in this sense, can only be established with permanent staff embedded in a web-of-support. This is exactly what Merseyside's HDAP, Los Angeles CAMP and Vancouver's AOT provide. These roles are not added onto other duties, but dedicated positions designed to sustain relationships professionally and with service users.

Whilst "continuity of care" has many clinical connotations, in the context of crisis response and chronic crisis management it emphasises the importance of a proactive, relational web-of-support. Programs like HDAP, CCSI, and AOT show that bridging crisis response to long-term care is far more effective when permanent professionals are in place to provide consistent, trusted relationships, during a vulnerable individuals transitional pathway to wellbeing.

Police Activated but Health Owned

Slate and colleagues (2021) note it is ironic, that for the last decade police and justice have been spearheading crisis response and judicial diversion initiatives, particularly in the US, to curb what they term the 'recycling' of individuals.[64] They point out chronic crisis cycling is often only identified institutionally, after a series of high-risk or criminal incidents.[65] So, it is unsurprising to find police initiating proactive programs to shift demand and find alternative therapeutic outcomes.

This highlights the unique 24/7 role police play in communities. Being the first point of call for many non-criminal incidents: collapsed persons (generally a health matter), vehicle fires (a fire brigade matter), to stray animals (local rangers). From a systems-thinking perspective, they are the agent best placed to act as the activators of coordinating a response from a web-of-support. This does not mean they are solely responsible for activation, just often the best placed, especially in remote and regional settings.

Whilst police may activate supports, in terms of treatment, funding, policy, coordination, essentially the longevity and maintenance of a web-of-support, remains distributed across sectors according to expertise.[66] Merseyside's HDAP exemplifies this: health and social service providers leverage on their expertise to design 24/7 crisis frameworks. Ensuring plans are communicated openly across the web-of-support, so each response is guided by the most appropriate care for the individual.[67]

Data and Information sharing

Co-responder programs have shown effective data sharing can improve crisis outcomes. For proactive chronic crisis cycling programs, information sharing is even more crucial in sustaining a broader, cross-sector web-of-support.[68] Merseyside's HDAP in the UK and Los Angeles' CAMP in the US illustrate how sharing information enables coordination of care beyond crisis. However, they remain reliant on manual data transfer, which can limit efficiency.

Establishing truly integrated, 24/7 cross-sectoral systems, requires secure data platforms. Platforms allowing frontline responders, emergency care providers, and ongoing care providers access to information quickly. Yet, such systems pose a raft of ethical and technical challenges. Pope et al., (2022) discovered people living with serious mental illness, often subject to crisis cycling, were generally supportive of a two-way exchange of data between health and justice, recognising the potential to improve care and judicial outcomes.[69]

A point Honey and colleagues (2024) made when they identified distress was often increased when individuals were forced to repeatedly tell their story due a lack of information sharing. Although it was emphasised data sharing needed to be transparent, accountable, and clearly to benefit the individual.[70]

Vancouver's *Early Warning System,* exemplifies this integrated data use.[71] Drawing information from police, justice, social services, and mental health agencies it combines historical data: such as situational triggers, substance use and cognitive health. Data which creates a dashboard that identifies those at high risk, enabling coordinated strategies across sectors.

Such systems will rely on two essential operational elements:

- Technology- As the world becomes more interconnected, frontline responders continue to call for centralised, accessible systems to improve speed and reduce errors from manual data transfers.[72] At the *Crisis Now III Summit* (Amsterdam 2024), global health leaders stressed how shared technology platforms could enhance collaboration and improve care outcomes.[73]

- Legislation- Laws must balance an individual's privacy and allowing practitioners to act responsibly. For example, Western Australia's *Mental Health Regulations* (Regulation 20) permits disclosure to prevent serious risk.[74] Similarly, the *U.S. Health Insurance Portability and Accountability Act* (Rule § 164.512) allows disclosure to police or other agents in imminent risk scenarios.[75]

Current laws however, are still focused on emergency crisis intervention. Failing to support preventative information sharing or post crisis collaborations aimed at interrupting chronic crisis cycling. As such agencies often hold off until there is an imminent risk to trigger data sharing.

Finally, Pope et al., (2022) noted participants believed *"that mental health information sharing might establish accountability on the part of a police officer".* Given, improved access to relevant information and alternative resources should improve standards in the decision-making process.[76]

Conclusion

This section has shown proactive chronic crisis cycling programs share six interlocking commonalities to build a "web-of-support". The first is *inclusivity*, which emphasises engagement over exclusion. Programs firstly see the risk posed by an individual's challenges, rather than focusing on diagnosis, for bringing them into a web-of-support. Second, as these individuals often impact many sectors, inclusivity also extends to *integrated referral pathways.* These pathways allow anyone who identifies an individual in need to nominate them for inclusion.

The next two factors are almost interdependent. Once included in a cross-sector program, individuals benefit from a period of *intensive case management*, delivered by teams of *dedicated staff.* Trauma-informed teams who are trained in de-escalation and collaboration. They provide sustained engagement to help support participants from patterns of crisis cycling to long-term care.

While a great deal of debate focuses on reducing police involvement, a systems-thinking perspective recognises police retain a critical role. Rather than 'gatekeepers', *police are activators*, uniquely positioned out-of-hours and community wide to initiate *health owned* plans. When other services are often unavailable, unaware of escalation or simply unable to respond due to risk.

Finally, such programs can only be enhanced by ethical ***information and data sharing platforms,*** which help identify individuals at risk, ensure continuity of care, and provide real-time feedback. All of which can only help to improve long-term collaboration and outcomes.

Together, these six elements illustrate proactive programs requires a systems-thinking approach. Rather than siloed or rigid lineal models, flexible "community ecosystems" are needed. Crisis care is not solely a health issue but a shared responsibility across sectors. Building a web-of-support based on inclusivity, integrated referrals, shared information, dedicated staffing, intensive management, and appropriate police activation, can interrupt crisis cycling and transition individuals to long-term care with dignity.

Fourth Emergency Service – Behavioural Health

Globally communities traditionally have three essential emergency services, ambulance, fire, and police. Each service began with a narrow 'core function' yet as communities identified new social emergency needs each services function gradually expanded. Fire brigades core function of fighting fires has evolved to include high-rise rescue, road-trauma extraction, hazardous materials containment, medical care, and a range of other non-fire emergencies.[77] Ambulance services have extended their core function to include teaching first-aid, conducting patient transfers, event safety, and supporting broader community health.[78] Changes in functionality which go beyond their initial design, yet society has come to accept this mission creep with little debate.

Policing has not been immune to similar evolution in functionality. While policing's core function is often held as preventing crime and maintaining order, police are now called upon to manage public safety, road safety, search for missing persons, mediate community/relational disputes, and coordinate disaster response.[79] Most relevant here, police have also absorbed responsibility for responding to behavioural health crisis.

This mission creep likely evolved as while long-term treatment for individuals able to manage their care became socially acceptable, urgent behavioural health crisis has been seen more negatively.[80] With some scholars identifying these individuals often are labelled as 'troublesome' by care providers, leaving police to manage incidents that are really health-related.[81]

This has raised concerns that individuals who repeatedly crisis cycle are being regularly criminalised for crossing social boundaries.[82] As such, unlike other expanded 'core functions' for ambulance, fire, and police, shifting a medical issue into the functions of policing and justice has been far more contentious, creating conflict for both those affected by crisis and policing agents tasked to respond.

Evolution of a De Facto Fourth Service

It is this conflict, police taking ownership for a health-based issue, that has seen communities develop alternative crisis response models. The police/clinician co-responder model was one of the earliest versions of this shift, as discussed in Chapter 4 Police Crisis Response Systems. Subsequent programs evolved rapidly across the globe, with many continuing to operate successfully for decades.

Parallel to co-responders, community-based programs such as Eugene's *CAHOOTS* and San Francisco's *Street Crisis Response Team* have become integral in frontline crisis care. While both aim to reduce police involvement, they demonstrate unique operational aspects. *CAHOOTS*, though a community program, operates with access to police communications and limited police data systems, enabling swift dispatch and information sharing directly from the emergency call centre.[83]

By contrast, San Francisco's *SCRT* is embedded even more firmly within the emergency services structure. Operated by the San Francisco Fire Department, SCRT teams are staffed with uniformed fire personnel paired with a clinician, responding in marked fire service vehicles with full emergency warning systems. They have access to both health and fire data systems, including 911 dispatch capacity.[84] Such integration gives *SCRT* parity with traditional emergency services operating in San Francisco.

A further shift in how communities support behavioural health crisis can be seen in the redesign of national emergency crisis call lines. In July 2022, the US federal Substance Abuse and Mental Health Services Administration (SAMHSA) launched "988", a simplified 3-digit number to replace the previous National Suicide Prevention Lifeline. In its first year, the service managed nearly 5 million contacts, an increase of nearly 150% compared to the previous year operating under 10-digit numbers.[85] Similarly, adopting easy-to-remember 3-digit emergency call lines has expanded globally, including 988 in Canada, 111 in the United Kingdom, and 113 in the Netherlands.[86]

In 2021 Austin, Texas took this concept a step further by integrating Mental Health as a fourth emergency service alongside Ambulance, Fire, and Police.[87] Call takers can now triage calls towards this option, creating a more consumer centric crisis response and reducing police engagement. Across all these jurisdictions the idea is clear, simple 3-digit numbers and frameworks similar to traditional emergency services improve public access to timely, non-police, support.

When looked at together these developments suggest society has already begun a gradual shift towards recognising behavioural health requires a stand-alone *fourth emergency service*. The rapid and expansive evolution of response alternatives shows both the need and capacity to formally establish, finance, and resource a 24/7 *Behavioural Health Service* alongside ambulance, police, and fire. Not as an adjunct or collaboration, but as an essential component of modern emergency services systems.

Time to Formalise a Fourth Emergency Service

SAMHSA in the US developed the *National Behavioral Health Crisis Care Guidance*, a framework to guide communities on behavioural health care systems. The framework is built on three elements deemed essential for success: Someone to Contact, Someone to Respond and A Safe Place for Help. The element of Someone to Respond calls for establishing a service capable of delivering rapid, on-site crisis interventions along with complementary prevention and postvention strategies.[88]

The United States is not isolated in setting national expectations and frameworks for crisis response. In the United Kingdom, both the National Health Service and Royal College of Psychiatrists have set frameworks for 24/7 mobile crisis systems, such as Crisis Resolution and Home Treatment Teams (CRHTT).[89] Similarly, the Mental Health and Wellbeing Commission of New Zealand in 2025 called for Health NZ to establish community crisis teams capable of delivering timely responses, inclusive of weekends and evenings.[90]

Key themes emerge from these national bodies: a need for rapidly mobile services that can equitably deliver specialist crisis intervention around the clock to all community members. However, to date, this integral element has largely been left for local communities to interpret and implement. This has seen an array of modalities and practices, with some areas establishing leading teams whilst others have an absence of service all together.

Given the prevalence and consistency of BHCFS, it is reasonable to debate whether national legislators should formalise behavioural health crisis response as an essential *fourth emergency service*. This ratification is more than just notional, establishing parity with the three traditional services- fire, ambulance, police – it affirms the societal expectations in recognising the impact behavioural health crisis is having upon communities. Formal ratification also acknowledges current emergency services and health systems lack capacity in terms of resourcing, staffing and specialist skillsets required to meet demand.[91]

Such calls for action have gained traction, for example, the U.S.-based *Fourth Branch Institute* states it is their mission "*to support municipalities, organizations, and communities in advocating for, developing, and implementing a fourth branch of the emergency response system for their community.*"[92] Establishing the fourth emergency service would also ensure parity in service delivery not only at community level, but also across state and federal systems. Over time, this parity would support development of global standards, through shared understanding, consistent frameworks and training which reinforces the idea behavioural health crisis response deserves the same professionalised response as other emergencies.

Formal recognition of behavioural health crisis response as a fourth emergency service will also provide benefits beyond the service itself but for the wider community. These benefits would be seen in several ways such as:

- **Efficiency** – A stand-alone service would not rely upon collaborative staffing models or community volunteers. Behavioural health teams would focus solely on a single demand stream, rather than triaging across competing demands such as crime (police co-responder), medical emergencies (ambulance co-responder) or broader social issues like housing or justice (community teams).
- **Public Trust** – A nationally ratified service brings a level of credibility and recognition, which in turn builds trust. Trust is essential for ensuring carers, communities or individuals are willing to access support during a heighted state of crisis.
- **Reliability** – Current community and co-responder models are often criticised in terms of lacking reliability. Present models are heavily dependent on limited resourcing and often tenuous collaborations. Parity with other emergency services would improve operational capacity and reliability, which in turn builds public trust
- **Safety** – Without a dedicated fourth emergency service, police remain a constant in crisis intervention to fill the gap. While police involvement will never be eliminated in crisis response, a behavioural health emergency service, having parity in capacity would reduce reliance on police. Thereby improving safety by reducing the negative effects of physical harm, trauma, and criminogenic outcomes for those experiencing a crisis.

Operationalisation of a Fourth Emergency Service

To attain parity with existing emergency services, behavioural health crisis response would need similar bureaucratic governance, ministerial oversight, funding security, insurance arrangements, and legislative protections. Yet, the unique aspect of behavioural health crisis work would require particular attention to several distinct fields:

- **Integration with Emergency Lines** – Unlike police or fire service, who are accessed generally through a singular emergency number (i.e., 000 Australia or 911 USA), behavioural health crisis will be reported across a myriad of call channels. These include traditional emergency call centres, not-for-profit lines, peer support lines, and national health crisis call lines. A further emergency service would need to centralise and streamline these pathways, ensuring urgent calls are effectively and safely routed to response teams.

- **Staffing and Training** – Recruitment and training would need to shift from a reliance upon degree based clinical personnel to a workforce more consistent with paramedics and police. Watson and colleagues (2025) recommend the establishment of a new first responder professional they termed "Community Behavioral Health Crisis Responder" (CBHCR), who is grounded in trauma-informed, person-centred, and culturally responsive practices, rather than focusing on academic qualifications.[93] This workforce design would increase accessibility and reflect the communities they operate within.
- **Vehicles and Priority Driving** – Crisis teams would require vehicles capable of rapid deployment, similar to other emergency vehicles. Fitted with appropriate communication and IT systems and rolled out with full emergency livery and warning system. San Francisco's Street Crisis Response Team vehicles provide a useful example.[94] Staff would accordingly be required to undergo sufficient training to operate these vehicles under priority driving conditions.
- **Involuntary Care** – A key concern many advocates hold in terms of crisis response is whether crisis teams should have legislated powers of involuntary care.[95] However, if a fourth emergency service is to attain parity and reduce reliance on other services, it must be able to act independently at critical moments. Watson and colleagues (2025) found consensus that a professional team with core competencies capable of involuntary interventions added to crisis systems, although acknowledging such coercive care should be used as a last resort.[96] One could argue that a specialist behavioural health team is more suited to apply involuntary care standards than deferring to police or ambulance officers.
- **Safety** – Behavioural health crisis can often be volatile and emotionally charged, making safety a critical consideration. Whilst this includes practical protections for staff, such as New York's recent mandate on body armour for paramedics, and Australian research into supplying body armour to paramedics.[97] A more important difference, is a dedicated behavioural health service enhances safety through the embedding of enhanced de-escalation techniques, trauma-informed practice and situational awareness, skills superior to part-time or ad-hoc crisis intervention programs.[98]

Conclusion

The global rise of non-police crisis response programs indicates governments have reached a time where they can no longer rely on a patchwork of localised interventions to meet a critical societal demand. What is apparent, is there is a clear case for a dedicated crisis response infrastructure, and emergency service in its own right. The *International Crisis Response Association* highlights that 'Community Responder Teams' operate differently to co-responder models, crisis intervention teams and mobile crisis-services.[99] Their professionalised 24/7 operations with links to emergency call centres aligns closely with an integrated fourth emergency service framework explored here.

As crisis response models expand globally, it would appear the time has arrived to formalise them at national levels. Recognising a fourth branch of the emergency services would provide stable funding, establish trust, establish consistent standards and oversight, and guarantee long-term capacity in service provision to address an issue already heavily impacting communities.

Importantly, ratification of a fourth emergency service must be viewed through a systems-thinking lens. This service will not stand alone. Rather it will operate as an integral role within a broader continuum of care. For decades, crisis response has struggled to fill the gap between health services and emergency services, seeing police fill the void. A dedicated behavioural health emergency service provides that professional solution to fill the gap and broader emergency services systems.

Although, there is need for caution. Establishing a fourth emergency service does not mean police, paramedics, fire services, or other agencies are removed of any responsibility in responding to behavioural health crisis. As with any crisis: whether fire, road trauma, domestic violence, or community threat, behavioural health will still cross into all services. Therefore, ongoing training, policy development, preparedness, and service improvements will still be essential.

From a systems-thinking perspective, the addition of a fourth emergency service enhances patient support and pathways to care, improves feedback loops, supports decision-making across sectors, and strengthens a community's web-of-support. A fourth emergency service would become a dynamic, and active actor within a broader system of community care, helping to simplify a complex societal problem, by providing a clear and logical crisis service.

Observational Summary

At the *Crisis Now III Summit* held in Amsterdam in 2024, over 100 global leaders in behavioural health crisis, called for improvements across the entire care-continuum. Stressing clinical intervention alone cannot address chronic crisis cycling. Instead, they emphasised the importance of cross-sectoral collaborations, what they called "community ecosystems", bringing together police, health providers, and social services.[100]

This emphasis on community ecosystems and collaboration clearly aligns with themes you've already read in this text. Crisis response is best approached through a systems-thinking lens: where all sectors play an integral role, yet no single sector can carry the weight of responsibility for success.

Systems-Thinking for Crisis – Webs-of-Support

The *Summit* also highlighted how much of today's debate remains locked in reactive modes, focusing narrowly on acute crisis interventions. To progress, communities need to adopt a broader systems-thinking perspective, building "webs-of-support" acting as a safety net across a fuller care-continuum. Webs-of-support recognise individuals do not move in a straight line towards wellbeing. Rather they may intersect across sectors, health, police, or justice, any time depending on varying needs.

The United Kingdom's *Prevention Concordat for Better Mental Health (previously Crisis Care Concordat)* exemplifies how a systems-thinking approach can not only be applied locally but nationally.[101] Formalising collaboration across sectors, it allows for shared planning of finances, infrastructure and policy, aimed at strengthening community webs-of-supports.

Systems-thinking perspectives help to clarify roles each sector plays in supporting wellbeing. Some sectors roles hold obvious benefits, while for other, like police and justice system, it can be harder to see. Yet, police can be "*activators*" within a web-of-support, with their 24/7 visibility across crisis systems to providing real-time feedback and connection.

Ultimately, when communities establish webs-of-support, they are building the kinds of community ecosystems called for at the Crisis Now III summit.

A Fourth Emergency Service

Supporting a broader community ecosystem, societies need to look beyond the "Tri-Partite" emergency model, of only Ambulance, Fire, and Police; a structure which has dominated public policy for decades. Current understanding of behavioural health and wellbeing points towards a missing piece of public safety: effective response to emotional and behavioural health crisis. Continuing to rely upon the traditional three emergency services risks repeating outdated outcomes. The time for a dedicated fourth emergency service focusing on behavioural health is becoming evidently more critical to strengthen the continuum of care.

Evidence for a fourth emergency service can be seen in ongoing debates about the gaps in crisis response, particularly the over-reliance on police.

Supported by the explosion in an array of crisis response models, such as crisis intervention teams (CIT), co-responder programs, mobile community and peer teams, and community responder teams, all showing both demand and capacity within communities to formalise a government endorsed emergency service.

Establishing a fourth emergency service would:

- Fill a clear gap in the continuum of care
- Enhance trust, credibility, and reliability within communities
- Bring professionalism and uniformity to a service designed for vulnerable individuals
- Align with systems-thinking principles, embedding crisis response into community ecosystems

Closing Thought

Sir Winston Churchill observed "*Out of intense complexities, intense simplicities emerge*".[102]

Behavioural health and chronic crisis cycling remain one of the most complex and pressing problems for society. Yet, adopting a systems-thinking approach offers a way to cut through complexity by its design. By building community ecosystems, we move beyond present debates locked on siloed and reactive models – debate which often creates division and impedes progress.

Building webs-of-support and recognising now is the time for a dedicated fourth emergency service, represents the logical next step in the evolution of crisis care. In doing so, those complexities can change into a simpler integrated continuum of care.

Notes

1 Office of Justice Programs. (2021, March). *Assessing the impact of co-responder team programs: A review of research* (NCJ 305544). U.S. Department of Justice, Bureau of Justice Assistance. www.ojp.gov/library/publications/assessing-impact-co-responder-team-programs-review-research.

2 Carpenter, R. A., Falkenburg, J., White, T. P., & Tracy, D. K. (2013). Crisis teams: Systematic review of their effectiveness in practice. *The Psychiatrist*, *37*(7), 232–37. https://doi.org/10.1192/pb.bp.112.039933.

3 Saunders, P., & Rahim, S . (2021, October). Mortality risk for mental health related frequent attenders at accident and emergency departments. *European Journal of Public Health*, *31*(Issue Supplement_3), ckab165.568, https://doi.org/10.1093/eurpub/ckab165.568; Fleury, M.-J., Cao, Z., & Grenier, G. (2024). Emergency department use among patients with mental health problems: Profiles, correlates, and outcomes. *International Journal of*

Environmental Research and Public Health, *21*(7), 864. https://doi.org/10.3390/ijerph21070864.

4 Saunders, P., & Rahim, S . (2021, October). Mortality risk for mental health related frequent attenders at accident and emergency departments. *European Journal of Public Health*, *31*(Issue Supplement_3), ckab165.568, https://doi.org/10.1093/eurpub/ckab165.568; Fleury, M.-J., Cao, Z., & Grenier, G. (2024). Emergency department use among patients with mental health problems: Profiles, correlates, and outcomes. *International Journal of Environmental Research and Public Health*, *21*(7), 864. https://doi.org/10.3390/ijerph21070864.

5 Crime and Justice Institute. (2024). *Behavioral health crisis response landscape analysis.* www.cjinstitute.org/assets/sites/2/2024/05/AV-Crisis-Response-Report.pdf.

6 Queensland Health. (2023). *Better crisis care: A framework for improving mental health crisis care in Queensland.* www.health.qld.gov.au/__data/assets/pdf_file/0031/1439482/qh-better-crisis-care-framework.pdf.

7 Crime and Justice Institute. (2024). *Behavioral health crisis response landscape analysis.* www.cjinstitute.org/assets/sites/2/2024/05/AV-Crisis-Response-Report.pdf; Queensland Health. (2023). *Better crisis care: A framework for improving mental health crisis care in Queensland.* www.health.qld.gov.au/__data/assets/pdf_file/0031/1439482/qh-better-crisis-care-framework.pdf.

8 McNab, D., McKay, J., Shorrock, S., Luty, S., & Bowie, P. (2020). Development and application of systems thinking principles for quality improvement. *BMJ Open Quality*, *9*(1), e000714. https://doi.org/10.1136/bmjoq-2019-000714.

9 Chappell, D. (Ed.). (2013). *Policing and the mentally ill: International perspectives* (1st ed.). Routledge. www.routledge.com/Policing-and-the-Mentally-Ill-International-Perspectives/Chappell/p/book/9780367866730.

10 Baldry, E., & Dowse, L. (2013). Compounding mental and cognitive disability and disadvantage: Police as care managers. In D. Chappell (Ed.), *Policing and the mentally ill: International perspectives* (pp. 219–34). CRC Press.

11 Jordans, M. J. D. (2024). Applying systems theory to global mental health. *Cambridge Prisms: Global Mental Health*, *12*, e2. https://doi.org/10.1017/gmh.2024.147.

12 Substance Abuse and Mental Health Services Administration. (2025). *Model definitions for behavioral health emergency, crisis, and crisis-related services* (HHS Publication No. PEP24-01-037). U.S. Department of Health and Human Services. https://988crisissystemshelp.samhsa.gov/sites/default/files/2025-08/SAMHSA_Model_Definitions_508_080525.pdf.

13 Bravo, J., Buta, F. L., Talina, M., & Silva-dos-Santos, A. (2022). Avoiding revolving door and homelessness: The need to improve care transition interventions in psychiatry and mental health. *Frontiers in Psychiatry*, *13*, Article 1021926. https://doi.org/10.3389/fpsyt.2022.1021926; Casey, M., Perera, D., Enticott, J., Vo, H., Cubra, S., Gravell, A., Waerea, M., & Habib, G. (2021). High utilisers of emergency departments: The profile and journey of

patients with mental health issues. *International Journal of Psychiatry in Clinical Practice, 25*(2), 172–80. https://doi.org/10.1080/13651501.2021.1904998.
14 Marcus, N., & Stergiopoulos, V. (2022). Re- examining mental health crisis intervention: A rapid review comparing outcomes across police, co- responder and non- police models. *Health & Social Care in the Community, 30*, 1665–79. https://doi.org/10.1111/hsc.13731.
15 Vancouver Coastal Health. (n.d.). *Assertive Community Treatment (ACT) Teams.* Vancouver Coastal Health. www.vch.ca/en/service/assertive-community-treatment-act-teams#overview; Vancouver Police Department. (n.d.). *Mental health initiatives.* Vancouver Police Department. https://vpd.ca/policies-strategies/mental-health-initiatives/.
16 Houston Police Department, Mental Health Division. (n.d.). *Chronic Consumer Stabilization Initiative (CCSI).* www.houstoncit.org/ccsi/; Blackwell, G. R. (2022). *Reducing recidivism in behavioural health crisis cycles.* The Churchill Fellows Association of Western Australia Churchill Fellowship [Report]. Churchill Trust. www.churchilltrust.com.au/fellow/glen-blackwell-wa-2020/.
17 Substance Abuse and Mental Health Services Administration. (2019). *The Sequential Intercept Model: Advancing community-based solutions for justice-involved people with mental and substance use disorders* (PEP19-SIM-BROCHURE). https://library.samhsa.gov/sites/default/files/pep19-sim-brochure.pdf; Mooney, S., Bunting, L., Coulter, S., & Montgomery, L. (2019). *Applying the Sequential Intercept Model to the Northern Ireland context: A selective review of practice innovations to improve the life chances of justice-involved young people and adults with complex needs.* Queen's University Belfast. https://pureadmin.qub.ac.uk/ws/files/279989394/NI_SIM_Main_report_12.12.19.pdf.
18 Substance Abuse and Mental Health Services Administration. (2019). *The Sequential Intercept Model (SIM): A framework for criminal justice and behavioral health systems* (Publication No. PEP19-SIM-BROCHURE). U.S. Department of Health and Human Services. https://library.samhsa.gov/sites/default/files/pep19-sim-brochure.pdf; Substance Abuse and Mental Health Services Administration. (n.d.). *Sequential Intercept Model (SIM).* U.S. Department of Health and Human Services. www.samhsa.gov/communities/criminal-juvenile-justice/sequential-intercept-model.
19 Embrett, M., Carson, A., Sim, M., et al. (2025). Building resilient and responsive health research systems: Responses and the lessons learned from the COVID-19 Pandemic. *Health Research Policy and Systems, 23*, 38. https://doi.org/10.1186/s12961-024-01229-0; National COVID-19 Health and Research Advisory Committee. (2022). *Strengthening Australia's health system post COVID-19* [Advisory report]. Australian Government Department of Health and Aged Care. www.nhmrc.gov.au/sites/default/files/2023-02/NCHRAC-Advice-30-Strengthening-Health-systems.pdf.
20 Jordans, M. J. D. (2024). Applying systems theory to global mental health. *Cambridge Prisms: Global Mental Health, 12*, e2. https://doi.org/10.1017/gmh.2024.147.

21 Jordans, M. J. D. (2024). Applying systems theory to global mental health. *Cambridge Prisms: Global Mental Health*, *12*, e2. https://doi.org/10.1017/gmh.2024.147; Nguyen, L.-K.-N., Kumar, C., Jiang, B., & Zimmermann, N. (2023). Implementation of systems thinking in public policy: A systematic review. *Systems*, *11*(2), 64. https://doi.org/10.3390/systems11020064.

22 Chappell, D. (Ed.). (2013). *Policing and the mentally ill: International perspectives* (1st ed.). Routledge. www.routledge.com/Policing-and-the-Mentally-Ill-International-Perspectives/Chappell/p/book/9780367866730.

23 Spanos, S., Wijekulasuriya, S., Ellis, L. A., Saba, M., Schroeder, T., Officer, C., & Zurynski, Y. (2025). Integrating non-clinical supports into care: A systematic review of social prescribing referral pathways for mental health, wellbeing, and psychosocial improvement. *International Journal of Integrated Care*, *25*(3), Article 21. https://doi.org/10.5334/ijic.9127; Drinkwater, C., Wildman, J., & Moffatt, S. (2019). Social prescribing. *BMJ, 364*, l1285. https://doi.org/10.1136/bmj.l1285.

24 Spanos, S., Wijekulasuriya, S., Ellis, L. A., Saba, M., Schroeder, T., Officer, C., & Zurynski, Y. (2025). Integrating non-clinical supports into care: A systematic review of social prescribing referral pathways for mental health, wellbeing, and psychosocial improvement. *International Journal of Integrated Care*, *25*(3), Article 21. https://doi.org/10.5334/ijic.9127; Drinkwater, C., Wildman, J., & Moffatt, S. (2019). Social prescribing. *BMJ, 364*, l1285. https://doi.org/10.1136/bmj.l1285.

25 Jordans, M. J. D. (2024). Applying systems theory to global mental health. *Cambridge Prisms: Global Mental Health*, *12*, e2. https://doi.org/10.1017/gmh.2024.147.

26 Pulido-Gómez, S., de Jong, J., & Rivkin, J. W. (2025). Cross-sector collaboration in cities: Learning journey or blame game? *Journal of Public Administration Research and Theory*, *35*(2), 117–32. https://doi.org/10.1093/jopart/muae026.

27 Pulido-Gómez, S., de Jong, J., & Rivkin, J. W. (2025). Cross-sector collaboration in cities: Learning journey or blame game? *Journal of Public Administration Research and Theory*, *35*(2), 117–32. https://doi.org/10.1093/jopart/muae026; Nguyen, L.-K.-N., Kumar, C., Jiang, B., & Zimmermann, N. (2023). Implementation of systems thinking in public policy: A systematic review. *Systems*, *11*(2), 64. https://doi.org/10.3390/systems11020064

28 McNab, D., McKay, J., Shorrock, S., Luty, S., & Bowie, P. (2020). Development and application of 'systems thinking' principles for quality improvement. *BMJ Open Quality*, *9*(1), e000714. https://doi.org/10.1136/bmjoq-2019-000714.

29 Alderwick, H., Hutchings, A., & Mays, N. (2024). Cross-sector collaboration to reduce health inequalities: A qualitative study of local collaboration between health care, social services, and other sectors under health system reforms in England. *BMC Public Health*, *24*, Article 2613. https://doi.org/10.1186/s12889-024-20089-5.

30 Cox, J. A. (2024). Systems thinking approach to mental health services. *Nature Reviews Psychology*. www.nature.com/articles/s44159-024-00329-6.pdf.
31 Carey, G., Malbon, E., Carey, N., Joyce, A., Crammond, B., & Carey, A. (2015). Systems science and systems thinking for public health: A systematic review of the field. *BMJ Open*, *5*(12), e009002. https://doi.org/10.1136/bmjopen-2015-009002.
32 Capra, F. (1996). *The web of life: A new scientific understanding of living systems*. Anchor Books.
33 Gadsby, E. W., & Wilding, H. (2024). Systems thinking in, and for, public health: A call for a broader path. *Health Promotion International*, *39*(4), daae086. https://doi.org/10.1093/heapro/daae086.
34 Gadsby, E. W., & Wilding, H. (2024). Systems thinking in, and for, public health: A call for a broader path. *Health Promotion International*, *39*(4), daae086. https://doi.org/10.1093/heapro/daae086.
35 Marcus, A., & Stergiopoulos, V. (2022). Crisis response models for people experiencing mental health emergencies: A rapid review. *Health & Social Care in the Community*, *30*(6), e2745–e2757. https://doi.org/10.1111/hsc.13731.
36 Mersey Care NHS Foundation Trust. (n.d.). *Psychotherapy and personality disorder hub*. www.merseycare.nhs.uk/our-services/liverpool/psychotherapy-and-personality-disorder-hub.
37 Blackwell, G. R. (2022). *Reducing recidivism in behavioural health crisis cycles: The Churchill Fellows Association of Western Australia Churchill Fellowship* [Report]. Churchill Trust. www.churchilltrust.com.au/fellow/glen-blackwell-wa-2020/; Merseyside Police. (n.d.). *Mental health policy*. www.merseyside.police.uk/SysSiteAssets/foi-media/merseyside/policies/mental-health-policy.pdf; Mersey Care NHS Foundation Trust. (n.d.). *Psychotherapy and personality disorder hub*. www.merseycare.nhs.uk/our-services/liverpool/psychotherapy-and-personality-disorder-hub.
38 Houston Police Department & The Harris Center for Mental Health and IDD. (n.d.). *Chronic Consumer Stabilization Initiative (CCSI)*. Houston Crisis Intervention Team. www.houstoncit.org/ccsi/.
39 Houston Police Department, Houston Health Department, & Mental Health Mental Retardation Authority of Harris County. (2010). *Chronic Consumer Stabilization Initiative: Submission for the 2010 Herman Goldstein Award for Excellence in Problem-Oriented Policing*. Center for Problem-Oriented Policing. https://popcenter.asu.edu/sites/g/files/litvpz3631/files/library/awards/goldstein/2010/10-13(F).pdf; Houston Police Department & The Harris Center for Mental Health and IDD. (n.d.). *Chronic Consumer Stabilization Initiative (CCSI)*. Houston Crisis Intervention Team. www.houstoncit.org/ccsi/
40 Police Assisted Addiction & Recovery Initiative. (n.d.). *Our law enforcement and public safety partners*. PAARI. https://paariusa.org/our-partners/
41 Police Assisted Addiction & Recovery Initiative. (n.d.). *Our law enforcement and public safety partners*. PAARI. https://paariusa.org/our-partners/.
42 Harris, J., Dalkin, S., Jones, L., Ainscough, T., Maden, M., Bate, A., Copello, A., Gilchrist, G., Griffith, E., Mitcheson, L., Sumnall, H., & Hughes,

E. (2023). Achieving integrated treatment: A realist synthesis of service models and systems for co-existing serious mental health and substance use conditions. *The Lancet Psychiatry*, *10*(8), 632–43. https://doi.org/10.1016/S2215-0366(23)00104-9.

43 Merseyside Police. (n.d.). *Mental health policy*. www.merseyside.police.uk/SysSiteAssets/foi-media/merseyside/policies/mental-health-policy.pdf.

44 Blackwell, G. R. (2022). *Reducing recidivism in behavioural health crisis cycles: The Churchill Fellows Association of Western Australia Churchill Fellowship* [Report]. Churchill Trust. www.churchilltrust.com.au/fellow/glen-blackwell-wa-2020/; Nguyen, L.-K.-N., Kumar, C., Jiang, B., & Zimmermann, N. (2023). Implementation of systems thinking in public policy: A systematic review. *Systems*, *11*(2), 64. https://doi.org/10.3390/systems11020064.

45 Slate, R. N., Frailing, K., Johnson, W. W., & Buffington, J. K. (2021). *The criminalization of mental illness: Crisis and opportunity for the justice system* (3rd ed.). Carolina Academic Press. Mansfield, D., & Jones, D. (2021, April 14). After the crisis: A co-response model for follow-up. *Police Chief Magazine*. www.policechiefmagazine.org/after-the-crisis/

46 Lim, C. T., Caan, M. P., Kim, C. H., Chow, C. M., Leff, H. S., & Tepper, M. C. (2022). Care management for serious mental illness: A systematic review and meta-analysis. *Psychiatric Services*, *73*(2), 180–87. https://doi.org/10.1176/appi.ps.202000473; Marshall, M. (2011). What have we learnt from 40 years of research on intensive case management? *Epidemiology & Psychiatric Sciences*, *17*(2), 106–09. https://doi.org/10.1017/S1121189X00002773.

47 Chappell, D. (Ed.). (2013). *Policing and the mentally ill: International perspectives* (1st ed.). Routledge. www.routledge.com/Policing-and-the-Mentally-Ill-International-Perspectives/Chappell/p/book/9780367866730

48 Chappell, D. (Ed.). (2013). *Policing and the mentally ill: International perspectives* (1st ed.). Routledge. www.routledge.com/Policing-and-the-Mentally-Ill-International-Perspectives/Chappell/p/book/9780367866730 Meyer, P. S., & Morrissey, J. P. (2007). A comparison of assertive community treatment and intensive case management for patients in rural areas. *Psychiatric Services*, *58*(1), 121–27. https://doi.org/10.1176/ps.2007.58.1.121; Dieterich, M., Irving, C. B., Bergman, H., Khokhar, M. A., Park, B., & Marshall, M. (2017, July). Intensive case management for severe mental illness, *Schizophrenia Bulletin*, *43*(4), 698–700. https://doi.org/10.1093/schbul/sbx061.

49 Dieterich, M., Irving, C. B., Bergman, H., Khokhar, M. A., Park, B., & Marshall, M. (2017, July). Intensive case management for severe mental illness, *Schizophrenia Bulletin*, *43*(4), 698–700. https://doi.org/10.1093/schbul/sbx061; Centre for Social Research and Evaluation. (2012). *Case management and importance of caseload size* [Evidence brief]. Ministry of Social Development. www.msd.govt.nz/documents/about-msd-and-our-work/publications-resources/research-archive/case-mangement-and-importance-of-caseload-size.pdf; Keiller, E., Masood, S., Wong, B.Hc., et al. (2023). Intensive community care services for children and young people in psychiatric crisis: An expert opinion. *BMC Medicine*, *21*, 303. https://doi.org/10.1186/s12916-023-02986-5.

50 Graham, S., Sebalo, I., et al. (2024). *Designing community services for people with borderline personality disorder to reduce hospitalizations.* Psychiatric Services. American Psychiatric Association. www.merseycare.nhs.uk/pd-journal
51 Houston Police Department. (2011, August). *Chronic Consumer Stabilization Initiative (CCSI)* [PowerPoint slides]. Houston Crisis Intervention Team. www.houstoncit.org/wp-content/uploads/2018/10/CCSI-Presentation-2011.pdf.
52 British Columbia Ministry of Health & Ministry of Public Safety and Solicitor General. (2018). *Interfaces between mental health and substance use services and police: A toolkit for police agencies and health authorities.* www2.gov.bc.ca/assets/gov/health/managing-your-health/mental-health-substance-use/police-interface-report.pdf; Blackwell, G. R. (2022). *Reducing recidivism in behavioural health crisis cycles: The Churchill Fellows Association of Western Australia Churchill Fellowship* [Report]. Churchill Trust. www.churchilltrust.com.au/fellow/glen-blackwell-wa-2020/.
53 Vancouver Coastal Health. (n.d.). *Assertive Outreach Team (AOT) – Mental health and addictions.* Pathways BC. https://vancouver.pathwaysbc.ca/programs/3571; Graham, S., Sebalo, I., et al. (2024). *Designing community services for people with borderline personality disorder to reduce hospitalizations.* Psychiatric Services. American Psychiatric Association. www.merseycare.nhs.uk/pd-journal; Mersey Care NHS Foundation Trust. (n.d.). *Psychotherapy and personality disorder hub – Liverpool.* Mersey Care NHS. www.merseycare.nhs.uk/our-services/liverpool/psychotherapy-and-personality-disorder-hub.
54 NHS England. (n.d.). *RECONNECT.* NHS Commissioning. www.england.nhs.uk/commissioning/health-just/reconnect/; Australian Community Support Organisation. (n.d.). *ReConnect.* ACSO. www.acso.org.au/residential-programs/reconnect/.
55 Slate, R. N., Frailing, K., Johnson, W. W., & Buffington, J. K. (2021). *The criminalization of mental illness: Crisis and opportunity for the justice system* (3rd ed.). Carolina Academic Press; Mansfield, D., & Jones, D. (2021, April 14). After the crisis: A co-response model for follow-up. *Police Chief Magazine.* www.policechiefmagazine.org/after-the-crisis/.
56 Midlands Partnership University NHS Foundation Trust. (n.d.). *Enhanced RECONNECT.* www.mpft.nhs.uk/services/health-and-justice-services/enhanced-reconnect; NHS England. (n.d.). *RECONNECT.* NHS Commissioning. www.england.nhs.uk/commissioning/health-just/reconnect/; Blackwell, G. R. (2022). *Reducing recidivism in behavioural health crisis cycles: The Churchill Fellows Association of Western Australia Churchill Fellowship* [Report]. Churchill Trust. www.churchilltrust.com.au/fellow/glen-blackwell-wa-2020/; Australian Community Support Organisation. (n.d.). *ReConnect.* ACSO. www.acso.org.au/residential-programs/reconnect/.
57 Vancouver Coastal Health. (n.d.). *Assertive Outreach Team (AOT) – Mental health and addictions.* Pathways BC. https://vancouver.pathwaysbc.ca/programs/3571; Graham, S., Sebalo, I., et al.. (2024). *Designing community services for people with borderline personality disorder to reduce hospitalizations.* Psychiatric Services. American Psychiatric Association. www.merseycare.nhs.uk/pd-journal.

58 Houston Police Department. (2017). *Chronic Consumer Stabilization Initiative (CCSI) brochure*. Houston Crisis Intervention Team. www.houstoncit.org/wp-content/uploads/2018/10/CCSI-Brochure-2017.pdf.

59 Ruud, T., & Friis, S. (2022). Continuity of care and therapeutic relationships as critical elements in acute psychiatric care. *World Psychiatry, 21*(2), 241–42. https://doi.org/10.1002/wps.20966.

60 Engström, I., Hansson, L., Ali, L. et al. (2023). Relational continuity may give better clinical outcomes in patients with serious mental illness – A systematic review. *BMC Psychiatry, 23*, 952. https://doi.org/10.1186/s12888-023-05440-1.

61 Engström, I., Hansson, L., Ali, L. et al. (2023). Relational continuity may give better clinical outcomes in patients with serious mental illness – A systematic review. *BMC Psychiatry, 23*, 952. https://doi.org/10.1186/s12888-023-05440-1.

62 Ruud, T., & Friis, S. (2022). Continuity of care and therapeutic relationships as critical elements in acute psychiatric care. *World Psychiatry, 21*(2), 241–42. https://doi.org/10.1002/wps.20966.

63 Ruud, T., & Friis, S. (2022). Continuity of care and therapeutic relationships as critical elements in acute psychiatric care. *World Psychiatry, 21*(2), 241–42. https://doi.org/10.1002/wps.20966.

64 Slate, R. N., Frailing, K., Johnson, W. W., & Buffington, J. K. (2021). *The criminalization of mental illness: Crisis and opportunity for the justice system* (3rd ed.). Carolina Academic Press; Mansfield, D., & Jones, D. (2021, April 14). After the crisis: A co-response model for follow-up. *Police Chief Magazine*. www.policechiefmagazine.org/after-the-crisis/.

65 Slate, R. N., Frailing, K., Johnson, W. W., & Buffington, J. K. (2021). *The criminalization of mental illness: Crisis and opportunity for the justice system* (3rd ed.). Carolina Academic Press.

66 Jordans, M. J. D. (2024). Applying systems theory to global mental health. *Cambridge Prisms: Global Mental Health, 12*, e2. https://doi.org/10.1017/gmh.2024.147.

67 Merseyside Police. (n.d.). *Mental health policy*. www.merseyside.police.uk/SysSiteAssets/foi-media/merseyside/policies/mental-health-policy.pdf.

68 Fisher, C., Thomas, S., & Clough, A. (2024). *Barriers and enablers to implementing police–mental health co-responder programs: A qualitative study*. Charles Darwin University. Retrieved November 11, 2025, from https://ris.cdu.edu.au/ws/portalfiles/portal/93686663/fisher_et_al_2024_barriers_and_enablers_to_implementing_police_mental_health_co_responder_programs_a_qualitative_study.pdf.

69 Pope, L. G., Labrecque, R. M., Chou, J. C., & Salyers, M. P. (2022). Information sharing across mental health service providers and criminal legal system stakeholders: Perspectives of people with serious mental illnesses and their family members. *Psychiatric Services, 73*(9), 927–34. https://doi.org/10.1176/appi.ps.202100355.

70 Honey, A., Hancock, N., Glover, H., et al. (2024). Collection and sharing of health information in mental health and related systems in Australia: Perspectives of people who access mental health services. *BMC Psychiatry, 24*, 932. https://doi.org/10.1186/s12888-024-06347-1.

71 Vancouver Police Department. (2023, March 8). *Mental health initiatives.* Vancouver Police Department. Retrieved November 11, 2025, from https://vpd.ca/policies-strategies/mental-health-initiatives/; Public Safety Canada. (n.d.). *Canadian Police College: A history.* Government of Canada. www.publicsafety.gc.ca/lbrr/archives/cnmcs-plcng/cn31963-eng.pdf
72 Birla, A. (2023, January 12). *How data sharing between police and mental health practitioners can improve outcomes.* Police1. Retrieved November 11, 2025, from www.police1.com/mental-health-outreach/articles/how-data-sharing-between-police-and-mental-health-practitioners-can-improve-outcomes-ca2WRSDb5UsmJL8U/.
73 Covington, D. W., Enomoto, K., & Hepburn, B. (2024, June). *Global behavioral health crisis care principles.* Crisis Now III Summit, Amsterdam. https://talk.crisisnow.com/wp-content/uploads/2024/12/Global-Crisis-Care-Principles_vFinalDec2024.pdf.
74 Western Australia. (2015). *Mental Health Regulations 2015: Regulation 20 – Prescribed authorised recording, disclosure or use of information.* State Law Publisher. Retrieved November 11, 2025, from https://classic.austlii.edu.au/au/legis/wa/consol_reg/mhr2015237/s20.html.
75 U.S. Department of Health and Human Services. (2003). *Standards for privacy of individually identifiable health information, 45 C.F.R. § 164.512 (Uses and disclosures for which consent, authorization, or opportunity to agree or object is not required).* Federal Register. Retrieved November 11, 2025, from www.ecfr.gov/current/title-45/subtitle-A/subchapter-C/part-164/subpart-E/section-164.512
76 Pope, L. G., Labrecque, R. M., Chou, J. C., & Salyers, M. P. (2022). Information sharing across mental health service providers and criminal legal system stakeholders: Perspectives of people with serious mental illnesses and their family members. *Psychiatric Services, 73*(9), 927–34. https://doi.org/10.1176/appi.ps.202100355
77 Cannuscio, C. C., Davis, A. L., Kermis, A. D., Khan, Y., Dupuis, R., & Taylor, J. A. (2016). A strained 9-1-1 system and threats to public health. *Journal of Community Health, 41*(3), 658–66. https://doi.org/10.1007/s10900-015-0142-x; San Francisco Fire Department. (n.d.). *Our organization.* https://sf-fire.org/our-organization; London Fire Brigade. (n.d.). *London Fire Brigade.* www.london-fire.gov.uk/.
78 London Ambulance Service NHS Trust. (n.d.). *Responding to less serious calls.* www.londonambulance.nhs.uk/about-us/what-we-do/responding-less-serious-calls/; St John Western Australia. (n.d.). *Ambulance and health services.* www.stjohnwa.com.au/ambulance-and-health-services.
79 Cooke, A. (2022). Foreword. In *State of policing: The annual assessment of policing in England and Wales 2021* (p. 5). Her Majesty's Inspectorate of Constabulary and Fire & Rescue Services. www.justiceinspectorates.gov.uk/hmicfrs/publication/state-of-policing-the-annual-assessment-2021/.
Emsing, M., Ghazinour, M. & Sundqvist, J. (2024). Police conflict management: A scoping review. *Journal of Police and Criminal Psychology, 39*, 499–508. https://doi.org/10.1007/s11896-024-09687-6; Ferguson, L., & Gaub,

J. E. (2021). Training police search and rescue teams: Implications for missing persons work. *Criminology & Criminal Justice*, *23*(3), 431–49. https://doi.org/10.1177/17488958211057380.
80 Quattlebaum, M., & Tyler, T. R. (2020). Beyond the law: An agenda for policing reform. *Boston University Law Review*, *100*(3), 1017–54.
81 Quattlebaum, M., & Tyler, T. R. (2020). Beyond the law: An agenda for policing reform. *Boston University Law Review*, *100*(3), 1017–54.
82 Slate, R. N., Frailing, K., Johnson, W. W., & Buffington, J. K. (2021). *The criminalization of mental illness: Crisis and opportunity for the justice system* (3rd ed.). Carolina Academic Press; Quattlebaum, M., & Tyler, T. (2020). Beyond the law: An agenda for policing reform. *Boston University Law Review, 100*(3), 1017–54.
83 White Bird Clinic. (n.d.). *White Bird Clinic history*. White Bird Clinic. https://whitebirdclinic.org/white-bird-clinic-history/.
84 San Francisco Fire Department. (n.d.). *Street Crisis Response Team*. San Francisco Fire Department. https://sf-fire.org/community-paramedicine/street-crisis-response-team.
85 SAMHSA. (2023). *Suicide & Crisis Lifeline*. www.samhsa.gov/find-help/988; SAMHSA (2023). *988 Lifeline's First Year*. www.samhsa.gov/sites/default/files/988-one-year-anniversary-fact-sheet.pdf.
86 9-8-8 Suicide Crisis Helpline. (2025). *Get help*. https://988.ca; 113 Suicide Prevention. (2025). *English*. www.113.nl/english; NHS England. (2023). *New mental health 111 services reduces A&E visits by a third*. www.england.nhs.uk/integratedcare/resources/case-studies/new-mental-health-111-service-reduces-ae-visits-by-a-third/.
87 Austin Texas. (2021). *Mental health option added to 9-1-1*. www.austintexas.gov/blog/mental-health-option-added-9-1-1.
88 Substance Abuse and Mental Health Services Administration. (2025, January 16). *National behavioral health crisis care guidance*. U.S. Department of Health & Human Services. www.samhsa.gov/mental-health/national-behavioral-health-crisis-care.
89 NHS England. (n.d.). *Crisis and acute mental health care*. www.england.nhs.uk/mental-health/adults/crisis-and-acute-care/ Royal College of Psychiatrists. (2022). *Practice guidelines for crisis line response and crisis resolution/home treatment teams*. www.rcpsych.ac.uk/docs/default-source/improving-care/ccqi/quality-networks/htas/practice-guidelines-for-crisis-line-response-and-crhtt's-2022.pdf?sfvrsn=b0bd5805_2.
90 Mental Health and Wellbeing Commission. (2025). *Crisis responses monitoring report*. www.mhwc.govt.nz/our-work/mental-health-and-addiction-system/crisis-responses-monitoring-report/.
91 Watson, A. C., McNally, K., Pope, L. G., & Compton, M. T. (2021, September 8). *The workforce for non-police behavioral health crisis response doesn't exist—we need to create it*. Health Affairs Forefront. https://doi.org/10.1377/hblog20210903.856934.
92 Fourth Branch. (n.d.). *About us*. www.4thbranch.org/about.html.

93 Watson, A. C., McNally, K., Pope, L. G., & Compton, M. T. (2025). If not police, then who? Building a new workforce for community behavioral health crisis response. *Frontiers in Psychology*, *16*, 1579787. https://doi.org/10.3389/fpsyg.2025.1579787.
94 San Francisco Government [sf.gov]. (2022). *Street Crisis Response Team pilot final report*. www.sf.gov/sites/default/files/2022-06/SCRT%20Final%20Report_FINAL-%201%20year.pdf.
95 Carpenter, R. A., Falkenburg, J., White, T. P., & Tracy, D. K. (2013). Crisis teams: Systematic review of their effectiveness in practice. *The Psychiatrist*, *37*(7), 232–37. https://doi.org/10.1192/pb.bp.112.039933.
96 Watson, A. C., McNally, K., Pope, L. G., & Compton, M. T. (2025). If not police, then who? Building a new workforce for community behavioral health crisis response. *Frontiers in Psychology*, *16*, 1579787. https://doi.org/10.3389/fpsyg.2025.1579787.
97 City of New York. (2024, May). *Mayor Adams signs two pieces of legislation providing extra protection for FDNY EMTs and paramedics*. Mayor's Office of the City of New York. www.nyc.gov/mayors-office/news/2024/05/mayor-adams-signs-two-pieces-legislation-providing-extra-protection-fdny-emts-paramedics; Charles Sturt University. (2024, May 28). Stab-resistant body armour research aims to improve paramedic safety. *CSU News*. https://news.csu.edu.au/latest-news/stab-resistant-body-armour-research-aims-to-improve-paramedic-safety.
98 MacIsaac, A., Baldwin, S., Semple, T., & Bennell, C. (2024). Exploring the relationship between officer safety and de-escalation in a simulated crisis encounter. *Police Quarterly*. https://doi.org/10.1177/10986111241289885; Watson, A. C., McNally, K., Pope, L. G., & Compton, M. T. (2025). If not police, then who? Building a new workforce for community behavioral health crisis response. *Frontiers in Psychology*, *16*, 1579787. https://doi.org/10.3389/fpsyg.2025.1579787.
99 International Crisis Response Association. (n.d.). *About us*. https://icraconnect.org/.
100 Covington, D. W., Enomoto, K., & Hepburn, B. (2024, June). *Global behavioral health crisis care principles*. Crisis Now III Summit, Amsterdam. https://talk.crisisnow.com/wp-content/uploads/2024/12/Global-Crisis-Care-Principles_vFinalDec2024.pdf.
101 Department of Health and Social Care. (2017). *Prevention concordat for better mental health: Consensus statement*. GOV.UK. www.gov.uk/government/publications/prevention-concordat-for-better-mental-health-consensus-statement/prevention-concordat-for-better-mental-health.
102 Churchill, W. (n.d.). *Out of intense complexities, intense simplicities emerge*. Quotosaurus. https://quotosaurus.com/q/4kbfa8/.

9 Conclusion

Conclusion

If you have made it here to the end of this book, thank you. By now, the purpose of this book should be clear: highlighting that behavioural health crisis is not simple and far from clinical. It is a topic filled with contradictions, unresolved debates, misaligned agendas across sectors, and frankly extremely complex. There is no more emotive, divisive, or persistent illustration of this complexity than the ongoing debate on policing's role within crisis.

The intention of this work has not been to take a singular position on that debate. Rather, it has been to show readers, through a perspective shaped by decades of operational experience, the real-world complexity of behavioural health crisis. To put a spotlight on those systemic, cultural, clinical, operational, and social factors often sidelined within those discussions, or perspectives not exposed to the realities of the frontline.

This final conclusionary chapter seeks to highlight several persistent themes identified throughout the text, emphasising key points in how the role of frontline responders, particularly police, are reimagined within a framework that needs to move beyond crisis response interventionist approaches towards broader systems-based crisis management models of continuous care.

A critical challenge in reimaging crisis systems is the dominance of academic and clinical terminology that over-delineates crisis. Labels such as "serious mental illness" and "persons with serious mental illness" may assist research and policy frameworks, but they narrow the understanding of crisis and embed narratives which lack real-world practicality[1] – narratives, that fail to reflect the true complexity and dynamic nature the frontline responders encounter.

This dominance of clinical language inadvertently excludes many individuals who experience crisis but do not fit neatly into diagnostic profiles. A problem grounded in the reality there is no definitive research that maps which diagnostic profiles and demographics – including neurodiversity,

DOI: 10.4324/9781003749585-9

substance use, situational crisis, or "less serious" mental illness – comprise *all crisis calls* regardless of causation and outcome. Further, police can be called to incidents coded as "mental health" only to identify onsite the issue is conflict or criminality and callers have misrepresented or failed to understand the situation, which can further challenge complete data collection. As the World Health Organisation cautioned, systems built too heavily on clinical frameworks may contribute to fragmentation and gaps in care for those who fall outside of those definitions.[2]

Such fragmentation can contribute to establishing a cohort of individuals where crisis becomes a reoccurring pattern, resulting in repeated interactions with police, ambulance, emergency departments, and community crisis services. Yet as they often do not fit clinical diagnostic profiles – or that research and policy frameworks do not allow for their presenting behaviours – individuals often become labelled with stigmatising terms such as "frequent flyers" or "high demand" by industry and researchers alike.[3]

However, such terms risk reinforcing implicit bias by focusing on the person rather than the pattern of chronic crisis cycling. Reframing the language with the term *Chronic Crisis Cycling* shifts the focus from assumptions individuals may *choose* a crisis lifestyle towards acknowledging how overly diagnostic frameworks, fragmented service delivery, and reactive crisis-intervention systems contribute to the cycling pattern.

There is no universal definition of what constitutes chronic crisis cycling or when someone should be considered to be in such a cycling pattern. The temptation is to define chronic crisis cycling by frequency: how many times someone enters acute crisis requiring urgent response. While high rates of contact may signal concern, frequency alone fails to show the real risk or complexity of a persons' situation. Some frequent callers simply need a conversation to reassure them, while others with far fewer calls require repeated lifesaving interventions. Numbers alone overlooks the diversity of needs and different levels of risk each individual presents.

To address this gap in crisis discussions, the author proposed the following definition as a starting point for discussion:

> Individuals whose repeated interactions with emergency services, particularly police and emergency departments, occurs in the absence of effective long-term care interventions, and which may involve a real and significant risk to themselves, to others, and/or to public safety.

This definition deliberately shifts the focus from the individual towards the systems within which crisis occurs. Acknowledging both the presentation of risk and the absence of effective long-term care, it reimagines chronic crisis cycling as a symptom of service provision, systems gaps, and complex unmet needs. Baldry and Dowse's (2019) *Complex Needs Web* powerfully shows this complexity.[4] It shifts attention away from narrow diagnostic profiles and individual choice to emphasising the interconnectedness of social, economic, environmental, and service provision as factors impacting upon a person's crisis cycling patterns. Through this perspective, chronic crisis cycling can be seen not solely as an individual's failing, rather an indication of systems-level fragmentation often due to design around siloed interventionist approaches.

Understanding chronic crisis cycling requires frequency to be overlayered with risk, unmet social needs, and environmental factors. A person repeatedly contacting crisis services is not always simply overusing services, it is likely a sign the system is failing them. In this sense chronic crisis cycling, through a systems perspective, acts to highlight how services are misaligned, siloed, or driven by sectoral self-interests rather than broad collaborative outcomes.

The opening chapter also raised a difficult but relevant question: should calls involving suicidality be classified within behavioural health crisis? Legal decisions such as the Australian case *Stuart V Kirkland-Veenstra [2009]*, and the United States ruling of *Adams v. City of Fremont* [1998], make it clear that police do not hold a duty of care to individuals who express suicidal thoughts, unless they are also displaying signs of mental illness or pose a threat to others.[5] Australian legislation further recognises suicidality can, in some circumstances, be used as a form of coercion in intimate partner violence, now treating such threats as a criminal element.[6]

Medical and ethical considerations further complicate the matter. Concepts such as Medical Assistance in Dying and the principle of autonomy, where adults of 'sound mind' can legally choose to refuse lifesaving treatment through directives such as 'do not resuscitate' orders.[7] These medico-legal positions indicate that individuals without cognitive illness may express or choose to end their life and will be supported in doing so. This creates a paradox for crisis response systems which are designed to focus on individuals who have a diminished cognitive capacity.

These distinctions have significant real-world implications for frontline responders. It affects the ethical, moral, legal, and operational landscape which crisis responders must navigate to ensure defensible outcomes. Crisis systems built for those with impaired decision-making may struggle to adjust for situations where suicidality presents in a person whose capacity appears intact, challenging long-standing default actions such as involuntary apprehension.

The discussion shifted over the next two chapters to look at how communities have established non-police crisis response systems and how policing itself has attempted to develop response models to address behavioural health demand. Exploring community response is simplified when viewed through the lens of the USA's *Substance Abuse and Mental Health*

Services Administration framework, which divides crisis management into three key stages[8]: Someone to Contact – Crisis Call Lines, Someone to Respond – Community Responder Teams, A Safe Place for Help – Crisis Stabilisation Centres.

Crisis call lines have expanded rapidly internationally in recent decades, substantially being dominated by the not-for-profit sector. They deliver services across a broad range of social and demographic groups, creating often narrow service provision or suicidality centric models, and often have limited-service delivery capacity.[9] A narrowing of service delivery which likely results from government and health policymakers historical view that crisis lines are merely supplementary rather than essential parts of the mental healthcare system.[10]

Operating in this environment has resulted in a fragmented and competitive landscape. The Australian Productivity Commission identified how present funding arrangements frequently set different sectors against one another for limited resources increasing division, duplication of service, reduced accessibility, and uneven service delivery.[11] As service providers continue to expand, so do concerns that the sector has become crowded and there is a need to consolidate resources for improved, reliable, and accessible 24/7 coverage.[12]

In response, globally there has been a shift, with governments consolidating services and simplifying access through three-digit crisis numbers such as USA's 988-Lifeline and England's NHS111. This shift recognises crisis call lines as integral components of a broader, coordinated, systems-based approach. Returning urgent crisis calls back into mainstream, government-led health services, enables crisis lines to act as key players in an integrated system, improving the continuum of care, and increases the opportunity to reduce unnecessary police interventions.

Community mobile crisis teams: whether peer-led, paramedic-led, or clinically staffed may have different operational models, yet ultimately, they have been established in communities with similar goals. Generally, they aim to reduce policing's role in crisis and improve therapeutic care on-scene. Two goals which these services have been widely shown to achieve along with broader benefits of reduced incarceration, improved follow-up care and wider social welfare benefit.[13] Although, operational variations affect service provision, community and peer-led teams are frequently recorded as having slower response times and narrow service provision, when compared to more formalised community responder or paramedic-led models which are often integrated more into emergency services frameworks.

Despite their demonstrated value, non-police response models face a similar barrier as crisis call lines, in being considered as supplementary programs rather than essential components of emergency service provision. This leaves them vulnerable to political and financial pressures. The recent withdrawal of CAHOOTS in Eugene, Oregon USA, regardless of its international acclaim, highlights how even effective 24/7 non-police response models are open to political agendas.[14]

Policing itself has pursued its own raft of initiatives to address both operational demand and public criticism. Globally agencies have adopted a range of strategies, with this text having focused on four prominent models to highlight common themes shaping police approaches.

The Crisis Intervention Teams (CIT) model is presented as a systems-level framework designed to bring communities together to tackle crisis.[15] In principle the ideology is to build integrated pathways between responder, hospitals, and long-term care. However, attainment of this systems-level integration in practice has regularly been questioned.[16] Rather across many jurisdictions CIT is implemented mostly as police training initiative, focusing on improving police officers' recognition and response to behavioural health crisis.

Academic evaluations reinforce this notion through a proclivity to assess CIT's effectiveness through police-centric outcomes, particularly training effectiveness. Research which does in itself highlight the effectiveness of CIT in improving officer self-efficacy, de-escalation skills, reduced use-of-force and criminal outcomes, benefits which are significant in themselves.[17] What has emerged in terms of community integration has been a mirroring of CIT style training being adopted in community services, schools and prisons, which ultimately focus on individualised skills enhancement and less on developing integrated health pathways as planned.

Co-Responder models, combining a police officer and mental health clinician, aim to bring clinical expertise and knowledge directly to the crisis. These teams seek to deliver more therapeutic engagement, reduce involuntary detentions, reduce use-of-force, and improve outcomes in real time – with research demonstrating significant positive impact in each of these areas.[18] Further there is evidence co-responder teams are a cost benefit to the communities they serve when examining initial attendance, hospitalisation, and judicial outcomes which have all been shown to reduce upon implementation.

Although some criticise the model's inability to reduce the involvement of police at crisis due to the embedding of police in the system and often models arising at the initiation of police agencies. Yet, emerging research from Australia has shown some service users prefer the co-responder framework over clinical response considering response times and de-escalation skills. Such strong support from service users, carers and policymakers alike can explain how co-response has expanded internationally more than any other police model.[19]

In the United Kingdom, the Serenity Integrated Mentoring program, operated with a more proactive approach, placing a police officer within

National Health Service clinics. The aim was to work with individuals identified as 'high intensity users' of emergency services and subject to excessive involuntary apprehensions. Gaining national recognition, it was rapidly expanded across the country after winning a National Health Service innovation award.[20] However, the program was dismantled almost as rapidly after only a few years due to national political pressure from service users and advocates raising concern about police involvement in health systems.[21]

Subsequently, the UK has turned to the Right Care, Right Person (RCRP) model, resulting in a shift in direction. RCRP seeks to withdraw police from crisis and behavioural health-related incidents, through a structured triaging process that redirects calls to ambulance and health services.[22] Policing leadership have reported significant reductions in policing hours spent on mental health calls, with estimates that as many as one million officer hours could be saved annually.[23] Such significant claims on policing resourcing efficiencies have contributed to the model's rapid expansion across the United Kingdom and adoption in Australia and New Zealand.

Yet, despite the success and growth RCRP has faced considerable controversy. Concerns emerged early regarding a lack of interagency collaboration and risks of service gaps from policing's rapid withdrawal.[24] Several high-profile coronial inquests have raised questions about how RCRP is implemented, along with the clarity and understanding of inter-sector roles and responsibilities. Criticism has also illustrated the lack of independent evaluation measuring information beyond police resourcing, such as actual outcomes to service users.[25] Despite these concerns from industry, public and judicial inquests, the model has continued to be rolled out across the nation with strong government support.

Together, these models reflect four distinct objectives: CIT emphasises training police; Co-Response builds collaborative practices; Serenity sought proactive engagement with individuals experiencing chronic crisis cycling; and Right Care, Right Person seeks to withdraw police from crisis altogether. In isolation though none of these themes are likely to break police free from crisis, as they only address a section of crisis cycling. However, when considered collectively, these themes are the foundation of a systems-based approach towards a sustainable and acceptable role for police in crisis.

Crisis Stabilisation Centres, were discussed earlier in the context of non-police response. They form the final phase of SAMHSA's crisis model and therefore warrant being re-examined here after revisiting non-police and police response systems.

They also support a systems-based approach. The effectiveness of crisis response extends beyond the initial crisis de-escalation, with crisis stabilisation centres providing first responders – whether police or community led – a pathway that supports, not undermines their efforts. Emergency departments, with their over stimulating environments and triaging practices, can often elevate distress in vulnerable persons inadvertently undoing the efforts of first responders.[26]

Recognising these limitations and gaps in crisis systems has resulted in considerable efforts to establish more therapeutic, dedicated alternatives to emergency departments within communities to provide consistent stable care.

The US federal government recently expanded its support for the Certified Community Behavioural Health Clinics program, which establishes 24/7 urgent crisis care clinics.[27] With similar models having been launched within Australian and England in recent years.[28] When available around the clock and prepared to accept both voluntary and involuntary presentations, they provide a genuine therapeutic support compared to traditional, overly stimulating hospital outcomes.

Early research suggests crisis stabilisation centres not only improve urgent care, but also impacts long-term outcomes. With improved patient referral, follow-up presentation, and decreases in urgent crisis care re-presentations rates, suggesting crisis stabilisation centres may be effective in interrupting the chronic crisis cycle.[29]

Following on from examining the operational developments in crisis response, the discussion turned to police training. This subject attracts substantial debate among academics, advocacy, the judiciary, policymakers, service users, and police practitioners themselves. Such debate is understandable, insightful, and at times constructive. However, this debate also continues parallel to often emotive discussions within these same sectors about reducing or even removing policing's role in crisis response altogether.

This juxtaposition is worth noting. On one hand, there are strong debates calling to reduce policing's role in crisis response; on the other hand, there are equally strong debates advocating for enhanced, diagnostic specific, specialised behavioural health training. While these positions seem difficult for police agencies to balance, they illustrate the complexity of the crossroads at which contemporary policing finds itself.

However, the author did address this topic earlier in the text and it is worth revisiting here, given internationally, training in this area is inconsistent or more honestly, non-existent for the majority of police. Where programs have been developed, they have often become heavily reliant on overly clinical or diagnostic specific content, that does not reflect the realities of dynamic, fast-moving, and at times high-risk calls for service.

In practice officers are better served being grounded in fundamental skills: procedural justice, relational and trauma-informed approaches, and effective de-escalation. Assumptions that more clinical content will improve outcomes by being able to somehow make clinical judgements while managing imminent harm, is misguided. Training development should focus on what officers on the scene will focus on: presenting behaviours, risk, cooperation, and criminality – not diagnostic profiles.

To embed these foundational skills, police training should be delivered initially within a structured continuous program of one week, or 40 hours. A commitment of this scale signals an organisations commitment and establishes credibility of purpose. Importantly, programs with sufficient length create the opportunity for meaningful experiential learning. Scenario-based training, delivered over a day or more, allows participants to adapt theoretical knowledge into practical skills within a controlled environment. A concept already adopted in police use-of-force training, in applying pressure to students before they engage in real-world situations where actions bring consequences.

Hand in glove with the debate of what police should learn is the question of who? Regularly the first call is for police academy recruits to be trained extensively in behavioural health crisis. However, recruits are still adjusting to policing culture, absorbing large amounts of legislation, policy, and paperwork, often with little practical concept of how everyday citizens interact with police – let alone those in crisis. The Los Angeles Police Department's practice of returning officers during their probationary period to undergo 40 hours of training is an innovative approach, allowing junior officers to scaffold on their real-world experiences while still in a formative stage in their career.[30]

Yet, training is not a one-and-done solution for police agencies. A culture of continuous crisis training, needs to be embraced in parity to continuous use-of-force training. For as CIT International highlight, such training can rejuvenate officers, and it further allows for officers to be updated in changes of legislation, policy and social pressures that drive crisis response.[31] With some jurisdictions already recognising this need, legislators have determined to mandate ongoing training through bodies such as California's POST and Texas TCOLE.[32]

The training discussion also illustrated a critical imbalance: far less attention is given to towards training health and service providers to understand police roles, powers, and constraints in crisis situations. Without this reciprocal understanding cross-sector collaborations can be difficult: with misaligned expectations, responsibilities are blurred, and families/service users may receive inaccurate advice about what police can lawfully do. Misunderstandings which often cause friction, frustration, or misguided blame primarily due to a lack of direct knowledge about policing realities. In many ways, this mirrors the very same concerns in the police training debate.

However, regardless of how extensive police training becomes, there are incidents where, even with the most skilled and empathetic officer on-scene, the only available outcome is non-clinical. Simply not all crisis can be resolved through de-escalation or referral to health services. As the text explored, policing and judicial systems seek to develop new approaches that reduce harm while recognising the limits of crisis interventions.

Los Angeles Police Department have introduced a contemporary new approach with "Tactical Disengagement" in an effort to reduce harm.[33] In its simplest form, this policy allows officers to delay contact or custody, at times by leaving, so that contact can be made when a more appropriate mental health response can be coordinated, inclusive of individuals making suicidal comments.[34] The idea is it seeks to preserve life, respect individual autonomy, and minimise harm, recognising police officers are not always the appropriate response.

Although some have questioned how this aligns with the notion police have a duty of care to individuals in crisis, the policy has emerged after a series of judicial directions that have held police to account when such incidents result in negative outcomes. Further the policy also reflects a broader principle in that police hold a duty of care to all present at the scene, not solely to one individual.

The text also robustly examined those circumstances where tactical intervention is unavoidable. While incidents that result in serious injury or death are often highly emotive and extensively publicised, they remain the statistical outliers. In most cases, such outcomes rarely are the preference of officers, but as a result of highly dynamic situations where other alternatives are no longer viable or available. This is not intended to absolve police actions from scrutiny: such incidents require rigorous and open review to maintain public trust. Rather, this discussion is intended to foster a more measured and nuanced understanding of the operational realities these events occur within.

One such emerging factor may be the effectiveness of non-police interventions, such as community responder teams. As these teams expand in service delivery, they are becoming more accepted in communities and increasingly addressing more lower risk calls for services. However, this success may have an inadvertent outcome: it leaves police responding predominately to more complex, dynamic, and higher-risk incidents. Simply, effective triaging to non-police options results in a concentration of the most dangerous calls remaining the responsibility of frontline police. As such, while many debate a police culture of force, focusing solely on officer culture may be overly simplistic and ignore broader systems changes, which need to also be examined as an operational shift as much as adjusting police culture.

One such systems issue illustrated in this context is the inconsistency in how police are equipped, as system reform concentrate police towards high-risk calls. Despite advancements in policing technologies and protective equipment, these developments have not always transferred into a broader use of less-lethal options for frontline police. Tools such as the remote tethering BolaWrap and conducted energy devices, better known by the brand name Taser, provide officers alternatives before lethal force. However, Taser accessibility still remains an example where long-standing, proven technology fails to be provided universally, particularly in the UK and USA.

This inconsistency in equipping officers is a critical consideration for policymakers and police leadership. Police are being triaged to a higher proportion of dangerous crisis calls, at the same time the public and judiciary rightly expect officers to exhaust less-lethal alternatives prior to lethal force. However, officers are regularly being deployed without the broadest range of options available to them as assumed in public debate. Leaving individual officers to operate within a narrower range of alternatives than public opinion demands. In this environment, discussion on police use-of-force needs to pivot, to a point, from narrow individual officer decision-making perspectives and examine organisational policy, equipment allocation, and training. Agencies carry a shared responsibility for outcomes as much as those officers who act within the limits placed upon them.

In summary, serious or fatal police encounters remain statistical outliers, rather than the norm. Yet, as triaging and non-police options improve, officers are increasingly concentrated towards those high-risk, dynamic, and complex calls for service. At the same time, many of those officers are deployed without access to the range of force options the public and judiciary expect. These factors – beyond individual officer control – demonstrate why debate must extend to the organisations and systems responsible for policy design, equipment allocation, training, and support. Broadening discussions allow for more nuanced assessments of the system frontline officers operate within, in turn enabling realignment of systems to support safer and more consistent outcomes, without reducing them to singular questions of culture or choice.

Throughout each area explored, the text has illustrated the same undeniable reality: crisis is complex, dynamic, and often overly simplified. Whether discussing police or non-police models, non-clinical outcomes, systemic barriers, language, and terminology, or even identifying patterns of crisis cycling, crisis is often examined through narrow clinical or interventionist approaches. Perspectives which risk reinforcing fragmented, siloed and at times divisive narratives that may result in creating the very patterns of chronic crisis cycling they aim to resolve. While some efforts have been attempted to bring sectors together, they often remain only dual-sector initiatives, vulnerable to political change and fail to create fully integrated systems.

The final chapter subsequently calls for crisis to be reimagined through a broader systems-based perspective. Crisis is rarely a single isolated incident;

individuals do not choose to be stuck in patterns of crisis and recovery does not always follow predictable clinical pathways. People move in and out of various supports with fluctuating degrees of risk, for many different reasons and their needs are not always clinical. Returning to Baldry and Dowse's "Complex Needs Web" crisis can be seen as emerging from overlapping social, environmental, health, and justice factors which can impact on a person's wellbeing at different times depending on circumstances.[35]

Understanding this dynamic and complex framework illustrates no single sector has the ability to resolve crisis alone. It requires multi-sector collaborations, operating as a coordinated web-of-support, that acknowledges shared demand, shared accountability and realisation working more integrated and collectively achieves broader benefits for all. Essentially crisis needs to be examined through a systems-based perspective beyond acute crisis interventionist models to build complete full continuum of care frameworks.

Through this systems-based lens it also raised the question: is retaining the tri-service emergency service model of police, fire, and ambulance sufficient for modern communities? As society evolves and understands the need for social and emotional wellbeing, calls for urgent support when individuals are in distress likewise grows. Placing a strain on traditional tri-services and causes confusion as to ownership of that demand.

From a critical perspective, it is clear communities have already begun on the pathway – albeit somewhat covertly – towards establishing a fourth emergency service. With the global expansion of police and community response models, such as co-responder teams, community crisis teams, and dedicated paramedic-led teams, it illustrates communities and policymakers alike are actively calling for and choosing to build a specialised, dedicated response service.

Therefore, it is time policymakers and communities openly debate the need for a fourth emergency service – Behavioural Health Response – positioned alongside those traditional tri-sector frameworks. Effectively, the workforce already exists: positioned across those various response teams and other localised initiatives filling the gap. All that is required is for policymakers to bring this covert service sector together, formalise their operational remit and recognise a dedicated emergency service.

To bring this covert service out into the open and formally recognise a fourth service several operational and organisational elements are required. As with those other services there is need for stable funding, clear governance, legislated authority, workforce protection, and inter-sector operational boundaries. Along with operational features such as, but not extensively, inclusion to emergency call service systems, purpose-built vehicles, emergency deployment authority, and carefully regulated powers for involuntary care apprehension.

This final consideration: granting involuntary apprehension powers may cause concern for some. However, to do so would provide two improvements on current practice. First, it would further reduce policing involvement in crisis response. Second, it shifts the responsibility and decision-making processes for such coercive actions into a more clinically informed setting, delivered by dedicated crisis responders.

Developing a sustainable and accessible workforce would also require reimagining the current reliance on degree-based clinical roles to hold such authority. Watson and colleagues (2025) support this shift, recommending the establishment of a new emergency professional – the "Community Behavioral Health Crisis Responder" – who is grounded in trauma-informed, person-centred practice rather than academic qualifications alone.[36]

The present tri-service model reflects an earlier time. As communities evolve, a systems thinking perspective reminds us emergency services also need to evolve. The addition of a fourth emergency service focusing on social and emotional wellbeing, is that next logical evolution. Behavioural Health Response, as that fourth emergency service, would provide a clear and logical crisis pathway and become a critical component within a broader system of community care: enhancing pathways to support, improving cross-sector decision-making and strengthening a community's web-of-support.

Final Observational Summary – Police Role in Crisis

We now arrive at the final observation in this work. From the outset, the aim has been to move beyond those dualistic narratives framing policing's role in crisis as either complete inclusion or complete exclusion, a debate increasingly being dominated by exclusion. These narratives, often shaped by narrow interventionist perspectives, simplify complex issues in ways allowing for quick policy change or assigning of blame, but ultimately creating division.

This divisive narrative has become a barrier to meaningful system-based reform. While energy is spent focusing on the virtues or failures of police in crisis, attention is diverted from examining more broadly crisis systems and the interconnectedness – or lack thereof – of sectors within them. A systems-based perspectives requires us to look beyond any single sector, or the point of acute crisis and consider the full crisis cycle.

Some readers may have expected a definitive answer by now as to what the police role *should* be. However, this text has illustrated both the over-reliance on police and under-utilisation of police can be problematic, depending on the context of the situation and how a community's web-of-support has been constructed.

There is undeniable evidence of the over-reliance on police in crisis response. This may arise from systemic gaps in health and social services, community expectations, organisational pressures, individual preference, or simply that police are the only 24/7 mobile service unable to decline a call for help. Crisis cycling is complex and it is possibly a combination of all these factors. Regardless, the current model is unsustainable and does little to build appropriate care pathways vulnerable individuals require. Police have neither the training, resourcing, or capacity to meet the needs of those experiencing chronic crisis cycling. Leaving police, even when paired with clinicians in co-responder programs, as the default crisis response is a disservice to all. Yet, caution is needed: police will never be entirely removed from crisis response. The dynamic, complex, and unpredictable nature of crisis means there will always be incidents where police remain the only service capable to respond, particularly when high risk or criminality is present.

On the other hand, police are noticeably absent from, systems-based approaches to addressing chronic crisis cycling. If communities are to build effective multi-sector, preventative, collaborations, excluding police from these systems risks fragmented and counterproductive outcomes. Police must be reimagined from the interventionist 'gatekeepers' role to becoming 'activators' operating in a broader, dynamic, 24/7 web-of-support.

Ultimately, the crisis discussion needs to move beyond the interventionist narrative that dominates today. Within a proactive crisis management model, police can reduce their footprint in acute crisis, while still contributing to the communities they serve. A systems-based perspective also supports police agencies, communities and other sectors understand how policing fits into a broader system of care, particularly in those times where they remain the only sector capable of responding.

By reimagining crisis itself fosters an environment where systems can be established to reduce fragmentation and division. A shift in narrative which also helps to move beyond the present fixation on the police role debate, an ongoing debate which could be seen as a symptom of broader systems failures, rather than the primary issue. Viewing crisis through a systems-based perspective opens dialogue which addresses reform through inclusivity, collaboration, and shared understanding, rather than fragmentation and reactive approaches.

Concluding Thoughts

The views and reflections throughout this work have drawn on the author's experience across policing, operating alongside mental health clinicians in co-responder roles, frontline behavioural health crisis engagement and time spent working within health settings. While these perspectives are not offered as a universal solution, they are informed by practice, reinforcing the need to live as much as study crisis response in order to understand its complexity. The text arrives from an ability to merge decades of operational experience with research and observations across international crisis systems. It is not a totally neutral vantage point, but the aim has been to provide real-world insight: recognising the strengths and limitations of perspectives formed solely from a distance, where the intricacies and complexity of crisis work can be difficult to fully appreciate.

Crisis stands at a crossroads. The time has come to decide on which direction we take. One path continues along the familiar, and often politically shaped divisiveness, where blame shifting, funding models and narrow interventionist models foster short-term gains. Approaches that address immediate needs or political will, but do little to address patterns of chronic crisis cycling affecting the vulnerable. It's a well-worn road, easy to follow, yet ultimately reinforces the very problems they seek to resolve.

The other road requires more from policymakers, sector leaders, and communities themselves. It identifies crisis as a shared responsibility beyond the moment. A path which requires crisis to be looked at through a systems-based lens and addressed with an integrated, web-of-support. A web that draws together genuine multi-sector collaborations with mutual understanding, capable of supporting a dynamic continuum of care, ensuring no single sector carries the burden.

The direction we choose at this crossroads will determine whether communities remain locked in reactive crisis response programs or progresses towards coordinated, sustainable crisis management systems. The pathway forward is ours to choose.

Notes

1 Slate, R. N., Frailing, K., Johnson, W. W., & Buffington, J. K. (2021). *The criminalization of mental illness: Crisis and opportunity for the justice system* (3rd ed.). Carolina Academic Press; Mansour, H., Mueller, C., Davis, K.A.S., Burton, A., Shetty, H., Hotopf, M., Osborn, D., Stewart, R., & Sommerlad, A. (2020). Severe mental illness diagnosis in English general hospitals 2006–2017: A registry linkage study. *PLoS Medicine, 17*(9), e1003306. https://doi.org/10.1371/journal.pmed.1003306.

2 World Health Organization. (2022). *World mental health report: Transforming mental health for all.* World Health Organization. https://iris.who.int/handle/10665/356119.

3 Akins, S., Burkhardt, B.C., & Lanfear, C. (2015). Law enforcement response to "frequent fliers": An examination of high-frequency contacts between police and justice-involved persons with mental illness. *Criminal Justice Policy Review*. Advance online publication. https://doi.org/10.1177/0887403414559268; House, A. (2023). Serenity integrated mentoring and the high intensity network: A scheme that raises serious questions for practice and governance in UK psychiatry. *BJPsych Bulletin*, *47*(1), 1–4. https://doi.org/10.1192/bjb.2022.6.

4 Chappell, D. (Ed.). (2013). *Policing and the mentally ill: International perspectives* (1st ed.). Routledge. www.routledge.com/Policing-and-the-Mentally-Ill-International-Perspectives/Chappell/p/book/9780367866730.

5 High Court of Australia. (2024). *Stuart v Kirkland-Veenstra [2009] HCA 15.* https://eresources.hcourt.gov.au/showCase/2009/HCA/15; California Court of Appeal, First District, Division 2. (1988). *ADAMS v. CITY OF FREMONT (1988) Nos. A074965, A075279.* https://caselaw.findlaw.com/court/ca-court-of-appeal/1288866.html.

6 Legislation Victoria. (2024). *Family Violence Protection Act 2008.* https://content.legislation.vic.gov.au/sites/default/files/2020-10/08-52aa053%20authorised_0.pdf.

7 Mendelson, D. (2014, October 10). Prevention of suicide: Police powers, parliamentary intent and judicial interpretation. *Journal of Law and Medicine, 2009*, 16. Available at SSRN: https://ssrn.com/abstract=2508274.

8 Substance Abuse and Mental Health Services Administration. (2025). *Model definitions for behavioral health emergency, crisis, and crisis-related services* (HHS Publication No. PEP24-01-037). U.S. Department of Health and Human Services. https://988crisissystemshelp.samhsa.gov/sites/default/files/2025-08/SAMHSA_Model_Definitions_508_080525.pdf.

9 Helplines. (2019). *Helplines partnership – Trends, changes and developments in the helpline sector 2017–2019.* https://helplines.contentfiles.net/media/documents/Helpline_Insight_Research_Report_2017-2019.pdf.

10 Draper, J., & McKeon, R.T. (2024). The journey toward 988: A historical perspective on crisis hotlines in the United States. *Psychiatric Clinics of North America, 47*(3), 473–90. https://10.1016/j.psc.2024.04.003.

11 Mental Health Association. (2021). *Submission to productivity commission into mental health.* (www.pc.gov.au/__data/assets/pdf_file/0012/243111/sub538-mental-health.pdf).

12 Mental Health Association. (2021). *Submission to productivity commission into mental health.* www.pc.gov.au/__data/assets/pdf_file/0012/243111/sub538-mental-health.pdf; Helplines. (2019). *Helplines partnership – Trends, changes and developments in the helpline sector 2017–2019.* https://helplines.contentfiles.net/media/documents/Helpline_Insight_Research_Report_2017-2019.pdf.

13 Dee, T. S., & Pyne, J. (2022). A community response approach to mental health and substance abuse crises reduced crime. *Science Advances, 8*(eabm2106). https://doi.org/10.1126/sciadv.abm2106; London Ambulance Service. (2025). *London Ambulance Service celebrates a decade of specialist care for mental health patients.* www.londonambulance.nhs.uk/2025/02/21/london-ambulance-service-celebrates-a-decade-of-specialist-care-for-mental-health-patients/; San Francisco Government [sf.gov]. (2022). *Street Crisis Response Team pilot final report.* www.sf.gov/sites/default/files/2022-06/SCRT%20Final%20Report_FINAL-%201%20year.pdf; Gillespie, S., Curran-Groome, W., & Rogin, A., (2024). *Evaluating alternative crisis response in Denver's Support Team Assisted Response (STAR) Program: Interim findings.* www.denvergov.org/files/assets/public/v/1/public-health-and-environment/documents/cbh/star/evaluating_alternative_crisis_response_in_denvers_support_team_assisted_response_program-interim_findings.pdf.

14 White Bird Clinic. (n.d.). *CAHOOTS: Crisis Assistance Helping Out On The Streets.* White Bird Clinic. Retrieved December 1, 2025, from https://whitebirdclinic.org/cahoots/; Oregon Public Broadcasting. (2025, June 4). *Eugene after CAHOOTS: The end of the crisis response program and the efforts to bring it back.* OPB. www.opb.org/article/2025/06/04/eugene-after-cahoots-the-end-of-the-crisis-response-program-and-the-efforts-to-bring-it-back/.

15 Watson, A., & Compton, M., (2019). What research on crisis intervention teams tells us and what we need to ask. *Journal of the American Academy of Psychiatry and the Law.* Online November 2019, JAAPL.003894-19; https://doi.org/10.29158/JAAPL.003894-19.

16 Watson, A., & Compton, M., (2019). What research on crisis intervention teams tells us and what we need to ask. *Journal of the American Academy of Psychiatry and the Law.* Online November 2019, JAAPL.003894-19; https://doi.org/10.29158/JAAPL.003894-19.

17 Compton, M. T., Bakeman, R., Broussard, B., Hankerson-Dyson, D., Husbands, L., Krishan, S., … Watson, A. C. (2014). The police-based Crisis Intervention Team (CIT) Model: I. Effects on officers' knowledge, attitudes, and skills. *Psychiatric Services*, *65*(4), 517–22. https://doi.org/10.1176/appi.ps.201300107.

18 Henry, P., & Rajakaruna N. (2018). *Western Australia Police Force mental health co-response evaluation report.* www.parliament.wa.gov.au/publications; Dee, t. Geiser, K. Gerstein, A. Pyne, J., & Woo, C. (2024). *Impact Report San Mateo County, California Community Wellness and Crisis Response Team Pilot Program: December 2021 through June 2024.* https://gardnercenter.stanford.edu/sites/g/files/sbiybj24036/files/media/file/impactreport_2024-10-15.pdf; Lamanna, D., Shapiro, G. K., Kirst, M., Matheson, F. I., Nakhost, A., & Stergiopoulos, V. (2018), Co-responding police–mental health programmes: Service user experiences and outcomes in a large urban centre. *International Journal of Mental Health Nursing*, *27*, 891–900. https://doi.org/10.1111/inm.12384.

19 Evangelista, E., Lee, S., Gallagher, A., Peterson, V., James, J., Warren, N., Henderson, K., Keppich-Arnold, S., Cornelius, L., & Deveny, E. (2016). Crisis averted: How consumers experienced a police and clinical early response (PACER) unit responding to a mental health crisis. *International Journal of Mental Health Nursing*, *25*, 367–76. https://doi.org/10.1111/inm.12218; Parliament WA. (2022, February 24). *Police — Mental Health Co-Response Program.* www.parliament.wa.gov.au/hansard/hansard.nsf/16ab30a0303e54f448256bf7002049e8/e2308818ee9e7c33482588bd00220b5e/$FILE/A41%20S1%2020220224%20p694d-695a.pdf; New Zealand Police. (2022, October 17). *Better outcomes for mental health.* www.police.govt.nz/news/ten-one-magazine/better-outcomes-mental-health; Kirubarajan, A., Puntis, S., Perfect, D., Tarbit, M., Buckman, M., & Molodynski, A. (2018). Street triage services in England: Service models, national provision and the opinions of police. *BJPsych Bulletin*, *42*, 1–5. doi: 10.1192/bjb.2018.62; Gov.UK. (2013, August 20). *Press release – Extending the street triage scheme: New patrols with nurses and the police.* www.gov.uk/government/news/extending-the-street-triage-scheme-new-patrols-with-nurses-and-the-police.

20 NHS England. (2017, June 23). *News NHS England kicks off international search for ground-breaking patient-care innovations.* www.england.nhs.uk/2017/06/international-search-for-ground-breaking-patient-care-innovations/.
21 Farrar, M. (2021). *Independent review of AHSN Network involvement in support to mental health trusts and police forces for the adoption of the Serenity Integrated Mentoring (SIM) model or equivalent.* https://thehealthinnovationnetwork.co.uk/wp-content/uploads/2023/05/Independent-Review-into-AHSN-role-in-SIM-Mike-Farrar-FINAL-V1.pdf.
22 Home Office (UK). (2024). *Policy paper National Partnership Agreement: Right Care, Right Person (RCRP).* www.gov.uk/government/publications/national-partnership-agreement-right-care-right-person/national-partnership-agreement-right-care-right-person-rcrp.
23 National Police Chiefs Council. (2023, July 16). *1M officer hours saved with new approach to mental health.* https://news.npcc.police.uk/releases/police-to-save-1-million-officer-hours-as-forces-adopt-new-model-to-ensure-specialist-care-for-health-incidents.
24 UK Parliament. (2023). *Urgent answers needed on funding for 'Right Care, Right Person' mental health strategy.* https://committees.parliament.uk/committee/81/health-and-social-care-committee/news/198473/urgent-answers-needed-on-funding-for-right-care-right-person-mental-health-strategy/.
25 Bird, H., Bryant, L., & Kadiri, H. (2024). Defunding the police is good for our mental health. *The Political Quarterly*, *95*, 474–79. https://doi.org/10.1111/1467-923X.13449.
26 Balfour, M. E., & Zeller, S. L. (2023). Community-based crisis services, specialized crisis facilities, and partnerships with law enforcement. *Focus*, *21*(1), 18–27. https://doi.org/10.1176/appi.focus.20220074.
27 Medicaid. (2025). *CCBHC demonstration background.* www.medicaid.gov/medicaid/financial-management/certified-community-behavioral-health-clinic-ccbhc-demonstration/ccbhc-demonstration-background.
28 NHS England. (2025). *Crisis and acute mental health care.* www.england.nhs.uk/mental-health/adults/crisis-and-acute-care/; Australian Government. (2024). *Department of Health and Aged Care – Medicare Mental Health Centres.* www.health.gov.au/our-work/medicare-mental-health-centres; Australian Government. (2025). *About Medicare Mental Health.* www.medicarementalhealth.gov.au/about-us.
29 Schwartz, S., Michel, J., Brown, E., et al. (2025). Assessing the impact of an innovate behavioral health clinic: A retrospective cohort study. *BMC Psychiatry*, *25*, 250. https://doi.org/10.1186/s12888-025-06669-8.
30 Blackwell, G. (2023). *Reducing recidivism in behavioural health crisis cycles.* www.churchilltrust.com.au/project/the-churchill-fellows-association-of-western-australia-churchill-fellowship-to-establish-diversionary-practices-for-mentally-and-intellectually-disabled-persons-engaging-police/.
31 Usher, L., Watson, A., Bruno, R., Andriukaitis, S., Kamin, D., Speed, C., & Taylor, S. (2019). *Crisis Intervention Team (CIT) Programs: A best practice guide for transforming community responses to mental health crises* (p. 128). Memphis: CIT International. https://citinternational.org/bestpracticeguide.

32 Texas Commission on Law Enforcement. (2024, December). *Training requirements.* Texas Commission on Law Enforcement. www.tcole.texas.gov/content/training-requirements; State of California Commission on Peace Officer Standards and Training. (2024, December). *Crisis intervention behavioural health training.* State of California Commission on Peace Officer Standards and Training. https://post.ca.gov/crisis-intervention-behavioral-health-training.

33 Blackwell, G. (2023). *Reducing recidivism in behavioural health crisis cycles.* www.churchilltrust.com.au/project/the-churchill-fellows-association-of-western-australia-churchill-fellowship-to-establish-diversionary-practices-for-mentally-and-intellectually-disabled-persons-engaging-police/; Lopez, R. (2022). *'But we can't just leave!' How LAPD SWAT implemented a strategic disengagement policy.* www.police1.com/swat/articles/but-we-cant-just-leave-how-lapd-swat-implemented-a-strategic-disengagement-policy-lHT6VGQ1dTv9UN4f/.

34 Lopez, R. (2022). *'But we can't just leave!': How LAPD SWAT implemented a strategic disengagement policy.* www.police1.com/swat/articles/but-we-cant-just-leave-how-lapd-swat-implemented-a-strategic-disengagement-policy-lHT6VGQ1dTv9UN4f/.

35 Chappell, D. (Ed.). (2013). *Policing and the mentally ill: International perspectives* (1st ed.). Routledge. www.routledge.com/Policing-and-the-Mentally-Ill-International-Perspectives/Chappell/p/book/9780367866730.

36 Watson, A. C., McNally, K., Pope, L. G., & Compton, M. T. (2025). If not police, then who? Building a new workforce for community behavioral health crisis response. *Frontiers in Psychology*, *16*, 1579787. https://doi.org/10.3389/fpsyg.2025.1579787.

Index

Note: Page locators in **bold** and *italics* represents tables and figures, respectively.

24/7 support: alternatives 50; challenges 191, 214–215; existing support 42, 43, 47–48, 195, 198, 217; lack of 51, 76, 184; need for 49–50, 165, 194–195, 214; role of the police 166, 190–191, 199, 222–223 *see also* access to services; crisis call lines
988 emergency line in Canada 39
988-Lifeline in the United States 36, 38–39, 40, 50, 194, 214

abuse: Adverse Childhood Experiences (ACEs) *16*, 129, **132**; Complex Needs Web *16*; emotional 21–22; by police 153; Substance Abuse and Mental Health Services Administration (SAMHSA) 3, 38, 47, 50, 177, 194, 195, 213–214, 216; substance abuse treatment 178 *see also* substance use disorders (SUD)
access to services: co-responder models 59–60; crisis stabilisation centres 51; demand 38; gatekeeping 103–104; integrated referral pathways 188; no wrong doors policies 75; trust 196 *see also* 24/7 support; crisis call lines
accountability: data and information sharing 155; justice 100–103, 105, 112; media 153; police 108, 127, 192; from policing to health 63; risk shifting 152–153; shared 151, 184, 221
acute stress (ICD-10 -F40-F49) 7–8
Adams v. City of Fremont [1998] 23, 95, 213
Adelaide 48
Adverse Childhood Experiences (ACEs) *16*, 129, **132**
advocacy 70, 74, 75, 80–81, 122, 150–151, 179, 217
Alexander, Paul, death of 72
Anderson, Chief Constable Paul 67–68, 161
anxiety 7, 8, 36, 40
arrests: deaths 108; effectiveness of crisis intervention 75, 77–78; mental health as predictor 129; non-arrest diversion pathways 187; procedural 9; re-arrests 17, 81, 189; reducing reoffending 189; substance use disorders (SUD) 8; success of co-responder programs 60–61; suicide 23 *see also* de-escalation; involuntary apprehension
Assertive Community Treatment (ACT) Team in Vancouver 178, 188, 189
Assertive Outreach Team (AOT) in Vancouver 186, 188–189, 190
Atlanta Policing Alternatives & Diversion Initiative (PAD) 41
Australia: Australian Productivity Commission 37, 151, 214; *Better Crisis Care* (2025) 174; chronic crisis cycling and incarceration 17; chronic crisis interruption 189; community

response teams 43; co-responder models 60, 62; crisis assessment and treatment teams in Australia 42; crisis call lines 12, 36; crisis recidivism 12, 39; crisis stabilisation centres 48; data and information sharing 192; emergency department presentations 7; Foetal Alcohol Spectrum Disorder 11; funding distribution 151; legal capacity of individuals 101; Mental Health Act 2014 (Australia) 155; missing persons 163; reduction of psychiatric hospital beds 11; Right Care, Right Person (RCRP) policy 69, 73; *Royal Commission into Violence, Abuse, Neglect, and Exploitation of People with Disability* 9; shootings 96, 107; substance use disorders (SUD) 8; suicide 20–23, 127–128, 213; tactical disengagement policy 99; tactical resolution (use of force) 108; therapeutic courts 103–104; walk-in services 48 *see also individual cities and states*
authority: attendance at suicide incidents 19, 22, 95, 126–128; fourth emergency service 197, 221–222; gatekeeping 157; high-risk situations 108; limitations 139–140, 154–155; operational paradox 95–96; policing non-criminal matters 161; procedural 99, 128; tactical resolution (use of force) 108–109
autism 11, 102, 122, 154
autonomy: care-planning 184; legal 101–102; listening to individuals in crisis 127; pace of negotiation 128, 130; suicide 19–24, 95–96, 213; tactical disengagement policy 98, 100, 219; therapeutic courts 102–103, 104; trauma-informed care **133**; wellbeing 179

Baldry, E., & Dowse, L., *Compounding mental and cognitive disability and disadvantage: Police as care managers* 2, 16, 176, 212–213, 221
Bari, Tcherno, death of 72
barriers: community response teams 45–46; crisis management 165–166; funding 150–152, 214–215; legislation 154–155; media and public opinion 153–154; narratives 222; resources 71; risk shifting 152–153; terminology 155–157, 160; therapeutic courts 103–104; trust 40
beds, psychiatric 11, 14
Behavioral Health Crisis Response Landscape Analysis (US) 174
Behavioral Health Emergency Assistance Response Division (BHEARD) in New York 43, 44
Behavioural Change Stairway Model (BCSM) *see* Behavioural Influence Stairway Model (BCSM)
Behavioural Health Call for Service: co-responder models 59–60, 80; crisis intervention teams 75; diversions 63; formalisation as an emergency service 193–198; judicial management 100; police attendance 44, 94–95, 106–107, 110, 112–113, 120; police risk assessments 71–73; reluctance to engage with the police 153; Right Care, Right Person (RCRP) policy 67–71, 73–74; tactical disengagement policy 98, 111–112; tactical resolution (use of force) 112; training 120–121; types of crisis presentation 18; use of term 9–10, 25, 156
behavioural health crisis: Behavioural Health Crisis Stabilisation Centres (CSC) 47, 217; Crisis Now III Summit 198; inclusivity 186–187; mental health as a distinct category 39; recognising complexity 180; role of the police 157–158, 163–164; systems approach 38–39, 41; unpredictability 109; use of term 6, 8–10
Behavioural Influence Stairway Model (BCSM) 130, **132**
Better Crisis Care (Australia) 174
Beyond Blue (Australia) 36
B-Heard program *see* Behavioral Health Emergency Assistance Response Division (BHEARD) in New York
bias: decision-making 127, 138–139; diagnosis 122; implicit 13, 19, 121, 128, 156, 212; problem of

terminology 7, 9; risk triaging 107–108, 110, 112; self-reporting data 43, 61; training challenges 76, 105, 137
Bittner, E., *The functions of the police in modern society: A review of background factors, current practices, and possible role models* 137, 139
blame: crisis recidivism 12, 14; divisive narrative 175, 179, 185, 222, 224; media portrayal of police 153; misguided 218; risk of framing the police 159–160; shifting risk 127–128, 152, 165
Boston 98–99

California: Case Assessment and Management Program in Los Angeles 188, 189, 190, 191; chronic crisis cycling 17; co-responder models 77; crisis call lines 36; legal capacity 101; Mental Health Intervention Training (MHIT) in Los Angeles 137; POST (Peace Officer Standards and Training) in California 138, 218; Psychiatric Mobile Response Teams (PMRT) Los Angeles 42; San Diego Mobile Crisis Response Teams (MCRT) 41; Street Crisis Response Team (SCRT) in San Francisco 12, 43, 44, 194, 197; suicide 20, 23, 95; Systemwide Mental Assessment Response Team (SMART) in Los Angeles 12, 60; tactical disengagement policy in Los Angeles 23, 98, 219; tactical disengagement policy in San Francisco 99; training 121, 218
calls *see* crisis call lines
Canada: Assertive Community Treatment (ACT) Team in Vancouver 178, 186; Assertive Outreach Team (AOT) in Vancouver 188–189, 190; community response teams 44; co-responder programs 60, 62; crisis stabilisation centres 48; data and information sharing 191; emergency call lines 39, 50, 194; Mobile Crisis De-Escalation Team (MoDe) in Vancouver 42; Toronto Community Crisis Service (TCCS) 41
capacity: authority in high-risk situations 108; autonomy in ending life 21, 22–23, 24; chronic crisis cycling **15**; cognitive 182, 213; collaboration 155, 176, 187–188; communities 94; co-responder teams 61; crisis intervention teams 77–78; delivery of 24/7 service 37, 48, 49–50, 51, 194–195, 214; diagnosis 9; emergency services 194; fourth emergency service 196, 198, 200; fragmented support 38; funding decisions 158; funding for crime fighting 159; legal capacity 101–102, 105; police 108, 139–140, 154, 156, 159–160, 161–162, 164, 184, 223; police attended incidents 11, 17, 24–25; psychiatric beds 11, 14; repeated use of emergency departments by individuals 12–13; Right Care, Right Person (RCRP) policy 70
Car 87 program 60
care: arrest 23–24; benefit of fourth emergency service 198; bridging programs 189; follow-up 37–38, 178; gatekeeping 13; inclusivity 186–187; police duty of care 22–24, 59, 68, 80, 95, 213; social prescribing 179, 189; trauma-informed 128–129, **132**, 189; welfare role of police 163, 190–191
Case Assessment and Management Program (CAMP) in Los Angeles 188, 189, 190, 191
charities 37, 70
child abuse *see* Adverse Childhood Experiences (ACEs)
children: Adverse Childhood Experiences (ACEs) *16*, 129, **132**; neurodivergence and crisis 9
Chronic Consumer Stabilization Initiative in Houston Assertive Outreach Team (AOT)178, 186, 187, 188, 190
chronic crisis cycling: care in emergency departments 46–47; Complex Needs Web 16, 176, 212–213; crisis call lines 39–40; distinction 25; examples 13–14; factors 14, 16, 223; impact 17; impact of collaborative models

65, 80; Intensive Case Management (ICM) 188–189; police initiatives 190; proactive strategy 178–179; risks **15**; successful models of interruption 189; suicidality 21; systems-thinking 182–185; understanding 212–213; use of term 156 *see also* recidivism
coercion: expectation of the police 163–164; intervention 21; perception of therapeutic courts 104; suicidality and coercive control 21–22, 213
collaboration: community ecosystems 198–199; Crisis Now III Summit 192, 198; funding distribution issue 151–152; importance of 178–179; information sharing 155, 191–192, 194; knowledge of referral paths 127; multi-sector systems thinking 178–179, 183–184, 187–188, 190; reluctance 179–180; strength of 189; two-sector 176, 180, 185, 188; web-of-support 178, 180–182, 183–184, 185, 189–191, 192, 221 *see also* co-responder models; crisis intervention teams; Right Care, Right Person (RCRP) policy; Serenity Integrated Mentoring (SIM)
College of Policing (UK) 69–70, 72, 99, 121, 134
Colorado 43, 44, 45
communication: access to police communications 194; de-escalation 95, 121, 126, 129–131, **132**, 139; failures 184, 185; integrated referral pathways 187; rapport building 40; scenario training 134
communities: changing the narrative 185; crisis intervention teams 76; demographic knowledge 123–124; ecosystems 198–199; embedding programs 181–182; gaps in support 12–13; integrated pathways 215; Memphis Model 74–75; mobile community mental health teams (MCMHTs) 42, 214; need for investment in support 17; non-police response models 12, 49–51; role of the police 162, 163–165, 190–191; support for therapeutic courts 104; tactical disengagement 100; tailored support for 37 *see also* community response teams
Community Behavioral Health: clinics 47, 217; crisis responder 197, 222
community response teams: benefits 44–45; crisis management framework 50; effectiveness 46; mobile community mental health teams (MCMHTs) 42, 50, 214; models 41, 213–215; obstacles 45–46; programs 42–43; reducing police attendance 44; reduction in criminal behaviour 45; unintended outcome 219
Complex Needs Web 16, 176, *177*, 212–213, 221
complexity of crises: challenge 220; need for integrated multi-sector teams 190; Right Care, Right Person (RCRP) policy 73; terminology 8–10
confidentiality 40
Conflict Management Using De-escalation, Communication, and Negotiation (UK) 121
Connecticut 17
co-responder models: about 12; aims 59–60; background 60; behavioural health as an emergency service 194; benefits 62–63, 215; criticism of 77; funding distribution issue 151; future 63; limitations 61, 80, 223; programs 60–61; rapid reform 175
Cotton, Sophie, death of 72
courts *see* therapeutic courts
criminal behaviour: mental health 100–102; reduction through community response team programs 45; role of the police 161–163; success of co-responder programs 60–61; therapeutic courts 102–105; victims 100, 104, 105
criminalisation of behavioural health: co-responder models 77; disability and policing 9; reducing 157–158; reduction of psychiatric hospital beds 11; suicide 19–20, 23–24 *see also* substance use disorders (SUD)
Crisis Assistance Helping Out On The Streets (CAHOOTS) program in Oregon 42, 44–46, 194, 215

crisis call lines: availability 37; background 35–36; confidentiality 40; crisis management framework 50; expansion of 214; institutionalisation 38–39, 194, 214; integrating with emergency lines 196–197; maintaining 36–37; outcomes 37–38; perception as supplementary care 37–38, 40–41; types of calls 36
Crisis Intervention Response Team (CIRT) in Houston 60
Crisis Intervention Team International (CITI) model of training 75–79, 80, 120, 123, 134, 215
crisis intervention teams 74–79, 80–81, 120
crisis management: calls for change 165; challenges for programs 181–182; data and information sharing 191–192, 193; demand for dedicated infrastructure 197–198; inclusivity 186–187; integrated referral pathways 187–188; intensive case management 188–189; models 178–179; narrative of law enforcement 163–164; programs 186, 192–193; role of the police 190–191; staffing 189–190; Substance Abuse and Mental Health Services Administration (SAMHSA) 195, 213–214; success factors 188–189; web-of-support 189–190
Crisis Now III Summit 192, 198–199
Crisis Outreach and Support Team (COAST) in Hamilton 60
crisis recidivism *see* recidivism
Crisis Resolution and Home Treatment Teams (CRHTT) in the UK 195
crisis response: complexity 2; moving beyond 175; pracademic perspective 2; preparedness 120–121; reimagining 4; response times 214; success factors 216–217; typical crisis presentations 18 *see also* Behavioural Health Call for Service; behavioural health crisis; community response teams; co-responder models; crisis call lines; non-police response models; tactical disengagement policy; tactical resolution (use of force)
Crisis Response and Intervention Training (CRIT) 123, 139
crisis stabilisation centres: 24/7 support 217; benefits 49; crisis management framework 51; development of centres 47; effect on emergency department presentations 48; global programs 48; importance of 46–47; lack of 45; suicidality 49; systems-based approach 216–217
criticisms: Right Care, Right Person (RCRP) policy 68, 70–71, 80, 216; Serenity Integrated Mentoring (SIM) 66; therapeutic courts 103–104

data: bias 61, 122; failures 183; incident coding 212; need for clearer 111; self-reporting 43, 46, 66, 73; sharing 155, 176, 180, 191–192, 193, 194
deaths of individuals: concerns about Right Care Right Person (RCRP), policy 71–73; ‘defund the police’ campaigns 157; fatal shooting by police 74–75, 96; media portrayal of police 153; shootings 106–107, 220; suicide by cop shootings 97 *see also* suicide
de-escalation: Behavioural Health Clinics 47; challenge of 95; co-responder model 59–60, 62, 80; crisis call lines 50; crisis intervention teams 77–78, 215; enforcement lens 164; fourth emergency service 197; Memphis Model 74–75; Mobile Crisis De-Escalation Team (MoDe) in Vancouver 42; operational paradox 95; reality 218–219; relational approach 128; safety 197; tactical disengagement policy 98–99; terminology 155; training 95, 111, 121, 123–126, 129–130, **132**, 134, 135, 215; trauma-informed care 129, 192
‘defund the police’ campaign 157–159
deinstitutionalisation 11, 14
dementia 8–9, 154
diagnosis: diagnostic profiles 7–8, 9–10, 24–26, 103–104, 126, 186–187, 211–213; diagnostic shadowing 9; expectations 154; lack of 8;

neurodevelopmental conditions in juveniles 11; terminology 123, 156, 211; training Beyond Blue122-126, 135, 138–139, 217–218 *see also* training
Diagnostic and Statistical Manual of Mental Disorders, 122
digital support 36
disability: case study 182–184; chronic crisis cycling **15**; Complex Needs Web *16*; crisis response from police 9; funding support 184; inclusivity 187; legal boundaries 155; legal capacity 101–102, 105; mental health courts 102–103; multi-sector systems thinking 176, 181; police knowledge 123–124, **132**
distancing approach 79–80, 81
diversions: community response teams 41–44; co-responder programs 63; crisis call lines 38; crisis intervention teams 76; emergency department 48; limitations 51; non-arrest diversion pathways 187; police knowledge of 127; Right Care, Right Person (RCRP) policy 68, 70, 159; sequential intercept model 178; substance use disorders (SUD) 187; therapeutic courts 103–104, 112
Drummond v. City of Anaheim (2003) 96
duty of care 22–24, 68, 80, 95, 100, 213, 219

efficiency 65, 162, 191, 196
emergency department: care of behavioural health 48–49; cost savings from reduced attendance 45; crisis recidivism of individuals 12–13; effect of crisis stabilisation centres 48; negative experience 46–47; reducing chronic crisis cycling 178; reducing presentation 44, 65; types of crisis presentation 7–9
emergency services: integrating with crisis call lines 196–197; reluctance to engage with 40 *see also* Fourth emergency service
empathy: co-responder model 62; crisis intervention training 78; training 126, 130, 135, 137, 139; trauma-informed care 126
engagement: avoidance 23; barriers 40; improving 188; inclusivity 192; interdisciplinary 78; outcomes 81; positive 44–45; reducing police 44, 80, 194; tactical disengagement policy 111–112; therapeutic 215; time-limited 189; use-of-force 106–107
ethics: attendance at suicide incidents 22, 213; autonomy 24, 25–26; data and information sharing 191, 193; gatekeeping 104; intervention 21; tactical disengagement policy 94–95; training 134, 139
evaluation: community response teams 43–44; co-responder teams success 61; Crisis Intervention Team (CIT) model of training 215; crisis intervention teams 76, 77–78; Right Care, Right Person (RCRP) policy 70–71, 73–74, 216; Serenity Integrated Mentoring (SIM), 66–67; tactical resolution (use of force) 111; therapeutic courts 104
exclusion 222 *see also* inclusivity

Fackender, Mr., death of 96
Family Violence Protection Act 2008 (Australia) 21–22
FBI Behavioural Change Stairway Model (BCSM), *see* Behavioural Influence Stairway Model (BCSM)
financial benefits: funding distribution issue 151–152; of reduced police intervention 45, 63
Florida 97
Foetal Alcohol Spectrum Disorder 11, 24–25
fourth emergency service: behavioural health 193–195; benefits of formalisation 199–200; evolution of 194; formalisation 195–196, 198, 221–222; operating of 196–197
frameworks: clinical 211–212; crisis intervention training 75–76; crisis management 50; *National Behavioral Health Crisis Care Guidance* 195; Substance Abuse and Mental Health Services Administration (SAMHSA) 177, 195, 214; therapeutic jurisprudence 105

frequency of support: reducing 44, 60, 65; risks 13–14, **15** *see also* chronic crisis cycling
frequent flyers *see* chronic crisis cycling
funding support: barriers 150–152, 165–166, 214–215; co-responder teams 61; crisis call lines 37, 40; 'defund the police' campaigns 157–158; increase in budgets 158–159; non-police response models 46; re-assessments of individuals 184; Right Care, Right Person (RCRP) policy 74; Serenity Integrated Mentoring (SIM), 65–66

gaps in support: 24/7 support 37, 40–41; addressing 12–13, 199–200; chronic crisis cycling 156, 176; complex cases 175; diagnostic profiles 211–212; effect of reduction of police attendance 158, 216; reduction of psychiatric hospital beds 11–12, 14; reliance on police 222–223; reliance on the police 68, 74, 157, 159, 165, 222–223
gatekeeping: bias in chronic crisis cycling 13; perception of police 157, 192, 223; therapeutic courts 103–104
Georgia 63, 78
government-led models: crisis call lines 38–39, 41, 214; Right Care, Right Person (RCRP) policy 68–69; Serenity Integrated Mentoring (SIM), 64–67
governments: consolidation of services 214; failure to support community response teams 45–46, scrutiny of Right Care Right Person (RCRP) model 70; support for co-responder teams 60–61

hallucination 135
Hamilton 60
High-Demand Action Plan in Merseyside 186, 187–188, 190, 191
High-Intensity Network (HIN) *see* Serenity Integrated Mentoring (SIM)
Horne v Anglo-Australian and Universal Family Life Assurance Company 19–20
hospitalisation: crisis stabilisation centres 35, 49; reducing 44, 62, 178; reduction through community response team programs 63 *see also* emergency department
Human Rights Act 1998 (UK) 68
Humberside Police 67–70 *see also* Right Care, Right Person (RCRP) policy

ideologies: co-response 63; crisis management 178; disengagement 99; enforcement lens 163–164; integrated pathways 120, 215; intensive case management 189; law enforcement 160–164; managing behavioural health crises 79–81; policing 138; role of the police 164
Illinois 49
Improving Responses to People with Mental Illnesses: Strategies for Effective Law Enforcement Training (US) 122–123, 134
incarceration: chronic crisis cycling 17, 189; intensive case management 189; police attended incidents 9, 11; preventing 42; procedural justice 127; reducing 151, 214; risks 104; trauma **132** *see also* arrests
inclusivity 9, 10, 186–187, 192
information sharing 50, 155, 191–192, 194 *see also* data
inpatient care: community response teams 45; crisis stabilisation centres 35, 47–49
insurance issues 19–20, 155, 192
Integrated Referral pathways 187–188, 192
integrated support: funding decisions 151; government-led models 38–39, 41, 42; integrated care pathways 187–188, 192; mobile community mental health teams (MCMHTs) 42, 214; training 79, 140; use of multiple approaches 77 *see also* community response teams; co-responder models; crisis intervention teams; Right Care, Right Person (RCRP) policy; Serenity Integrated Mentoring (SIM)
intensity of support: chronic crisis cycling 13–14, **15**; Isle of Wight Integrated Recovery Programme 64;

Serenity Integrated Mentoring (SIM) 64, 65–66
Intensive Case Management (ICM) 186, 188–189, 192
International Commission of Jurists 101–102
International Co-Responder Alliance (ICRA) 63
International Crisis Response Association 198
intervention: case study 182–185; coercive 21, 23–24; failures 71–73, 80; legal boundaries 154–155; unavoidable 94; voluntary euthanasia 20–21; who benefits financially? 151–152 *see also* community response teams; co-responder models; Right Care, Right Person (RCRP) policy
intimate partner violence (IPV) 21, 24, 25, 213 *see also* violence
involuntary admission 9, 19, 44, 47, 62, 197
involuntary apprehension: benefit 222; de-escalation training 130, 135; powers 222; procedural knowledge 126–128; reducing 60–62, 64, 216; sectioning 154–155; suicidality 19, 25, 152, 213; suicide incidents 213; tactical disengagement policy 98–99
Isle of Wight Integrated Recovery Programme 64

Jennings, Police Sergeant Paul 64–67
judicial approach: chronic crisis cycling 17, 189; criticism of Serenity Integrated Mentoring (SIM) 80; legal capacity 100–102; listening to individuals in crisis 128; management 112; police attended incidents 8, 9, 11; shift to health systems thinking 178–179; success of co-responder programs 60–61, 63; therapeutic courts 102–106 *see also* law enforcement role of the police; therapeutic courts

Kansas 99

Las Vegas 96
law enforcement role of the police: crisis management 163–164; framing 156; legislation as barrier 154–155; Peelian principles 161–164; procedural knowledge 126–128; shifting risk 152–153; suicide 19–20, 22–23, 25–26, 95–96, 127–128; suicide by cop shootings 97; tactical disengagement policy 98–99; use of term 160–161, 165
liability 14, **15**, 19–20, 22, 40, 95–96, 127–128, 152–153
Lifeline Australia 36, 39
listening 127, 128, 130, **132**
longitudinal approach: benefits 44, 184–185; management 65; need for 181–182; outcomes 38, 49
Los Angeles: Case Assessment and Management Program (CAMP) 188, 189, 190, 191; chronic crisis cycling 17; psychiatric mobile response teams (PMRT) in Los Angeles 42; Systemwide Mental Assessment Response Team (SMART) 12, 60; tactical disengagement policy 23, 98, 219; training 121, 137, 218

media 153–154, 157, 159, 165
Medical Aid in Dying (MAID) 20–21
Medicare Mental Health Centres in Australia 48
Memphis Model of crisis intervention 74–75, 79
Mental Health Act 1983 (UK) 64, 70, 154
Mental Health Act 2014 (Australia) 155
Mental Health Australia 37
Mental Health Call for Service (MHCFS) 6–7, 156
mental health courts *see* therapeutic courts
mental health crisis: diagnosis by police 122, 124–126; *Inquiry into Mental Health* (Australia) 37; Mental Health Joint Response Car in London 43, 44, 45; Mental Health Treatment Requirement (MHTR) 103; police attended incidents 8; presentation in Australian emergency departments 8–9; use of mental illness term 211; use of term 6–7, 156
mental health professionals 43, 64, 72, 75, 123, 127, 139–140 *see also*

community response teams; co-responder models; non-police response models; Right Care, Right Person (RCRP) policy
Merseyside 67, 178, 186–188, 190, 191
Metropolitan Police 66, 68–70, 73, 109, 159, 161
misrepresenting behaviours: effect of focused training 124; fragmented communication 185; terminology 9, 212; training risks 134–135 *see also* terminology
missing persons 72, 163
mobile crisis teams 41, 42, 50, 106, 195, 198, 214
models: Behavioural Change Stairway Model (BCSM), 130; community response teams 41–43, 213–215; crisis management 178; ideologies 79–81; impact of co-responder teams 63; Memphis Model 74–75; objectives 216; person-centred care 48–49; reducing judicial engagement 45; Serenity Integrated Mentoring (SIM), 64–67; tri-agency 61; use of multiple approaches 77
mood disorders (ICD-10 – F30–F39) 7
morality of intervention 19, 22, 25–26, 95–97, 155, 213

narratives: changing 185, 223; divisive 179, 222; law enforcement 121, 161–164; media portrayal of police 153–154, 157, 159, 165; mental illness 135, 153, 211; personal safety 121
National Alliance on Mental Illness (NAMI) in the US 74–75, 78
National Behavioral Health Crisis Care Guidance 195 *see also* Substance Abuse and Mental Health Services Administration (SAMHSA) in the US
National Suicide Prevention Strategy in Australia 37
negotiation 99, 121, 130, 134, 155
Netherlands: community response teams 44; emergency call lines 39, 194
neurocognitive disorders 187
neurodevelopmental conditions 7, 11, 103
neurodivergence 9–10, 59, 100, 102–103, **132**, 151, 211–212
New South Wales: Mental Health and Cognitive Impairment Forensic Provisions Act 2020 101; Police Force 8, 69; State of New South Wales v Talovic [2014] 127–128, **133**
New York 43, 44, 158, 197
New Zealand: co-responder team 61; Mental Health and Wellbeing Commission 195; policing 160; Right Care, Right Person (RCRP) policy 69, 216; voluntary euthanasia 21
NHS: 111 number 38–39, 214; alternatives to emergency departments 48; Innovation Accelerator funding initiative 65–66; Isle of Wight Integrated Recovery Programme 64–65 *see also* United Kingdom
non-police response models: barriers 214–215; ‘defund the police’ campaigns 157; demand for dedicated infrastructure 197–198; establishment in the United States 158; Memphis Model 74–75; unavoidable use of force 106, 110–111 *see also* community response teams; crisis call lines; crisis stabilisation centres

operational paradox 95–97, 213
Oregon: assisted suicide 20–21; community response models 42–43; Crisis Assistance Helping Out On The Streets (CAHOOTS) program 42, 44, 46, 194, 215
organic mental disorders 8–9
Ouslem, Ryan, death of 71
outcomes: benefit of therapeutic courts 102; concerns about Serenity Integrated Monitoring (SIM) 66–67; co-responder model 61, 63; crisis intervention teams 78; follow-up care 37–38, 48; government-led models 38–39; ideal 94; improving training 121–122; limitations of therapeutic courts 103–104; longitudinal 37–38, 44, 49; non-clinical 113; positive engagement with non-police models

44; Right Care, Right Person (RCRP) policy 69–73; risk shifting 152; self-reporting 43, 73; success of Serenity Integrated Mentoring (SIM), 64–65; systems-thinking 182; tactical disengagement policy 219; web-of-support 184–185
oversight 73, 108, 151, 153, 183, 196, 198

Palmquist, Paul, death of 97
Paramedic Response Teams 12, 41, 42–43, 61, 106, 127, 197, 214, 221
parens patriae 95, 96
Peel, Sir Robert 161–164
peer support 41, 75, 180, 196
Personality Disorder Hub 186–187, 188–189
Persons with Serious Mental Illness (PwSMI) 7, 156, 211
phone based support *see* crisis call lines
physical intervention: 'defund the police' campaigns 157; dominant narrative 121; expectation of the police 163–164; forcible entry into home 96; reduction with co-responder models 62 *see also* law enforcement role of the police; use-of-force
police: behavioural health crisis skills 59; blaming 159–160; budgets 158–159; criminalisation of behavioural health 11; deaths of individuals 71–73, 80, 220; 'defund the police' 157–159; disability related incidents 9; duty of care 22–23, 68, 80, 95, 100, 213, 219; effect of austerity in the UK 158; escalating incidents 107–108; fatal encounters, impact on police officers 110; fatal shootings 74–75, 106–107; first response 10, 17; framing 156, 160–161, 163–164; gatekeeping 157, 223; major incidents 163; media 153, 157, 159, 165; non-lethal tools 109–110, 219–220; paradoxical position 2; Peelian principles 161–164; reducing police attendance 44, 49–50, 51, 75–76, 77–78, 214, 215; role, contemporary 162; role, reimagining 164–165; role, understanding 124, 222; role, welfare 163, 190–191; role as activator 157, 191, 192; role in the community 190–191; substance use disorders (SUD) responses 8; suicide by cop shootings 97; training in crisis intervention 75, 76, 80–81; training in tactical disengagement 99; use of resources 67–68 *see also* co-responder models; Right Care, Right Person (RCRP) policy; Serenity Integrated Mentoring (SIM); suicide; tactical disengagement policy; tactical resolution (use of force); training
Police Ambulance Clinical Early Response (PACER) in Victoria 60
police response systems 79–81 *see also* co-responder models; crisis intervention teams; Right Care, Right Person (RCRP) policy; Serenity Integrated Mentoring (SIM)
policy: effect on response 154; funding non-police models 158; impact of media 153; increase in budgets 158–159; unpredictability 180; vulnerability of community response teams 45–46
POST (Peace Officer Standards and Training) in California 138, 218
Post Traumatic Stress Disorder (PTSD) 21, 110
practical perspective 1–2
presentation of crises 7–8, 13–14, 18, 122, 124
prevention: co-responder model 80; crime 162; frameworks 195; *Preventing Future Deaths (PFD) report* (UK) 71; Prevention Concordat for Better Mental Health (UK) 199; suicide 36–37, 49, 194; systems thinking approach 177, 185
proactive strategy 17, 178–179, 185 *see also* reactive model of response
procedural knowledge 126–128, **132**
psychiatric: assessment 19; beds 11–12, 14; inpatient care 49
psychiatric emergency services in Houston 47
psychiatric mobile response teams (PMRT) in Los Angeles 42
psychoactive substance use (ICD-10 F10-F19) 7

public: expectation of the police 163; media portrayal of police 153–154; perception of police use of force 108; relationship with the police 161–162

quality of life 21
Queensland: *Better Crisis Care* (2025) 174; Queensland Mental Health Co-Responder (MH-CoRe) 43

Rapid Review (UK) 71
reactive model of response 175, 176, 178, 185
realities: case study 182; diagnostic profiles 211–212; factors in chronic crisis cycling 179; preparedness 121; problem of terminology 9–10, 24–25; scenario training 134; training needs 124–126, 128, 131, 136–137, 139; unavoidable use of force 106, 110–111; welfare role of police 163–164
recidivism: crisis 12–13; crisis call lines 37, 39–40; police involvement 11, 67; Serenity Integrated Mentoring (SIM), 80; therapeutic courts 102, 104 *see also* chronic crisis cycling
Reconnect programs 189
referrals: appropriate 78; cross-sector decision-making 187–188; integrated pathway 187–188, 192; knowledge for police officers 127
reforms to crisis response 174–175
Reith, Charles 162
relational approach: continuity of staffing 190; police response 126, 128, 130; training **132**, 139, 217
reliability of services 196
responders: Community Behavioral Health Crisis Responder 197, 222; effect of terminology 10; reflecting realities 9–10
Responding to Persons Experiencing a Mental Health Crisis 124
responsibility: criminal behaviour 101–102; outcomes 220; Right Care, Right Person (RCRP) policy 71–73; therapeutic courts 102–103, 105
Right Care, Right Person (RCRP) policy: approaches 68; benefits 69–70, 159; concerns 70–71, 216; deaths of individuals 71–73; future 73–74; global programs 69, 158; ideologies 79–80; implementation 67–68; police risk assessments, concerns about 71–73; risk shifting 152
risks: anti-police narrative 159; de-escalation 129; inclusive programs 186–187; misrepresenting behaviours 9, 124, 134–135, 185, 212; operational experiences of crises 18; operational paradox of police intervention 95–97; police duty of care 68; police risk assessments, concerns about 71–73; reactive model of response 155; risk shifting 127–128, 152–153; shared assessment 188; tactical disengagement 98; tactical resolution (use of force) 99–100; training scenarios **125**; triaging 107; types of 14, **15**; use of deadly force 74–75; use of force 106
Royal Commission into Violence, Abuse, Neglect, and Exploitation of People with Disability (Australia) 9

safety: behavioural health as an emergency service 196; benefit of a fourth emergency service 197; concerns about Right Care Right Person (RCRP), policy 70; crisis stabilisation centres 47; de-escalation 129; immediate role 9, 24; improving 75–76; increase in police budgets 158–159; operational paradox of police intervention 95–97; reducing police intervention 39; relational approach 128; risk triaging 107–108; tactical disengagement 23, 98; use of force 106 *see also* risks
Salt Lake Mobile Crisis Outreach Teams (MCOT) 41
Samaritans (UK) 35–36, 39
San Diego Mobile Crisis Response Teams (MCRT) 41
San Francisco: Street Crisis Response Team (SCRT) 12, 43, 44, 194, 197; tactical disengagement policy 99
schizophrenia 7, 124
Scott v. Smith (2024), US 96

scrutiny 11, 66, 70–73, 74, 95, 97, 110, 112, 219
Sequential Intercept Model 178, 179
Serenity Integrated Mentoring (SIM): concerns 66–67, 80; dismantling of 73, 215–216; expansion of program 65–66; *A Feasibility Assessment of Serenity Integrated Mentoring (SIM) Implementation in London, England* 66–67; longitudinal support 65; strategic impact 65; success 64–65
Serious Mental Illness (SMI) 7
Shorter v Hodges 14 NSWLR 1988 20
situational distress 7
social convergence 11
social prescribing 179, 189
social workers 10, 67, 74, 127
society: benefit of non-police model 45, 51; increased funding for preventative support 158; reintegration 103; role of the police 59, 162, 163–165; systemic gaps 159–160 *see also* communities
somatoform disorders 7
Spokane Regional Stabilisation Center 47
staffing: Authorised Mental Health Practitioners (AMHPs) 59–60; Community Behavioral Health Crisis Responder 197, 222; community response teams 41; crisis call lines 37, 197; importance of 192; low staff-to-client ratios 188; Memphis Model 70; stability 189–190
stakeholders: competing priorities 76; crisis management 178; Merseyside High-Demand Action Plan 187–188; relations 136; reluctance 179–180; Right Care, Right Person (RCRP) policy 68, 70; training **133**; web-of-support 180–182, 183
State of New South Wales v Talovic [2014] 127–128, **133**
stereotyping 134–135
stigma 13, 73–74, 77, 78, 104, 154
Stockholm Psykiatriambulans (PAM) 43, 45
Street Crisis Response Team (SCRT) in San Francisco 12, 43, 44, 194
Street Triage in the United Kingdom 60–61, 62, 64
stress: impact of fatal encounters on police personnel 110; types of crisis presentation 7
Stuart V Kirkland-Veenstra [2009], Australia 22–23, **133**, 213
Substance Abuse and Mental Health Services Administration (SAMHSA) in the US 3, 38, 47, 50, 177, 194, 195, 213–214, 216
substance use disorders (SUD): diagnostic shadowing 9; drug courts 103; factor in fatal police incidents 109; incarceration 17; non-arrest diversion pathways 187; non-police response models 45; police attended incidents 8; psychoactive substance use (ICD-10 F10-F19) 7
suicide: autonomy 25–26, 95–96; coercive control 21–22; by cop 97; criminalisation 19–20; crisis call lines 36, 37–38, 40; crisis presentation 7; crisis stabilisation centres 49; decriminalisation 20; disclosure of suicidal thoughts 40; police duty of care 22–23, 213; procedural knowledge 126–128; question of mental illness 23–24; Suicide Act 1961 (UK) 20; tactical disengagement policy 98–100; training scenarios **125**; voluntary euthanasia 20–21, 213; wills 20 *see also* crisis call lines
Support Team Assisted Response (STAR) in Denver 43, 44, 45
Sweden 43, 45
systems-based thinking: absence of police 223; bigger picture of crisis 177–178; case study 182–185; crisis 223; crisis, reimagining 4; crisis intervention teams 80–81, 215; data and information sharing 191–192; expanding throughout the health system 185; fatigue 174; fourth emergency service 198; funding distribution 151–152; importance of 200; improving crisis response 175, 220–221; from justice to health 178–179; longitudinal approach 181–182; maintaining 179–180; mobile community mental health teams (MCMHTs) 42; need to

embed crisis lines 38–39, 41, 214; police in the web-of-support 190–191; risk shifting 152–153; Substance Abuse and Mental Health Services Administration (SAMHSA) framework 50; success of co-responder programs 63–64; terminology 10; web-of-support 180–181

tactical disengagement policy: attendance at suicide incidents 95–97; complex situations 94–95, 111–112; defining 219; global policies 99; introduction of policy 98; operational paradox of police intervention in self-harm 95–98; suicide by cop shootings 97; United States 23
tactical resolution (use of force): acknowledging realities 106, 112; improving police response 109–110; risk 99–100; risk triaging 107; tools 109, 219–220; unavoidable use of force 108
Taheri, S. A., *Do crisis intervention teams reduce arrests and improve officer safety? A systematic review and meta-analysis* 77
teams *see* community response teams; co-responder models; Serenity Integrated Mentoring (SIM)
terminology: barriers 155–157, 165; behavioural health crisis 6; challenges 211–212; changes 8–9, 24–25; effect on response 10; legal definition of mental illness 154; mental health crisis 6–7; risk of diagnostic shadowing 9; training 123; unhelpful use of 7–8 *see also* law enforcement role of the police
Texas: Chronic Consumer Stabilization Initiative in Houston 178, 186, 187, 188, 190; crisis call management 39; Crisis Intervention Response Team (CIRT) 60; Houston Jail Diversion program 103; mental health as a fourth emergency service in Austin 194; Psychiatric Emergency Services in Houston 47
therapeutic courts: approaches 102–103; benefits 112; benefits and challenges 105–106; inconsistencies 103–104; lack of legal rigidity 104–105
time: building webs 185; embedding programs 182; managing conflict situations 99, 130, **132**; response times 214; time-limited engagement 189
Toronto Community Crisis Service (TCCS) 41
training: behavioural health crisis skills 59; benefits 121; crisis call lines 197; crisis intervention teams 75, 76, 78, 80–81, 120, 121; de-escalation 129–130; deficiencies 71; devising 124–126; framework 130–133; getting the content right 138–139, 217–218; improving police response 109; most beneficial 121–122; need for comprehensive 120–121, 135–136, 218; ongoing approach 137–138, 218; practical 122–123; procedural knowledge 126–128; real-world policing context 136–137, 218–219; relational approach 128; risk of stereotyping 134–135; scenarios **125**, **132**, **133**, 134–135, 218; tactical disengagement 99; trauma-informed care 128–129; understanding the role of the police 124, 217
transportation of service users 62, 197
trauma-informed care 126, 128–129, **132**, **133**, 135, 139, 189, 192, 197, 217, 222
Trends, Changes, and Developments in the Helpline Sector (UK) 37
tri-service model 221–222
trust: behavioural health as an emergency service 196; crisis call lines 40; relational approach 128; welfare role of police 159

United Kingdom: alternatives to emergency departments 48; chronic crisis interruption 189; co-responder models 60–61, 62; decriminalisation of suicide in England 20; defending outcomes 158; historical criminalisation of suicide in England 19–20; integrated

referral pathways 187–188, 189, 190, 191; local collaborative models 67; Mental Health Act 1983 64, 70, 154; Mental Health Joint Response Car in London 43, 44, 45; NHS 111 First Response for Mental Health 38–39, 194, 214; past trauma in patients 129; Peelian principles 161–164; programs 186–187; risk shifting 152; Serenity Integrated Mentoring (SIM), 64–67, 215–216; systems thinking approach 178, 182, 187; tactical disengagement policy 99; tactical resolution (use of force) 108, 109–110; therapeutic approach to justice 103 *see also* College of Policing (UK); Merseyside; Right Care, Right Person (RCRP) policy
United Nations Convention on the Rights of Persons with Disabilities (CRPD) 101–102
United States: 988 Suicide & Crisis Lifeline 36, 38–39, 40, 50, 194, 214; adoption of Behavioural Health 8; *Behavioral Health Crisis Response Landscape Analysis* (US) 174; Behavioural Influence Stairway Model (BCSM), 130; chronic crisis cycling 17; community response teams 42–44, 45, 215; co-responder programs 12, 41, 60, 62, 63; crisis call management 39; crisis intervention 78, 121; crisis response 195; crisis stabilisation centres and suicidality 49; data and information sharing 191; development of crisis stabilisation centres 47–48, 217; framing of police as law enforcers 160–161; funding of police 158; *Improving Responses to People with Mental Illnesses: Strategies for Effective Law Enforcement Training* 122–123; insurance 155, 192; integrated care pathways 188; intensive case management 189; intervening in suicide 23, 213; judicial management 103, 190; legal boundaries 155; liability 95–97; Medicaid support for Certified Community Behavioural Health Clinics (CCBHC) 47–48; past trauma in patients 129; peer support 41; progressive training approach 137; reduction of psychiatric hospital beds 11; shootings 106–107; Substance Abuse and Mental Health Services Administration (SAMHSA) 38, 47, 177, 194, 195, 214; suicide by cop shootings 97; systems approach 178, 187; tactical disengagement policy 96, 98–99; tactical resolution (use of force) 108, 109–110; voluntary euthanasia legislation 20–21 *see also individual states and cities*
unpredictability 2, 109, 134, 176, 180, 223
Urgent Mental Health Care Centre in Adelaide 48
use-of-force: 'defund the police' campaigns 157; dominant narrative 121; expectation of the police 163–164; justice approach 11; outcomes 43; reducing 62, 139, 215; responsibility 220; scenarios **133**, 134; shift away from 111; suicide incidents 97–98; training 136, 138, 218; unavoidable 106–108, 110 *see also* tactical resolution (use of force)

Vancouver: Assertive Community Treatment (ACT) Team 178, 188, 189; Assertive Outreach Team (AOT) 186, 188–189, 190; Car 87 60; Early Warning System of data use 191; Mobile Crisis De-Escalation Team (MoDe) 42
Victoria 60
violence: Complex Needs Web *16*; family 9, 59, 163; fourth emergency service 198; intimate partner violence (IPV) 21, 24, 25, 213; judicial management 100, 102, 104; media portrayal 153–154; police responsibility 42, 51, 75, 107–108, 129
voluntary admissions 35, 47
voluntary euthanasia 20–21

walk-in services 47, 48, 51
Washington 47

web-of-support 178, 180–182, 183–184, 185, 189–191, 192, 221
Western Australia: juvenile detainees 11; legal boundaries in information sharing 155; legal capacity of individuals 101; Mental Health Co-Response (MHCR) program 60–62; Mental Health Regulations 155, 192; Right Care, Right Person (RCRP) policy 69, 73; therapeutic courts 103; unusual police incidents 163
women 11
World Health Organisation 7, 151, 154, 212

young people: disclosure of suicidal thoughts 40; mental health and offending 17

For Product Safety Concerns and Information please contact our EU representative GPSR@taylorandfrancis.com
Taylor & Francis Verlag GmbH, Kaufingerstraße 24, 80331 München, Germany

www.ingramcontent.com/pod-product-compliance
Ingram Content Group UK Ltd.
Pitfield, Milton Keynes, MK11 3LW, UK
UKHW022351190926
475702UK00015B/2233
9781041262169